Organizational Survival

Organizational Survival

Profitable Strategies for a Sustainable Future

GREGORY BALESTRERO

AND NATHALIE UDO

New York   Chicago   San Francisco   Athens   London
Madrid   Mexico City   Milan   New Delhi
Singapore   Sydney   Toronto

1 2 3 4 5 6 7 8 9 0   DOC/DOC   1 9 8 7 6 5 4 3

ISBN   978-0-07-181712-7
MHID   0-07-181712-3

e-ISBN 978-0-07-181718-9
e-MHID   0-07-181718-2

SEEE™ and the SEEE model™ are trademarks of International Institute for Learning, Inc.

This publication is designed to provide accurate and authoritative information in regard to the subject matter covered. It is sold with the understanding that neither the author nor the publisher is engaged in rendering legal, accounting, securities trading, or other professional services. If legal advice or other expert assistance is required, the services of a competent professional person should be sought.

> —From a Declaration of Principles Jointly Adopted
> by a Committee of the American Bar Association
> and a Committee of Publishers and Associations

Library of Congress Cataloging-in-Publication Data

Balestrero, Gregory.
  Organizational survival : profitable strategies for a sustainable future / Gregory Balestrero and Nathalie Udo.
     pages cm
  ISBN 978-0-07-181712-7 (alk. paper) — ISBN 0-07-181712-3 (alk. paper)
  1. Sustainable development. 2. Management—Environmental aspects. 3. Social responsibility of business. I. Udo, Nathalie. II. Title.
  HC79.E5B3483   2014
  658.4'012—dc23
                                                                    2013028476

McGraw-Hill Education books are available at special quantity discounts to use as premiums and sales promotions or for use in corporate training programs. To contact a representative, please visit the Contact Us pages at www.mhprofessional.com.

Contents

Foreword

On Midway Island, halfway across the Pacific Ocean, I recently contemplated a nesting Laysan albatross sheltering her single egg. Observers who have documented her return to this place since the 1950s call her Wisdom. A serene gray and white bird, Wisdom began a lifetime of flying over the surface of the ocean at about the same time I launched myself into decades of exploring the depths below. Over the years, we have both witnessed the appearance of masses of drifting plastics, slicks of oil, and an increasing abundance of ships—as well as a steady decrease in the number of squid and fish necessary for Wisdom's survival, and that of her future hatchlings. Both Wisdom and I have experienced an era of unprecedented changes, but she cannot understand the causes, nor could she know what to do to about them even if she did understand. But humans can.

Owing to the advances of technology in the past century, humanity has learned more about the nature of the world and the universe beyond than during all the preceding time. By some accounts, at the same time, more has been lost. Since the middle of the twentieth century, half of the planet's coral reefs have disappeared or are in a state of sharp decline. Populations of many fish and other ocean species have decreased by 90 percent. Only five percent of North America's old growth forests remain from their former expanse across the continent. Globally, mangrove forests, coastal marshes, kelp forests, and sea-grass meadows have declined by as much 60 percent. Oxygen-generating, food-producing phytoplankton populations are changing, with hundreds of dead zones in some coastal regions and reduced levels of production in others. Measurements of ice decline in polar regions are coincident with increasing temperature, sea level rise, and ocean acidification—all closely coupled with the swiftly increasing emissions of carbon dioxide generated by burning vast reservoirs of fossil fuels—coal, oil and gas—that were millions of years in the making.

Astronauts in training learn everything they can about the systems that keep them alive during journeys in the hostile environment beyond Earth's atmosphere. While flying through space, they take care of their air, water, food, and temperature control as if their lives depend on it, because they so clearly do. Less obvious to most people is that we are all aboard a great, blue spacecraft hurtling through an otherwise inhospitable universe. Until recently, we could take for granted the processes that generate oxygen, maintain favorable temperatures, yield water, furnish building materials, provide food, and much more. But complacency is no longer an option. Now we know: the world is not too big to fail.

From the smallest microbe to the largest whale, all living things impact the world around them, but never before has a single creature—humankind—so swiftly and so comprehensively altered the nature of the entire planet, with consequences that put much more at risk than profits on a balance sheet. Increasingly, there is evidence that our actions are eroding the underpinnings of the natural systems that keep us alive.

What about "Tomorrow's Child?" That is the message I heard from Ray Anderson, founder and CEO of Interface Inc., a highly successful carpet company, at a conference early in the twenty-first century. In a voice resonating with soft, drawn-out vowels, Anderson said he personally had come to recognize that what is taken from nature, or alters, contaminates, or destroys land, air, water, and wild plants and animals must be recognized as costs that we deal with or they will become debts passed along to our children. Leaders in business and industry not only have the power, he suggested, but also the responsibility to reverse the disastrous trends currently in motion. He challenged his colleagues to find ways to be successful in business using approaches that not only did not degrade the integrity of the natural world, but also helped restore what already has been lost.

In this work, authors Greg Balestrero and Nathalie Udo provide provocative examples and thoughtful strategies on how companies can embark on a path to sustainability based on understanding the need to find an enduring place for ourselves within the natural systems that sustain us. They share stories of companies like Interface Inc. that have transformed in order to excel in a sustainable future—not just for the organization's survival, but also for the future of humankind. And they provide insights about how you can achieve similar goals. At a time when many despair about the near and distant future, here you will find engaging stories, practical solutions, inspiring examples—and plenty of reasons for hope.

Sylvia A. Earle
National Geographic Explorer in Residence
September 3, 2013

Preface

> *The world needs dreamers, and the world needs doers.*
> *But above all, the world needs dreamers who do.*
> —SARAH BAN BREATHNACH

GREG—After a long and successful career, I have come to the embarrassing conclusion that I may be a slow learner. It took over 30 years and three big "aha" moments to get to the point of writing this book. It boils down to the fact that unless people sense a real crisis, they most likely won't react. If you see a bus coming toward you, you step out of the way. If something is flying at your face, you duck. The right question is, how far ahead should you plan to avoid these risks to life and limb before they are upon you?

My first "aha" moment came in October 1980, when I was offered a position as program manager of a national program for improving energy efficiency in the industrial sector. Eight years in energy conservation had prepared me for this job, and the program was expected to have a dramatic effect on national industrial energy consumption. The funds for the program came from the newly created U.S. Department of Energy (DOE), formed in 1977. Although the start date was delayed until after the November presidential election, I was ecstatic and wildly optimistic about the future.

Then Ronald Reagan was elected, and he lived up to his campaign pledge. Funding was diverted from the DOE and other areas to rebuild the economy and the country's defense. At first I was confused and angry. How could anyone make this trade-off when the data was crystal clear? Energy consumption was growing exponentially; production was flat. How could the government be so blind? My frustration gave way to understanding as I realized that the economic and defense crises were right in front of us. The bus was coming, and we needed to step out of the way. Government acts when the crisis is upon us.

My next "aha" moment came 10 years later. Working for the Institute of Industrial Engineers (IIE), an association dedicated to performance and productivity improvement, I watched one U.S. industry after another die on the vine due to shortsightedness about the challenges posed by emerging international competitive and technological trends. Shipbuilding, the auto industry, electronics, computers, and more were fast being eroded due to this lack of foresight. How could this happen again? I thought U.S. companies were recognized for their powerful strategic planning. I came to realize that the "strategic horizon" of U.S. companies tended to be about three to five years, and unless the crisis was upon them, most would not react.

Now fast-forward to 2011 for "aha" moment number three. I was preparing to retire as CEO of the Project Management Institute (PMI) and was reflecting on my nearly nine-year tenure. I had spent my career as an advocate for business excellence through project, productivity, and performance improvement. I'd had a great run. The turn of events in 1980 encouraged me to spend my career in the not-for-profit sector, bringing people together to solve common problems without government involvement and hopefully helping companies become more successful. I had traveled to nearly 70 countries, meeting wonderful, ordinary people who were doing extraordinary things.

However, I had been extremely restless for the last five years. I believed that there was a conversation we needed to have, but I couldn't quite put my finger on it. Beyond meeting thousands of wonderful people around the world, I had witnessed a world converging on a point in the future that was going to have a long-lasting negative impact on business and personal prosperity. My travels had shown me firsthand the dilemma of an expanding population in an era of declining resources. Seven years of scenario planning and reading signpost reports for PMI had made me acutely aware of the problems that could emerge by the middle of the twenty-first century.

To confirm my conclusions, I picked up a copy of *Limits to Growth: The 30-Year Update* by Donella and Dennis Meadows and Jørgen Randers, and I read it carefully. The original set of scenarios, produced in 1972, was the result of the first computer-generated models showing how the competition played out between a rapidly growing population and a resource-limited planet. The book proved that sometime before the mid-twenty-first century, there would be a "kink" in the supply hose for society and businesses. Something had to give, or a global adjustment would put thousands of companies out of business, put millions of people out of work, and do long-term damage to global prosperity. Is no one listening or watching?

I decided to put sustainability on my own public agenda. I spoke globally on the pending dilemma and the changes that needed to be made. I engaged business and government leaders around the world in the conversation, and I began to see changes were brewing—significant changes—that might be able to effect a course correction. I was driven to get someone to listen to me, to act.

I did learn that great environmental entrepreneurs such as Ray Anderson of Interface Inc. and Yvon Chouinard of Patagonia were exercising their own initiative and taking a revolutionary approach to business. I owned BMW motorcycles and cars for years before I learned that the company was also a powerful force for fighting the AIDS epidemic. Companies like Whole Foods were demonstrating that growth with a commitment to building sustainable communities is not only possible but profitable as well. Thousands of individuals were proving that social innovation wasn't a fad but a powerful trend altering the way people interact and prosper.

These companies were transforming the traditional commitment of business capitalism from turning profits and maintaining market share to building global prosperity and improving the planet. But clearly they were in the minority. I realized that this was the conversation we needed to have. Hope is built not in the political mechanisms that regulate solutions but rather in the boardrooms of the world. The initiative and innovation of businesses can be directed to building a sustainable future while still making money and staying in business. It was time to act. I was going to make people wake up and listen.

The idea of this book began to take shape. I was convinced that studying the transformations that were going on would reveal common approaches that could be shared and utilized. The information was out there, waiting to be mined, sorted, and shared. But I couldn't do it alone. I needed both the opportunity and a development partner. The opportunity came from a friend and colleague who is the epitome of a business entrepreneur—and a person whose default state is "action." That person was E. LaVerne Johnson, founder, president, and CEO of the International Institute for Learning (IIL). I knew from personal experience that she was committed to building sustainable communities and helping society. She understood the idea of shifting from profits to prosperity. We agreed that we would somehow work together, and in 2012 we committed to this book project.

I also realized I needed a balanced approach to this task. I needed to avoid my own linear view and try to be critical. I needed another strong perspective to uncover and tell the stories and to find the common thread that would transform companies. I needed someone to test my limits and understanding by sharing a strong opinion, a global opinion. I found that person in Nathalie Udo. Together, using the opportunity presented by LaVerne Johnson, we have carried on the conversation about shifting from profits to prosperity. We hope you continue the conversation after reading this book, with one important provision: that you act on it.

Years ago, I attended a workshop by futurist Joel Barker and picked up a saying that has affected my career and helped me motivate others: "Vision without action is a dream. Action without vision is simply passing the time. Action with vision is making a positive difference." Help your organization develop a vision and take action. That is all we ask. Just do it.

NATHALIE—I was very honored when Greg asked me to be his co-author. Growing up in the Netherlands—one of the most densely populated Western countries in Europe—I was keenly aware of the limited availability of untouched nature. Don't get me wrong; we have forests in the Netherlands, but the trees are all in nice, neat rows, almost manicured. In high school I was a member of Greenpeace and dreamed of becoming an activist to protect our planet's nature and wildlife from the exploitation of ruthless corporations. When I was in university, I longed for unlimited wealth so I could buy up large sections of the Amazon forest—the lungs of our planet—and put armed guards around those areas to punish anyone who wanted to cut down a tree. Then my working life began, and the day-to-day reality of paying bills pushed everything else to the side. I felt overwhelmed by the scale of changes needed for us and our descendants to continue to enjoy the world and all its natural wonders.

I have traveled a lot in my life, both for pleasure and work, and in the process I developed a healthy distrust of corporate intentions regarding nature, wildlife, and people, simply from seeing the damage done by corporations on land and under water. When I heard more and more companies talking about corporate social responsibility but could not see real progress, either due to lack of transparency or lack of action, it sounded to me more like a marketing tool than true intentions to sustain our environment and societies. My personal awakening came around 2008, when I started to work closely with Japanese corporations.

Corporations rooted in Japanese culture have long-term visions covering multiple generations. They are concerned with the sustainability of their organizations, but they also care about the societies in which they operate, since that affects the company's sustainability. Working closely with these corporations, learning their histories, hearing their executives talk about sustainability and how it is part of their value system, seeing how they support their words with actions and how they raise the awareness of their employees in this area made me realize two things. First, I realized I was not taking any action in this area that was critically important to me. Second, I realized that corporations hold the key to the social, environmental, and ethical improvements needed to change the course we and the planet are on. They have the necessary reach through their value and supply chains, and they have the necessary resources.

The feeling of being overwhelmed by the gigantic problem we are facing had muted my "I'm in control" mentality. Experiencing the real passion some Japanese organizations have for improving the communities they touch convinced me that I needed to do something. So here I am writing this book with my dear friend Greg Balestrero. I want to do my part to raise awareness and inspire more companies to transform their organizations to become more sustainable. In the process, they will improve the health of the planet and of society at large—and also the health of their bottom line, as you will read in this book!

The Dalai Lama says, "If we make consistent effort, based on proper education, we can change the world. We are selfish, that's natural, but we need to be wisely selfish, not foolishly selfish. We have to concern ourselves more with others' well being, that's the way to be wisely selfish. We have the ability to take the long-term benefit into account. I think it is possible to make real change in this century." I also believe that real change is possible, even before the middle of this century!

Introduction

Why would we write a book on the relationship between global sustainability and corporate strategy when there are already so many other sustainability books out there? In part, we did so because we want to continue a meaningful conversation about the change that needs to happen. The massive global library of information on sustainability is not merely a virtual shelf filled with discrete, unrelated bytes of information. On the contrary, each book and every article contributes to shaping our beliefs about the future of business and the planet. Just as creating this book has shaped our beliefs, we hope reading it will shape yours and encourage you to act.

More important, we believe leaders at the corporate, business, and government levels continue to assume that we have plenty of time to change course. In reality, time is running out. We are now well into the second decade of the century, and while we have seen remarkable transformations taking place, there still isn't sufficient progress to avoid catastrophic damage to our businesses, our societies, and global prosperity. We want to raise the level of urgency in the conversation and spur rapid, transformational changes.

But we also believe the changes we need aren't just about the environment or natural resources. Most sustainability books focus on those angles, and no doubt they are critically important, but the change we need today is far more complex. Consumers expect companies to do the right thing and to help the society they serve. Ethics and trust have never been higher on the lists of important criteria for successful companies.

In addition to making profits and protecting their value chain, corporations have to stand up for society and demonstrate ethics above all. These changes have to be embedded at the very heart of the business philosophy.

We want to explain the common traits and actions that we have uncovered at the core of companies making this transition successfully and profitably—from entrepreneurial businesses to multinational titans. These organizations have identified the problems we face and have made real, meaningful commitments to changing the way they do business. Those changes have resulted in huge benefits to the organizations, to their brands, and ultimately to their long-term survival. We want to point the way: a way that is not only the right thing to do but also a way of surviving and thriving in a rapidly approaching future.

How This Book Is Organized

One of the common themes you will find in these pages is that *you cannot accomplish this change alone*. You will need to build alliances and partnerships to meet your goals. To that end, we have gone to great lengths to help you develop a strong argument for change and to build a common belief across your organization that change is no longer an option but a mandate for survival—a belief that will result in changes to strategy and execution.

The Case for Change

In Chapters 1 to 3, we lay out the case for change, not just from an environmental standpoint but also from a practical one. Of course you know that our global population is growing, but did you know that a huge percentage of that growth comes from an emerging middle class in developing countries? New cities are springing up all over the world, and people are migrating to these urban centers in record numbers, searching for a better way of life. The resulting demand for middle-class goods and services will put enormous strain on resources and supply chains that are already stretching to the breaking point.

The message of these chapters is crystal clear: there is no longer any doubt that global demand will become unsustainable by 2050. Sustainability is no longer a choice. It is an imperative. Businesses are in a unique position to meaningfully alter the shape of our future. The new paradigm has to be based on the belief that organizations' long-term prosperity is joined at the hip with global prosperity. Bea Perez, Coca-Cola's chief sustainability officer, is very clear on this issue: "There will be no companies 100 years from now if companies do not focus on sustainability!"

The Awakening of Organizational Leadership

The rapid demographic, economic, and environmental shifts we are facing will present unprecedented challenges—and also unprecedented opportunities for businesses willing to embrace sustainability in their strategic planning. In Chapters 4 to 6, we share our research into companies worldwide that are making dramatic changes and realizing dramatic successes as a result.

The organizations discussed in these chapters were carefully researched and chosen based on a set of very specific criteria. (See Appendix A for additional discussion on our selection process.) We hoped to find companies that either were founded on the values of sustainability or acted on the trends discussed in Chapters 1 to 3 by implementing strategic changes to reposition themselves for a sustainable future.

The companies we identified and researched have put sustainability at the core of their business. For some, sustainability was built into strategy and decision making from their founding. For others, sustainability has moved from the margins to the center of the corporate agenda. And for others still, new business paradigms are being created through social innovation that will shape an entirely new economic model. All of these companies believe that profits will follow sustainable business practices and have proven that this is the case.

We quickly found that these companies were making dramatic and innovative strategic changes throughout their supply and value chains, leading to impacts that could change entire industries. It is this corporate performance and strategic change that we highlight in these chapters. Their stories show how organizations build respect, improve stakeholder loyalty, and increase profitability by doing the right thing and exercising leadership in their sector.

Payback Is Real

While consumers, employees, and society are scrutinizing companies more and more about their sustainability strategies, there is a widely held belief that Wall Street has not caught up yet. The prevailing view is still that investing in sustainability comes at the expense of the bottom-line results. One of the issues companies face is that the business case for long-term sustainability can seem ambiguous—the return on investment is not always immediately clear. Chapters 7 to 10 describe the value and payback elements of the transition to sustainability, dispelling the myth that sustainability comes at the expense of profits. These chapters show that the payback is real, puts money in the bank, and builds a valued brand.

The success stories shared earlier in the book may seem both remarkable and unrealistic to many in your organization, and you may be confronted with skepticism and roadblocks along the way. In Chapter 7, we provide a practical guide to anticipating and responding to the myths and questions that you may encounter during your transition. We will help you analyze the success stories and be prepared to respond directly to these challenges.

Chapter 8 shows that the stocks of those companies that have adopted a sustainable strategy consistently outperform those that haven't. Chapter 9 explains how companies can change the conversation by tailoring it to the values, ethics, and cultures of specific communities in which the company operates. We describe how the conversation with the financial community needs to change to recognize and reward sustainable behaviors, which would inspire many more organizations to adopt sustainable strategies.

Finally, Chapter 10 focuses on collaboration and the common traits we (and others) have observed in sustainable companies. This will help you self-assess which traits you need to develop to guide your company through the transition. Cultivating these traits will allow you to successfully transform your business into an organization driven by sustainability while benefiting from the financial payback it provides.

A Road Map for Changing Our Future

The core of this book is a new approach to assessing and developing a strategy to transform your business. This approach focuses on using risk management, scenario planning, and the SEEE model™ we have developed in conjunction with International Institute for Learning, Inc.—a framework that takes into account the Social, Economic, Environmental, and Ethical factors of strategic change. This new model will help you integrate sustainability into your strategic plan and to create and instill a new, sustainable outlook throughout your organization that will enable real and lasting change. The last chapters of the book introduce the tools you need to make this change successful. We help you answer key questions like: Where do I start? How do I build an agenda for change? How do I create and balance the portfolio of change? And how do I make sure that this change survives me—that it becomes sustainable beyond any one person, management team, or board? All of these questions are critically important to the leader in transition. This will not be an exhaustive treatment, but it will be a guide to real progress and a compass, if you will, to get started on this important change process.

To build a successful, profitable, and sustainable company with a solid reputation, you must weave sustainability into business strategy and day-to-day decision making. When sustainability is incorporated in organizational strategy, the decision processes for all initiatives will include a basic question: How does this affect our plans for sustainability? More important, sustainability becomes a variable in the formula for determining value in all company operations.

At any company, an integrated strategy that affects the entire value chain of the organization is critical to success. Figure I-1 displays a framework for establishing sustainability integration using the SEEE model:

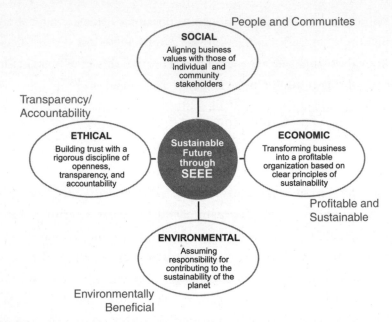

FIGURE I-1   The SEEE model makes sustainability an integral part of strategic decision making throughout the organization.

© 2013 International Institute for Learning, Inc.

the Social, Economic, Environmental, and Ethical elements of strategic change. Strategy development and the associated strategic decisions must embrace all four of these elements:

- *A social commitment* that integrates key individual and community stakeholder interests into the company's strategy and aligns them with the business values and principles. This requires a clear understanding of the key stakeholders in the organization and of the impact that the organization has (and can have) on its stakeholders.
- *An economic commitment* that transforms the organization into a profitable business based on clear principles of sustainability. This goes beyond the cost savings from concepts like zero waste. It embraces an economic model with a long-term vision that avoids trading sustainability for profits during economic challenges and that values

commitment to sustainability as a corporate principle with intrinsic value.

- *An environmental commitment* that takes responsibility for contributing to the sustainability of the planet. This requires the organization to take a full and complete look at its impact on the planet throughout its entire value chain, accept responsibility for its products and services throughout their life cycle, and take action accordingly.
- *An ethical commitment* that builds trust through openness, transparency, and accountability. This requires an organization to set clear measures of change, to assign objectives based on clear metrics, and to provide public reporting on progress against these objectives. It also requires the organization to own the impact of its mistakes by taking responsibility for failure and committing to overcome it and change.

The SEEE approach covers a lot of territory, but it takes effort and perseverance to implement a profitable sustainability strategy. One of the common traits of truly successful sustainable companies is that they work toward long-term change. Most of the organizations we discuss in this book have based their plans on a 10-year horizon. Obviously, such a long-term view requires an investment in ensuring that the change is real and substantive. Strategies must be built on a solid foundation of knowledge. Accumulating this knowledge requires conducting detailed analyses of value and supply chains, engaging stakeholders in discussions about key issues in their communities, understanding the most critical risks in the future and how those risks drive strategic change, and embracing partnerships to address critical supply issues that are beyond the resources of the company. The last section of this book addresses the strategic changes needed. Chapter 11 goes into more detail about how to create this long-term view and collect the required information, and Chapter 12 describes the process of integrating them into your company's strategy and decisions.

A successful sustainability strategy must be built carefully, so the SEEE approach uses phase-based strategy development. Figure I-2 shows an example of the different stages the change can go through.

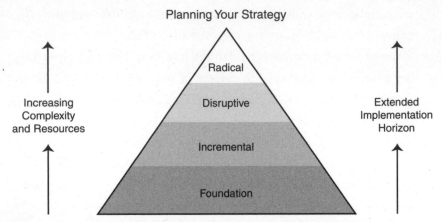

FIGURE I-2   The SEEE approach and the four stages of change: an information-gathering foundation that establishes a foundation or baseline, incremental changes to begin the transformation, a period of disruptive change moving the organization into the future, and finally a radical transformation of company operations and perceptions in the market.

Establishing a progressive step-by-step framework for strategic changes that embrace sustainability allows you to consider all of the changes needed to become a sustainable company. As you begin the process of strategic change, you will progress through four stages:

- *The foundation.* In order to build a socially responsible company, you first need to understand and meet the minimum required level of sustainability. The organization should understand, embrace, and comply with all legal and regulatory requirements for each element of the strategy. Compliance is the operative word for this level.
- *Incremental change.* In this stage, you ensure that the right steps are taken to begin the transformation, such as engaging stakeholders in discussions, measuring the organization's environmental footprint, and evaluating reporting methodologies. During incremental change, companies focus on finding efficiencies like reducing their carbon or water footprint and energy use.
- *Disruptive change.* Initiating deliberate, measurable change will disrupt the organization, but in a positive way. This is where the

organization moves from certainty to uncertainty, from the present into the future. In this stage, innovation is used to drive change. Strategic goals, for example, might include targeting a zero environmental footprint in carbon and water, or using only renewable energy sources and contributing to the communities in your value chain.

- *Radical change.* This is where aggressive changes occur that propel the organization into the future, not only in the way it operates but also in the way it is perceived. This could mean dramatic changes in product design, or taking an approach that actually removes more carbon from the atmosphere than your value chain adds.

THE CENTRAL MESSAGE

This book is a story of hopefulness rather than gloom and doom. It is intended to show that there is a reason to change—a burning platform, if you will. More important, however, this book is intended to show that it literally pays to change, by providing many great examples of how companies changed, made a difference, and ensured survivability well into this century.

In addition, this book presents a model for changing strategy that integrates the elements of economics, social responsibility, environmental sensibility, and a long-term commitment to building public trust through a rigorous devotion to ethical behavior. Thus, the real leverage of this book is in a truly integrated model for strategic change. We believe that the model described in this book will help companies navigate the critical era ahead of us and contribute greatly to positive change in society and the planet.

Part 1

The Case
for Change

Chapter 1

THE DOUBLE MEANING OF SUSTAINABILITY

Before you start some work, always ask yourself three questions: Why am I doing this? What might the results be? Will I be successful? Only when you think deeply and find satisfactory answers to these questions should you proceed.
—CHANAKYA, INDIAN TEACHER, PHILOSOPHER,
AND ECONOMIST (370–283 BCE)

GREG—Waking at six o'clock in the morning on the last day of our trip into the Amazon River basin and the Peruvian rainforest was both exciting and sad. My wife and I jumped out of bed and ran to the board ramps for the skiffs to begin our last expedition of the trip. We didn't want it to end, but we knew we needed to drink in the world around us one last time. We had spent eight days aboard a small riverboat with 25 other passengers, searching out and witnessing life and biodiversity in this amazing place. Our expectations weren't just surpassed; they were blown out of the water.

The rainforest is an incredible place. I relished the scents, the sounds, the feeling—a remarkable experience. Each day we spent six to eight hours in small skiffs, riding through the estuaries and tributaries, walking through the rainforest, and watching for signs of prey and predator alike. My mind ran through the huge variety of experiences we'd had and what this rainforest and others like it represent to the world.

The rainforests of the Amazon River basin cover parts of seven countries: Venezuela, Peru, Brazil, Bolivia, Colombia, Ecuador, and Guyana—approximately 40 percent of the continent. Though the percentages vary according to the source, experts estimate that the Amazon rainforest produces between 15 and 40 percent of the world's supply of oxygen, second only to the oceans of the world.

Oh, and let's not forget the biodiversity. More than one-half of Earth's millions of species of plants, animals, and insects live in rainforests throughout the world. In the Amazon basin alone, more than 1,500 species of birds are found. A recent study identified 1,500 plant species, 750 species of trees, and 900 tons of living plants in one hectare (2.47 acres). Nearly 500 reptiles find a home in the rainforests of the Amazon River basin. The river itself supports over 2,500 species of fish.[1] Can you imagine? I couldn't believe that I was there, witnessing this abundance and diversity of life.

And of course there is the Amazon River itself—nearly 6,500 kilometers (4,000 miles) long—stretching from its beginning just east of the Pacific Ocean in the Peruvian Andes to the massive estuary emptying into the Atlantic. The water passing through the Amazon in one day would meet the needs of the entire U.S. state of New York for a full year! Truly amazing.

But the marvels of the Amazon Basin aren't limited to wildlife. The river and forest people are wonderful. They are beautiful and friendly and very accepting of outsiders. They are extraordinarily resourceful, using the land, the water, and the wildlife to live, eat, and thrive. From the palm wood they use to build their homes, to the fish and animals they eat, these people owe their lives to Mother Earth, or Pachamama, as the Incas say.

The government of Peru invests in the education of its people, including the river and forest people. Every village, however small, has a state-funded school building to educate children through the eighth grade. Literacy among these river and forest communities is nearly 98 percent. To continue their education, children must travel to and stay in a city with a high school. Many children make this journey, seeking more education and more opportunities for prosperity. As their knowledge of the world grows, their own desires change, encouraging them to look for more opportunity. More than anything, the people of Peru are its greatest resource.

THE STORY OF OUR FUTURE

Storytelling is a remarkable means of sharing important parts of our lives. It has formed the basis of passing on traditions and principles of life and society over the millennia. However, in the era of broadcast, cable, and social media, it is difficult to tell which story is the right one to listen to, especially when you're trying to make concrete decisions. When one tries to understand the implications of climate change, the reports disputing and supporting the science pile up on either side. Each report, whether by a newscaster or a scientist, tells a story that is embellished by a host of facts, analyses, conclusions, and more important, opinions. To those of us trying to make a decision about strategic change to address the impacts of climate change, this presents a great challenge: a very complex subject, not yet fully understood, contested and supported by thousands of opposing sources. It's tempting to tune them all out and just live day by day.

The story of Peru represents another set of observations, more points of reference that clarify the challenges facing us in the world today and well into the twenty-first century. It helped reinforce our thinking that there are indeed very complex challenges in the future, for which many of us—individuals and organizations—remain unprepared. If organizations don't embrace change, then in all likelihood, their very survival will be in question in a few short years. In other words, the sustainability of companies in the next 40 years is inextricably linked to the sustainability of communities and the planet.

A Precious Link in Global Supply Chains

Leading organizations today have expanded their view to include the complete value chain of their products and services. The **value chain** is often defined as the successive stages in which value is created when producing, distributing, or servicing a product. The **supply chain,** on the other hand, is part of the value chain and is often defined as the integrated list of suppliers that provide everything from raw materials to semifinished goods to cleaning services and paper towels. When organizations scrutinize their value and supply chains to ensure that they are robust, it can allow them to ramp up and deliver without surprises. These leading companies also look at the supply chains of the *indirect* resources that contribute to their overhead, such as headquarters facilities, administrative personnel, energy to power the administrative offices, and so forth.

Looking more closely at Peru provides a sense of how the rainforest is tapped to provide input to global supply chains. Beginning with its natural habitat, the biodiversity of the Amazon River basin has been under attack for many years. Climate change, deforestation, commercial farming, city growth and overcrowding, pharmaceutical harvesting, and commercial fishing are doing tremendous damage. Since 1970, the Brazilian rainforest alone has lost over 600,000 square kilometers (230,000 square miles) according to satellite surveys by the Brazilian National Institute for Space Research (INPE).[2] This massive deforestation has stripped away countless species, some of which might have provided remedies for illnesses. Many prominent zoologists, such as Nigel Stork of Griffith University in Australia, warn that deforestation is responsible for the loss of thousands of plant, insect, and animal species per year. Some estimates place the rate of destruction at a staggering 50,000 species per year—an average of 137 species every day.[3]

Globally, there are many coordinated efforts to move toward net zero deforestation. One prominent effort is the UN-REDD Programme, a United Nations Collaborative initiative on Reducing Emissions from Deforestation and forest Degradation (REDD) in developing countries.[4] Launched in

September 2008, this program assists developing countries, with the help of several other UN programs, in preparing and implementing national REDD+ strategies. (REDD+ extends beyond deforestation and degradation to address conservation, sustainable management of forests, and "enhancement of forest carbon stocks in reducing emissions.")[5] The World Wildlife Federation is also working toward a goal of net zero deforestation for the Amazon rainforests by 2020. These programs and others like them are making a difference, but we are still a long way from reversing the destruction.

Why is so much effort expended to strip the forests in the Amazon River basin? We know this area represents a treasure trove of raw materials, food, medicines, and other supplies that can feed, cure, house, and clothe people throughout the region and the world. It is also the location of new cities and agricultural centers. And yet both the river basin and the forest have become exploited links in many supply chains, with insufficient attention paid to making these links sustainable. Recent efforts in Peru and Brazil have slowed this process, but a broad range of industries have been affected by these restrictions, since the Amazon River basin is the raw material link in hundreds of supply chains. This could result in a backlash of lobbying to remove restrictions.

In addition, the domestic transformation of the people of Peru provides a microcosm of the future workforces of the world. Peruvian villagers demonstrate a passion for improving themselves and building expectations of prosperity. Each of the villages has an odd thing in common: satellite TV. Yes, each of the villages has access to the world outside of the region and their country through TVs powered, not surprisingly, by diesel generators. It isn't hard for the villagers to see the numerous and exciting opportunities in the larger cities of Peru and in other developed nations. For them, local education is an answer, but it also provides motivation to move to the cities. They believe they need more education to become more prosperous, so they move to the cities, where they live with families and friends who are willing to house them. There in the cities, the bounty associated with educated middle-class people may very well be available to these relocated villagers.

The Race to the Cities

According to the UN Department of Economic and Social Affairs, 76 percent of Peru's 29 million residents live in cities, and the influx is growing, leaving small villages and agro-communities abandoned. By 2050, UN projections indicate that Peru will have a population of nearly 38 million, while the global population will have swelled to approximately 9.5 billion. If the percentage of Peruvian urbanites doesn't change, more than 33 million will be living in cities—nearly eight million more people than the current total population of Peru![6]

Globally, about 51 percent of the population lives in cities today, a first for humankind. Eduardo Lopez Moreno, in a recent report for UN-Habitat, calculated that there are more than 193,000 "city dwellers" added to urban areas across the globe *each day*—that's two every second.[7] The needs to supply this massive urban population grow by the minute: food, building materials, automobiles, public transportation, sanitary facilities, clean water, foodstuffs, educational institutions, and more. The Amazon River basin and forest and others like it are among the primary supply chains for many of the basic and raw materials to meet these needs.

THE EXPLODING MIDDLE-CLASS MARKET

In the past, developing nations were considered a great source of inexpensive, high-quality labor. Companies throughout the developing world became the low-cost assembly providers for autos, cellular phones, computers, televisions, and more. Along with this burgeoning industry came greater prosperity and—as is the case in India, Africa, and China—a new emerging middle-class market for domestic goods.

So not only is the urbanization of countries like Peru creating more demand on supply chains; so is the growth of consumption of this new worldwide middle class. Throughout the developing world (Latin America, Africa, Asia, and India) there is a passion to move more people than ever before out of poverty and into the middle class.

The 2012 report of the United Nations Millennium Development Goals (UN MDG) for 2015 included preliminary estimates indicating that the global poverty rate has already fallen to less than half of the 1990 rate.[8] If these results are confirmed, the first target of the UN MDGs—cutting the extreme poverty rate to half its 1990 level—will have been achieved well ahead of schedule. This was a massive collective effort by business, government, nongovernmental organizations (NGOs), church groups, and other not-for-profit institutions. It is a remarkable success.

However, this report defines the income threshold for emergence from extreme poverty to the lowest strata of the middle class at US$1.25 per day. This number may seem remarkably low, but it is a commonly accepted threshold. The economics of this new middle class in the developing world are very different than any in the developed nations. A special 2009 report by *The Economist* titled "Burgeoning Bourgeoisie" highlights these differences in the way the middle class is measured.[9] In the early 2000s, global economists tended to measure middle-class economics by reflecting on the existing middle class. The result was a daily earning power range of US$12–$62. This traditional middle class definitely contributes greatly to the engine of consumption, buying the things they have come to expect as a result of their economic status. However, the growth of a middle class in that range of earning power is in the single digits.

The new global middle class—and its measure of growth—is dramatically larger than the traditional middle class. A study by India's National Council for Applied Economic Research found that from 1995–2005 there was a movement out of poverty, emerging into a new middle class.[10] The new range was between US$2–$12 per day at 2005 purchasing power parity (PPP), and the percentage of the population that moved up from poverty into this range of earning potential grew from 18 percent to a jaw-dropping 41 percent!

As a result, the World Bank and the UN have formed a consensus to use a different figure to measure the daily earning potential of the class of people moving out of poverty: US$10.68 at 2005 PPP. With this number in mind, the new emerging middle class is massive. Today, India, Africa, and China are leading the world in middle-class expansion. Based on the revised statistics, Africa, India, and China *each* have a middle class in 2012 that numbers 300–500 million! Any one of those new middle classes represents a population rivaling that of Europe or the United States.

> **GREG**—The dream of having a better life is not limited to the developing world of today. People have always dreamed of gaining affluence and prosperity. Both of my parents were Italian immigrants who moved to the United States as children immediately following World War I. My grandparents received education only to the third grade, while my parents ended their education at the eighth grade. They were brought to the United States to seize the opportunity, the "dream," of moving out of poverty and into the middle class.
>
> My parents were union workers. They wanted a home, a car, freedom from want, and the opportunity for my generation to attend university. To them, these were the hallmarks of being in the middle class.
>
> Those same beliefs exist today in the minds of low-income earners throughout the world, along with the passion to have readily available transportation, a cell phone, a TV, a computer, clothes for every occasion, and the middle-class luxury of spare time to invest in activities not related to pure survival.

This rapidly escalating middle-class demand is wonderful for the global marketer or for the domestic marketer in the affected countries. However, the unexpected consequence of this improvement is a growing consumption of all things "middle class" and growing expectations for more products at prices far lower than ever before. The growth in this desire is exponential in developing nations. Mario Pezzini of the Organization for Economic Cooperation and Development (OECD) calls the middle class "the motor of consumption."[11] The African Development Bank calculated that while annual global population growth is down to 2.6 percent, the middle class continues to grow annually at 3.1 percent. In his article on the middle class, Pezzini noted that in Brazil, documented poverty has dropped from 40 percent of the population in 2001 to 25 percent in 2009, a shift with important consequences.

Regardless of your measuring stick, this new, emerging urban middle class represents a massive global engine of consumption, most of which is domestic to the respective countries. And with that market comes a series of expectations that will create a demand for goods and services unprecedented in our history:

- Sanitary facilities (including clean water)
- Clothing
- Readily available food supplies
- Connectivity for family and work (cell phones, Internet)
- Mobility for work and necessities (inexpensive cars, motorcycles, public transport)
- Healthcare for families (medicines)
- Homes, hospitals, and educational institutions (building and construction materials)
- Entertainment (TVs)

A Paradox of Opportunity

All of this would seem to be a boon for manufacturers and service providers. If the UN predictions are correct, the population of the world will be approximately 9.5 billion in 2050, up more than 35 percent over 2011. Though various assumptions and projections surround the size of the middle class in 2050, it appears that there is some consensus that it will be well above 50 percent of the global population, with a vast majority of the global population (70 percent) residing in cities.

Why shouldn't business leaders be excited and aggressively pursue this burgeoning market? This is a great market opportunity for retail goods and services and for the movement and creation of fixed capital. It would mean creating a strategic plan to scale up capacity and distribution in those regions of the world. In other words, how quickly can business scale up and provide the goods and services necessary to meet that growing demand?

All of us have read about companies that are following their marketing research and instincts and building capacities in developing regions of the world. At first, the move to set up manufacturing and assembly plants in the developing world was made to take advantage of low-cost, high-quality labor. Businesses believe there is a golden opportunity in Africa, India, and Asia to take on a share of these emerging domestic markets. Companies like Ikea, BMW, Samsung, and Ford Motor Company have been moving quickly to capitalize on this new market. This is less news than it is history.

A Distant, Fragile Middle Class

However, there are implications of this new, emerging middle class that create potential hazards for companies and organizations alike. First, this metamorphosis in the urbanization, population, and economic condition of humanity is not occurring in the same places as in the past. In fact, the highest growth in the middle class is moving east, with the largest contribution in Asia, India, and Africa. Homi Kharas, a Brookings Institution scholar appointed by UN Secretary-General Ban Ki-moon to lead the panel to develop the UN MDG for 2015, presented a compelling paper at the World Economic Forum in 2012.[12] He shared a projection that indicates 64 percent of the middle class in 2030 will be in Asia, while the middle class in Europe and the United States—today composing some 50 percent of the world's middle class—will fall to 22 percent in 2030. In addition, his research projected that 40 percent of global middle-class consumption in 2030 will come from Asia.

Second, and more important, this new middle class is fragile, dependent heavily on freedom to work, improvement in healthcare, improvement in education, a strong economy, and interlinked with issues such as national governance, domestic racism, and more. Those in the lower part of the US$2–$12 per day range are particularly vulnerable to all of these factors. Also, there has been little reduction in what the UN calls *vulnerable employment*—that is, unpaid family members or own-account workers. Vulnerable workers account for 58 percent of all employment in developing regions. UN and World Bank studies have proven earnings in this income range are quite fluid, sliding up and down the scale and easily falling out of middle class and back into abject poverty. It is a difficult market to target and stay with.

The reality of this new middle class is that it is shifting from the traditional Western, developed nations to Latin America, Asia, and Africa. And this movement is not due only to a shift in percentages. While the new paradigm of the middle class proliferates in the developing world, the old paradigm of the middle class in the developed world appears to be shrinking. For example, a 2012 joint study by the Bertelsmann Foundation and the German Institute for Economic Research (DIW) found that "Germany's once robust middle class has been shrinking rapidly for years" and "confirmed that low-income earners in Germany hardly ever move up the social ladder."[13] Once the backbone of society, the German middle class has dwindled over the past 15 years:

> Based on a poll of 20,000 adults, the study found that [at the end of 2012], middle-income earners accounted for 58 percent of the overall German population, down from 65 percent back in 1997. In absolute numbers, the middle class thus decreased by 5.5 million over the period under revision to total 47 million people.
>
> At the same time, four million more people were added to the army of low-income earners, the survey said, while adding that once relegated, a renewed promotion to the higher income league was the exception rather than the rule.[14]

This convergence between the shrinking traditional middle class and the growing new low-earner middle class may very well mean a "motor of consumption" that will be greater than any we have witnessed in our history.

UNRELENTING DEMAND AND DIMINISHING SUPPLIES

There is no question that this emerging motor of consumption and its associated urbanization is growing exponentially. Over the next 40 years, with continuing prosperity and proper supply, it will present a tremendous opportunity to provide thousands of classes of goods and services such as housing, clothing, food, transport, medicines, consumable goods, communication devices, and more. Even with the knowledge that the new market is in the developing world—and that it is also quite fragile, expanding and contracting with the cycle of fluctuating prices and changes in local and global economies—it remains a powerful magnet for new and existing providers of these goods and services throughout the world.

But this unrelenting demand is not affecting only the finished goods that are available. All one has to do is look up the supply chain to the source of the raw materials that are the genesis of most goods and materials. From the most fundamental resources such as water and wood, to the most enjoyable resources such as cocoa for chocolate, to the most exotic materials for telecommunications devices, supplies are diminishing and will continue to diminish at alarming rates unless something is done soon. Chapter 2 will address the issue in depth and how this demand will challenge nearly all supply chains, but a brief preview here will begin building a stronger case for the need for a new, more sustainable strategy.

Quenching a Global Thirst

In the 2012 UN MDG report, much attention was directed to one of the most critical goals: broad use of safe drinking water. The report indicates that while 19 percent of the rural population of the developing world used unimproved sources of water in 2010, the rate in urban areas was only 4 percent. However, the report further indicates that since safety, reliability, and sustainability are not factored into tracking progress on this goal, it is likely that these percentages overestimate the number of people using safe water supplies. Worse, nearly half the population in the developing world—*2.5 billion people*—still lacks access to improved sanitation like toilets and proper bathing facilities. With rapid urbanization on the horizon, safe drinking water and sanitation become critical to a healthy and strong populace and global workforce.

Industry and manufacturing are the greatest competitors for fresh drinking water in the world today. Manufacturing, energy, and production must compete for a share of water not used in agriculture, drinking, or sanitation. When water is permanently polluted in the manufacturing process, the total clean water available—whether on the surface or below ground—is reduced. The need for water in agriculture will grow in developing nations, even if agriculture becomes more sustainable and productive throughout the world. The hidden competition for water among industry sectors anywhere in a food-related supply chain will become intense throughout the century.

The 2012 UN MDG report also indicated that progress in diminishing food deprivation had slowed or been reduced in many regions of the world. In fact, even though there have been dramatic improvements in moving people out of abject poverty, undernourishment rates—especially in sub-Saharan Africa and in Southern Asia (outside of India)—have not improved. Nearly one-fifth of children in the developing world remain undernourished. The battle for water is under way and with a growing population may very well become a battle for life.

Water is an undervalued resource. It sustains our people, it irrigates our crops, it cools our machines, it helps produce our energy, it creates our refreshment drinks, and it nourishes our animals. In short, freshwater is the most valuable of all resources on the planet. We often limit our thinking about water usage to drinking, cooking, and agriculture, but it is the factories and offices that will create an ever growing need for water as these engines of production attempt to meet the demand of the massive population of the mid-twenty-first century.

Supplying the Raw Materials

In his landmark 1970 book *Future Shock*, Alvin Toffler predicted that developing nations might very well leapfrog over mature technologies and use new and emerging technologies in ways previously unheard of. Nothing proves this theory more than the use of cellular phone technology. The 2012 UN MDG report indicates that in 2011, more than 75 percent of mobile cellular subscriptions were in developing regions, up from 59 percent in 2005. In sub-Saharan Africa, mobile cellular penetration is 50 percent, while landlines are at only 1 percent! The International Telecommunications Union (ITU) 2012 statistical report confirms this growth. For consideration, in 2011:

- Mobile cellular subscriptions reached a global penetration of 86 percent
- 80 percent of the 660 million new subscriptions were in the developing world
- 142 million new subscribers were added in India alone
- 144 million broadband subscribers were added in the BRICS (Brazil, Russia, India, China, and South Africa), which is 45 percent of total global subscription growth
- 105 countries—including nations such as Botswana, Namibia, and Gabon—had more cellular subscriptions than inhabitants[15]

This increased use will drive greatly increased demand for the materials used to manufacture these products. Chapter 2 highlights the challenges in finding and accessing the raw materials to meet this demand—not the rosiest of futures for the information and communications technology (ICT) field, or for any other industry sector. The sources are few, and the locations are volatile, from both an economic point of view and a governance point of view. Regardless of the associated technology business, a clear understanding is required of the trade-offs and "deals" that have to be brokered to ensure some sort of supply in the future, and this brokering will challenge business ethics.

Outsourcing—What About Accountability and Ethics?

No doubt, the supply chains spanning the globe today will only stretch further in the years to come. Constant vigilance and negotiation will be required to ensure that these supplies are readily available. However, a challenge that continues to grow is deciding who is ethically responsible for the work done by suppliers in other parts of the world. This question, or the lack of a suitable response, has made headlines for years.

GREG—In 2007, while I was in Singapore for my association, I was asked to be a subject matter expert on CNBC regarding a dilemma involving Mattel. That year, there were seven Mattel product recalls (toys) due to quality and safety problems.[16] All seven recalled toys were manufactured in China as part of Mattel's outsourcing processes. Mattel, by the way, had been outsourcing in Asia since 1959, and by 2007, more than 65 percent of its toys were manufactured in China. By most measures, Mattel was a very successful outsourcer.

Mattel's initial response to the recalls was to blame China, and frankly, the press tried to do the same. When I was asked about the so-called outsourcing responsibility, I was compelled to answer with the question, "Who owns the brand?" As I saw it, the responsibility sat squarely in Mattel's executive suite—a view later shared by Mattel's leadership. Mattel's products could be outsourced, but not Mattel's brand—and it was the brand that was tarnished by the situation. Mattel had become somewhat complacent due to its very significant success, and the company failed to maintain due diligence in supplier inspections. In many cases, Mattel allowed its trusted suppliers to do their own inspections.

This is not new, nor is it a surprise. Today the question focuses on where responsibility for the brand ends. Also, does that responsibility involve only product quality and safety, or does it also involve the way that employees are treated?

Apple, Inc. is one of the most remarkable ICT companies in the world. The successes of its iPod, iPad, iPhone, and Mac computers have become legend in the industry. In the interest of full disclosure, Greg, like millions across the globe, owns an iPod, iPad, iPhone, and an Apple Mac Pro. In 2012, Apple stock prices hit an all-time high for any company in the history of publicly traded firms—valued for a time at nearly US$750 billion!

To produce these millions and millions of products, Apple—like many of its industry competitors—outsources some manufacturing and final assembly to Asia, Africa, and Latin America. In 2011, a problem surfaced that affected not only Apple but also its competitors. Specifically, the problem involved the quality of work-life practices at Foxconn, a provider of inexpensive, high-quality labor used to produce, manufacture, and assemble, among other ICT products, the iPad and iPhone product lines. Though Foxconn was founded and headquartered in Taiwan, the company has factories throughout the world. Fifteen of the world's largest ICT providers had outsourced the assembly and manufacturing of many of their products to Foxconn.

To some extent, many of these providers viewed Foxconn as responsible for the care and well-being of its employees. Typically, some of these client firms (but not all) have supplier codes of conduct and ethics, and they ask that contractors be responsible for maintaining their policies in accordance with the codes. It is up to the clients to verify compliance, but many do not.

In early 2011, the Foxconn factory in Chengdu, China, was targeted by two different Chinese fair labor practice NGOs for safety violations, employee suicides, and an explosion that killed three employees.[17] Unfortunately, Apple did not react quickly and publicly enough, and the problem went viral when employees at the plant began tweeting and publishing reports of problems on the Internet.

Apple was forced to act—and acted aggressively. Apple was also forced to provide a list of its outsourcing providers, and all of Foxconn's other ICT contracts were also vulnerable. The public's reaction to these events has shifted accountability for compliance with supplier codes from the outsourcing providers to their clients, and has created a need for companies to be transparent about such activities. The novel element of this situation is that the NGOs were Chinese nationals investigating labor practices in their own country, and the entire affair became public through social media, which served as the whistle-blowers' tool to reach the public.

With social media, it is now virtually impossible to keep a problem of this magnitude quiet.

THE DOUBLE MEANING OF SUSTAINABILITY

We hope that this first chapter grabbed your attention and set up the *why* when you're considering a new strategy for your company. However, it is important for us to reiterate that this book—and more specifically, this chapter—is not intended to be a harbinger of doom. This book is intended to be an eye-opener, representing the contours of the playing field for your organization in the future. More so, we hope this book can help you develop a long-term strategy for your organization that will help maintain marketplace sustainability well into the twenty-first century while creating a strategy that is inextricably linked to survivability and sustainability for communities and the planet.

As we researched the book, it became clear that the *why* was attacking the very core of a company's strategy. The traditional model of sustainability was for a company to continue to maintain a lead in market share while providing the necessary return on investment to its stockholders and its board. Over the last three decades, companies have moved beyond the economic qualifier for success and have added environmental qualifiers. For some companies, sustainability has been about minimal compliance with regulations, while for other companies, it has been about creating a mission that would not be harmful to the planet.

Still other companies pursue sustainability with the "triple bottom line," as first defined by John Elkington in his book of the same name. The triple bottom line involves a strategy that somehow embraces social responsibility in the day-to-day operation of a business. For some companies, this means contributing funds or workers' time to a worthy cause; for others, it means recycling plastics; and for others, it means building an organization that creates real and continuing value in the world.

Today, however, there is an evolving fourth element of sustainability that must be addressed in all aspects of business: the ethics of strategy.

Like it or not, organizations today are custodians of the public trust. People expect companies to do the right thing, to protect their interests, and to provide safety and quality in the products and services they offer. Protection of this trust is watched over and reported on by all measures and types of stakeholders through broadcast, print, and social media. We are all reporters, we are all whistle-blowers, and we are all responsible.

This means that successful companies of the future will have an integrated strategy, driven by a mission, that meets all of these criteria:

- *Social responsibility.* The company will open its doors to a new stakeholder mentality, starting internally with its own labor force, the supply of future labor, the communities supporting the creation of the organization, and most important, the global social fabric of which we are all a part.
- *Economic performance.* The company must generate surplus money to support and maintain its investors, its employees, and its enterprise, and it must reduce costs and eliminate waste—not only in the office or on the shop floor but also throughout its supply chain, in partnership with all of its suppliers.
- *Environmental responsibility.* The company must focus on protecting the environment in all that it does throughout its value and supply chains, whether in the direct investment in products and services or in the creation of the indirect infrastructure to support the creation of value in its product and service line, including the utilization of raw materials and the removal of carbon from the atmosphere.
- *Ethical behavior.* Finally, the company will thrive on extreme transparency and accountability to a set of stakeholders far larger than the traditional list of stakeholders and customers. It will have to define its brand by ethical behavior throughout its value and supply chain, not just in the internal processes that define its direct work content.

There are many people in the world who genuinely believe that our efforts to date are sufficient and that innovation will solve the problems of the world. There is no question that much progress has been made. However, the real question is when is enough, enough? It is well beyond the scope of this or any one book to highlight all of the initiatives, regulations, and laws that have contributed to the better world that we live in. Instead, we would like to refer to one of the most noted and profound studies done to project the impact of people on the planet.

In 1970, a man by the name of Jay W. Forrester, considered by many to be the father of system dynamics, quietly received a project contract to conduct a study called "Limits to Growth" for the Club of Rome. The Club of Rome is a global think tank founded in 1968 that deals with a variety of international political issues, and it sponsors and conducts research on root causes of the crises facing the world, particularly in growth, development, and globalization.

Forrester gathered some of the great systems thinkers of the time, including Dennis L. Meadows, Donella II. Meadows, and Jørgen Randers. The team developed a computer model for analyzing population and urban growth, current and future demands on the planet and its resources, and potential future scenarios. The results of the study were published in 1972 in a book titled *Limits to Growth*—the first landmark study on the subject.

Since that time, four 10-year updates have examined the progress made on the planet. The last living author is Randers. His recent book, *2052: A Global Forecast for the Next Forty Years*, looks ahead and provides "an educated guess," in his words, as to where we will end up in 2052.[18] He looked back at the original Limits to Growth study and highlighted the conclusions. At the time, the group's main conclusion was that "without big changes, humanity would grow dangerously beyond the physical limits of the planet."[19] But the required changes would take time: time to recognize that the problem is real, time to come up with realistic solutions, and time to implement those solutions. Even though the clock was ticking, consider that it took nearly 30 years before the United Nations could bring business and government leaders together to develop a set of global goals (the previously mentioned Millennium Development Goals) to coordinate action.

Though it presents a different picture and forecast than the original study, *2052* does not promise a happy future. Randers characterizes his view of the future as "gloomy."[20] In fact, his projection indicates that we may very well overshoot our use of planetary resources, like overfishing streams and oceans. We can do it for a while, but it will eventually cause irreparable damage. He believes that we need to consider different paradigms about the way the world will operate—different underlying principles. In short, we need to think differently about our future 40 years from now.

We remain optimistic that business and industry can still make a difference, in ways that can have a significant impact on the future of planetary resources, while still thriving in business. Hundreds of organizations are already succeeding along these lines. Later in this book, we will present examples of large and small organizations alike. Size doesn't matter; the actions in this book are scalable and actionable regardless of how challenging they may seem. As you will see, partnerships are the rule. You don't have to change alone, since this challenge affects all of us, competitor and partner alike.

Corporate sustainability is not about perfection but rather about deliberate progress in an integrated fashion. Each year, hundreds of companies around the world "get it" and begin to change. We want this book to change your mindset by sharing some of the many examples of successful transformation across the globe and the skill set that many have adopted to make this strategic change. Finally, we want to provide you with the tools to assess and change your organization. This book is about a realistic approach to change. We believe this book can build hope that change is possible, and can present a new perspective on what hope looks like.

I am not an optimist in the sense that I believe everything
will go well. But neither am I a pessimist in the sense that I believe
everything will go wrong. I am hopeful. For without hope, there will be
no progress. Hope is as important as life itself.[21]
—Vaclav Havel

CHAPTER SUMMARY

This chapter has provided much food for thought. In review, these are some of the complexities you will be dealing with in the future:

- Growing population will be dramatically more urban and will require all of the trappings of an urban environment, competing for the same supply chains companies need to produce goods and services.
- A new global middle class, more than double the size of the middle class of today, is emerging, and it may well represent the majority of the population of 2050.
- Middle-class growth dominates in developing nations, particularly in China, Southern Asia, and Africa, and not in the traditional markets we know.
- This new middle class will create an unheard-of demand for goods and services, without the robust prosperity that has accompanied the traditional middle classes of the past. This may lead to broader ranges of price without sacrificing quality.
- This new middle-class market will be fluid, fragile, and in many cases still teetering on the edge of poverty.
- The combination of urbanization and this new middle class will place great strains on governments around the globe to provide the education and social welfare needed to support the population and future workforces of the world.
- From water to food to exotic raw materials, supply chains in the future will be taxed more than ever in human history, and they will require innovation and entrepreneurial responses that have never been seen before.
- Companies must and will change, in an integrated fashion, to support:
    - Social responsibility
    - Economic performance
    - Environmental responsibility
    - Ethical behavior

Chapter 2

Dwindling Supplies and Growing Demand

When the well's dry, we know the worth of water.
—Benjamin Franklin

NATHALIE—One of my passions is scuba diving. I have been diving all over the world for more than 15 years. Seventy percent of the planet is covered by water, and it is awe-inspiring to float around and admire an ecosystem where we humans cannot survive without technology.

In 2012, I spent eight days on the Nautilus Swell, a beautiful wooden dive boat converted from a 1912 tugboat. It was an amazing trip, exploring Alaska above water as well as below. Alaska definitely feels like the last frontier. The scenery is stunning and spectacular, with astounding wildlife. The country is rugged—some towns are reachable only by air or water—and large stretches are still unexplored. We watched crumbling glaciers, played around and on icebergs, soaked in hot springs, and observed feeding humpback whales, bald eagles, and running salmon. Underwater, the show continued: prehistoric-looking prowfish, lots of extremely colorful rockfish, basket stars with hundreds of small tentacles, playful Steller sea lions, impressive shipwrecks like the *Princess Sophia* and the *State of California*, and walls so covered with brightly colored corals that you can't touch a single square inch without touching something that is alive.

In the short time I have been diving, I have seen the changes in the aquatic ecosystem with my own eyes: fewer large predators, more bleached corals, foreign species replacing native species, floating trash "islands" the size of the state of Texas, pollution, diminishing visibility, shoreline erosion, toxic algae blooms, and much more. As a scuba diver with a passion for this planet, seeing this change hurts my heart. As a business owner, I might think, "This does not affect my business; why should I care or take action?" As a consumer, I might not like fish, so perhaps it doesn't affect me. However, the changes that are taking place on our planet, not only in our oceans but also in the air and on land, affect us all! This chapter explains how current patterns of consumption and production threaten your business's bottom line—and potentially its survival—unless we make significant strategic changes. It will also highlight examples of companies that made these strategic changes and the benefits they reaped.

As Chapter 1 explained, we are faced with a growing world population, a skyrocketing number of people in the middle class who will send consumption rates soaring globally, and an environment that is cracking under the pressure. If we continue down the current path, it is not a matter of *if* but *when* we will run out of resources to run our businesses and to support the population. Let's take a look at the state of several raw materials—some basic and some more exotic—used in most businesses and in our daily life.

ON THE ROAD TO SCARCITY

Of all the resources in the world, water is the most critical. Freshwater is essential for human life, agriculture, and industry. Without it we, and most of the animal and plant world, would not exist. Ninety-seven percent of the earth's water is in the ocean, and the ocean supplies almost all the water that falls on land as rain and snow. Of the approximately 3 percent that is freshwater, a little over three-quarters is frozen, 20 percent is inaccessible groundwater, and a mere 1 percent remains as accessible surface water (Figure 2.1).[1]

Most critically, the supply of freshwater on our planet is finite and irreplaceable. This means that when water gets contaminated by raw sewage, factories, power generation, or natural disasters, it must be cleaned or it is a threat to human, animal, and plant life. Desalinization is not an answer since desalination plants tend to be very energy intensive, adding

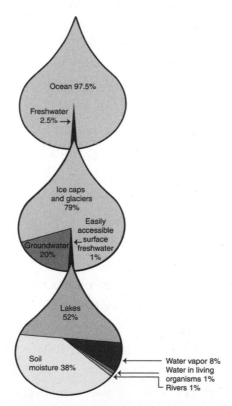

FIGURE 2.1 Earth has abundant water, but only a very small percentage of it is freshwater, and even less is easily available for human use. This figure shows the relative distribution of freshwater in terms of total water supply. Most communities get their water from river runoff and other surface water supplies (0.03 percent of the total planetary supply).

Source: AAAS Atlas of Population and Environment, http://atlas.aaas.org.

to the global warming problems of the world. In addition, the brine and chemical discharges from the plants negatively impact coastal water quality and marine life. The oceans are the source of livelihood for a significant portion of the people on this earth and are already under considerable stress from overfishing, pollution, invasive species, coastal habitat loss, and acidification. Large-scale desalination would only add to these stresses. Since we cannot create additional freshwater, it is even more critical to conserve the water we have.

Sadly, we are not good stewards of this scarce resource. Studies show that agriculture accounts for about 70 percent of global freshwater use each year.[2] Since the hydrological cycle is closed, this means that all other industries (manufacturing, energy, production, etc.) and the world population must compete for the rest. Agriculture is also a main contributor to water pollution from excess fertilizers, pesticides, and other pollutants. When water is polluted, the total clean water available, whether on the surface or below ground, is reduced. Agriculture is expected to produce even more food, feed, fuel, fibers, and building materials in the coming years to support the increasing world population and escalating consumption rates. Even if agriculture becomes more sustainable and productive throughout the world, the competition for water will become more intense during the century. Almost every industry and company will be impacted, either directly because agriculture is one of the ingredients or indirectly because they will need to fight over the remaining water.

Companies will have to actively manage their **water footprint** to protect their supply chains from future water scarcity, from the water needed by their raw materials to the water used in their factory operations. The water footprint is the volume of freshwater used to produce a product, measured over the full supply chain, from raw ingredients until it leaves the factory. It is a multidimensional indicator, showing water consumption by source and pollution amounts by type of pollution. The water footprint of a business consists of an equation of green, blue, and gray water. To produce goods and services, a business consumes a certain amount of the global green water resources (rainwater) and of the global blue water resources (surface water and groundwater). In the process, it creates a certain volume of polluted water (gray water).[3] A business can lower its water footprint by purifying the water used in the sourcing and production process and returning it to nature in an as clean or cleaner form than it was withdrawn.

Every company is dependent on water, either directly or indirectly. For those interested in the details of global water management, an excellent analysis is provided in the UN World Water Development Report *Managing Water under Uncertainty and Risk.* (UNESCO, 2012). In this book, we will focus on what companies can do to manage the risk to their supply chain.

Let's look at how this precious resource is linked to everything we do. Every time you turn on a light, you use water—and a lot of it. Yes, it sounds crazy, but without water, our energy and power generation systems would come to an abrupt stop. A recent study by the Virginia Water Resources Research Center in Blacksburg, Virginia, provides some startling statistics.[4] The study compared the water use for producing different fuels and different power generation methods. Just to give you an idea, the thermoelectric industry in the United States alone uses more than 132 billion gallons (almost 500 billion liters) of freshwater *each day* to produce electricity to meet the daily demand—enough to fill six million swimming pools.[5] This translates to 95 liters of water (about 25 gallons) to produce one kilowatt-hour of electricity—the electricity needed to keep a 60-watt incandescent lightbulb lit for about 18 hours!

Why so much? According to the study, "Water is used in many ways when producing fuels and power, including pumping crude oil out of the ground, helping remove pollutants from power plant exhaust, generating steam that turns turbines, flushing away residue after fossil fuels are burned, and keeping power plants cooled." Table 2.1 shows the differences in water use efficiency between different fuels and power generation methods. From a water efficiency point of view, nuclear power is one of the least efficient ways to generate power, due to the need for special cooling and steam turbines to produce the electricity. However, the most

TABLE 2.1 Water Use Efficiency of Power Generation and Fuel Sources

Fuel Source	Efficiency (Gallons/MBTU)	
	Low	High
Coal	41	164
Natural Gas	3	n/a
Petroleum/Oil	1,200	2,420
Corn-Ethanol	2,510	29,100
Soy-Biodiesel	14,000	75,000
Hydroelectric	20	n/a
Fossil Fuel Thermoelectric	1,100	2,200
Geothermal	130	n/a
Nuclear	2,400	5,800
Solar Thermoelectric	230	270
Hydrogen	143	243

Calculated water use efficiency for various energy sources. Water is used in a variety of ways for energy production, including mining of the source material, irrigation for biofuel crops, steam generation, coolants, cleaning, and more. Table 2.1 details the relative efficiency of various energy sources in terms of gallons of water used per one million BTUs (British Thermal Units).

Source: Virginia Water Resources Research Center.

surprising one is biodiesel. When you look at the full life cycle to grow and produce it, biodiesel becomes the least efficient way to produce energy.

In developed nations, regulations have been imposed on the power generation sector to protect and clean water used in the process. This has helped maintain a continued supply of fresh drinking water. But in the developing world, the attention to restoring gray (polluted, undrinkable) water to drinking water purity is not nearly as intense, and industry is far less heavily regulated. Any manufacturing or production plant that utilizes electricity is consuming water upstream in the so-called life cycle of power and should show interest in protecting it no matter where in the world the plant is located.

What about product-specific uses of water? Think of that nice, cold beer or soda you might enjoy on a hot day. The water footprint of one liter of soda is 338–618 liters, depending on where the sugar originates![6]

Anywhere from 61 to 180 liters of freshwater is needed for your nice, cold beer, depending on where the barley is grown.[7] The vast majority of the water footprint is not in the manufacturing factories or bottling plants. In fact, most modern bottling companies throughout the world have reduced the operational use of water to less than 10 liters per liter of final product.[8] When one looks at the entire supply chain, most of the water is used in the fields where ingredients like sugar, barley, rye, and tea are grown (99.7 percent to 99.8 percent). These numbers get contested at times if the agricultural footprint is shared with multiple product companies using the same agricultural supplier, but even if that is the case the numbers are still staggering. As mentioned earlier, agriculture is the single biggest consumer of water, so any industry that depends on it has a large water footprint and should actively assess and manage that footprint to limit supply chain disruptions.

The United Nations projects that two-thirds of the world's population will face water scarcity by 2025.[9] One reason not discussed yet is climate changes that could create more severe weather and disrupt rainfall patterns.

Feeling the Heat

Climate change is a real business risk. It causes extreme weather events, including excessive rainfall and extreme droughts, affecting agriculture yields, livelihoods, and supply chains. It causes significant changes in the forests around the globe, impacting their ability to photosynthesize and their overall health. It is changing both the temperature and acidity of our oceans, directly affecting marine life and world coral reefs.

NATHALIE—I grew up in the Netherlands, where more than one-quarter of the country is below sea level, so since my youth I have heard about the dangers of climate change and rising oceans. Though climate change has been contested for decades, even the staunchest opponents of the idea that the human race is heating up this planet have finally conceded and agree that we are, if not the sole cause, at least part of the cause. At the end of 2012, the World Bank released a report titled *Turn Down the Heat* that highlights the devastating effects of a temperature increase of just 4°C.[10] Four degrees might not seem like much, but it can create a vastly different world. During the last ice age, most of the northern hemisphere was frozen solid, and global mean temperatures were only 4.5–7°C (7–12°F) lower than today. The 4°C scenario is not a hypothetical analysis; it is a very likely reality by the end of this century if we continue down our current path.

When the average world temperature rises 4°C, sea levels are expected to rise between one-half and one meter, inundating coastal areas. Scientists believe more extreme heat waves will become the norm, increasing the number of wildfires. Many regions will have to deal with increased water scarcity while others will become wetter with more frequent floods, and more severe weather will affect more people all around the world. You only have to look at today's headlines to know this trend has already started. In 2012 part of Australia was experiencing major floods, forcing thousands of people to leave their homes, while other areas were parched and fighting bushfires because of severe rainfall deficiencies for at least nine months. That same year, the sea ice covering the Arctic fell to record lows not seen since satellite tracking began 33 years ago, igniting a political quarrel about who owns the oil rich soils under the once vast icepack and opening new Arctic shipping routes.

No matter who or what is causing it, the effects of a warmer earth will directly impact businesses and economies globally through increased frequency and severity of extreme weather events. The 2011 Thailand floods—the region's worst in 50 years—disrupted automotive, electronics, and retail supply chains all over the world, creating global part shortages.

In addition to disrupting supply chains through flooded factories or failed crops, the trends noted earlier—growing global population, increasing wealth in the developing world, and climate changes—could also cause several direct threats for businesses. Raw materials could become scarce due to crop losses caused by changing climates, or loss of arable land caused by rising oceans and changes in rainfall patterns. Local governments could hike prices or cut off supplies to foreign factories. Global reputations could be tarnished when local communities revolt against water shortages they perceive to be caused by factories. Coca-Cola experienced this firsthand in India, where local farmers blamed several Coca-Cola bottling factories for depleting groundwater and aggravating drought. One case still in Indian courts involves the Plachimada community in the Indian state of Kerala, which claimed that ever since a bottling plant was opened on their land in 2000, they have faced polluted and depleted groundwater, causing crops to fail. A scientific study has found even though the plant had "aggravated the water scarcity situation," the most significant factor was lack of rainfall.[11] Coca-Cola's reputation and brand, however, were damaged by this event, especially in India. Critics continue to question the ethics of locating bottling plants in drought-stricken areas. In March 2004, the local government decided to shut the plant down.

Supply chains could be further impacted by regional conflicts caused by large-scale migrations, which will take place when people are either forced to move because of permanent flooding or because the land can no longer support increasing demands for food due to depletion of the soil, water pollution, or water scarcity. The latest UN World Water Development Report (WWDR) highlights these challenges, indicating the immense threats posed by natural disasters.[12] Droughts, for example, strain agricultural production, leading to price increases and shortages of basic foods. Desertification, land degradation, and drought (DLDD) have already degraded, often irreversibly, nearly two billion hectares of land (nearly eight million square miles) worldwide—an area twice the size of China. Nearly 1.5 billion people live in DLDD-affected areas, putting them at risk of water insecurity and malnutrition.[13] The WWDR underscores other widespread effects of scarcity, including population displacement, disruption of livelihoods, regional conflicts, and health epidemics.

The Ethical Dilemma of Our Mobile World

The criticality of water, food, and agriculture is often discussed in the media. But there are other, less visible raw materials that we rarely talk about that are used in products our businesses and daily lives now depend on.

No matter where you are in the world today, almost everyone around you has a cell phone. In developed countries, some people even have two or three. The "ingredient" list of a cell phone reads like an alchemist's shopping list, with many precious metals most of us have never heard of (Table 2.2).

TABLE 2.2 Selected Rare Minerals Used in Cell Phone Manufacturing

Mineral	Use
Aluminum	Wiring on circuit boards, housings
Beryllium	Heat dissipation of conductors in electronics
Cobalt	Rechargeable batteries, coatings for hard disk drives
Copper	Conductors in electronics
Gallium	Integrated circuits, optical electronics, LEDs
Germanium	Transistor components
Gold	Solders, conductors, and connectors
Indium	LCDs, photovoltaic components
Iridium	Surface acoustic wave (SAW) filters
Lithium	Rechargeable batteries, surface acoustic wave (SAW) filters
Neodymium	Neodymium (NdFeB, NIB, Neo) magnets
Niobium	Microcapacitors
Palladium	Conductors in electronics
Platinum	Hard disk drives, TFT LCDs, etc.
Sapphire	LEDs
Silver	Wiring on circuit boards
Tantalum	Capacitors and conductors
Tin	Lead-free solders
Tungsten	Makes cell phones vibrate

This table lists just some of the minerals used in manufacturing cell phones and other electronics. Most of these are base chemical elements rarely found in native deposits. For example, lithium is usually extracted from brines and clays, and indium is obtained from zinc ores. Neodymium is a rare earth element, primarily mined in China. The familiar gemstone sapphire has a variety of industrial uses, though synthetic forms are sometimes used.

If you are old enough, you might remember the large bricks we used to carry around that we called cell phones. We have the rare metal tantalum to thank for the small phones we use today. Tantalum is extracted from the ore columbite-tantalite (coltan). It is virtually corrosion proof and is used in the manufacture of capacitors, which regulate voltage, store energy, and are used in many electronic devices. Tantalum is an extremely good conductor of both heat and electricity, so it can be used in small components and withstands pressure. This makes it ideal for phones and other small electronic devices such as handheld game consoles, laptops, and digital cameras.[14]

The rare earth elements (REEs) also fall into the category of most important raw materials you have never heard of. REEs are found in ores. Although plentiful in the earth, they are not concentrated in large enough quantities anywhere, hence the name "rare earth." Lanthanum, one of the rare earth elements, is critical in the manufacturing of modern batteries. Each Toyota Prius, for example, needs about 10 pounds of lanthanum for its nickel-metal hydride (NiMH) battery. Where is lanthanum in the NiMH? It is the "metal" in metal hydride and makes the battery one of the most powerful on the road. Another rare earth element—europium, a phosphor—was used in the cathode ray tubes (CRTs) in older TVs and computer monitors. Today, it is used in the manufacture of LED lighting. Erbium, another REE, is used as an amplifier in fiber optic technology to speed transmission of data along the line.[15]

As you read in Chapter 1, there is no doubt the demand for cell phones and low-priced electronics will grow exponentially along with the population and new global middle class. A 2010 article, "How a Handful of Countries Control the Supply of the Earth's Most Precious Resources," by Kate Rockwood, reemphasizes this point:

As our gadget dependency grows, so does our appetite for these bits of earth. In fact, demand for the 14 most-critical minerals for today's electronic technologies may as much as triple over the next 20 years, according to the European Commission. . . . "The era of access to easy resources is over," says mining analyst Paul Bugala of Calvert Investments.[16]

This growth brings varied challenges. Only 30 milligrams of tantalum are used in a cell phone. But with billions of cell phones currently in use (there were six billion cell phone subscribers, based on SIM card count, at the end of 2011)[17] and many more expected, that's a lot of tantalum. The primary sources of the metal have been Australia, Brazil, and Canada, but due to the growing demand (and thus price), the Democratic Republic of the Congo (DRC) and Saudi Arabia have become new suppliers. Unfortunately, the receipts from the sale of tantalum have been used to fund opposing sides in the DRC's civil war, which has killed more than five million people since 1998, marking DRC tantalum as a conflict mineral (similar to "blood diamonds"). Neighboring countries have also been accused of smuggling the metal out of the DRC.[18]

The REEs, on the other hand, present a different business problem. Ninety-five percent of the world's supply is from China. The reformist Chinese politician Deng Xiaoping once observed that these minerals are to China what oil is to Saudi Arabia. His comment seems to be more accurate than once believed. In 2010, China suddenly restricted the export of raw ore for REE, seemingly for political reasons. This restriction had an immediate impact on the global electronics industry and initiated a worldwide search for new REE sources.[19] Complicating the picture is the fact that rare earth deposits require extensive processing to yield usable ores. The extraction and purification process is waste-intensive and uses radioactive materials. Plants are often located in the developing world where there are less strict regulations of waste treatment, permanently impacting the environment and surrounding communities.

Organizations need to take these supply chain constraints and ethical issues into account when looking for raw materials. Even if your raw materials are plentiful right now, that can change suddenly due to political issues or an exponential increase in demand. In addition, companies should implement programs to recycle existing rare earth elements to help ensure a shortage-free transition to a reliable and sustainable international supply chain.

Replenishing Raw Materials

We've investigated the exotic raw materials mined from deep in the planet's crust. Now let's move back to the surface and look at a more traditional natural resource: wood. Since the beginning of humanity, forests have been a source of raw material for buildings, transportation, communication, and fuel for cooking. As Ahmed Djoghlaf, executive secretary of the Convention on Biological Diversity, said in the foreword of the 2009 *Forest Resilience, Biodiversity, and Climate Change* report:

> The world's forest ecosystems provide environmental services that benefit, directly or indirectly, all human communities, including watershed protection, regional climatic regulation, fibre, food, drinking water, air purification, carbon storage, recreation, and pharmaceuticals.[20]

Continent after continent, forests have succumbed to population growth. According to the UN's Food and Agriculture Organization (FAO), over 13 million hectares (30 million acres) of forests are destroyed by human activity every year.[21] Leading causes are illegal logging, poor forest management practices, growing demand for forest and agricultural products, and human-related fires. The destruction of the world's remaining forests is a major concern. The world's rainforests are said to be the source of more than one-third of Earth's oxygen, the remainder being produced by the world's oceans.[22]

Aside from the direct problems caused by deforestation—flooding, loss of nutrient-rich soil, desertification ("persistent degradation of dryland ecosystems by human activities . . . and by climate change"[23]), biodiversity extinctions, and deaths during land disputes caused by illegal logging—wood is also a main raw material for many industries such as housing, furniture, transportation, sanitation, paper, clothing, art, and musical instruments. These industries compete with approximately two billion people who still depend on wood to cook and preserve their food. Additionally, forests play an important role in the global carbon cycle. After our oceans, forests are the biggest absorbers of carbon dioxide. Deforestation is a double whammy; it leaves fewer trees to provide oxygen, and removing the trees releases stored carbon back into the atmosphere.

Population growth, urbanization, water scarcity, and the changing climate are all affecting the world's forests by increasing the demand for wood and reducing the available supply. In addition, we should expect that a sustainable global economy will use more wood for energy, shelter, and an increasing array of products. This is possible only if we practice sustainable forest management.

Forestry has been practiced for thousands of years. Sustainably managed forests can redirect demand from nonrenewable rainforest hardwoods to renewable, sustainable supplies. In addition, sustainably managed forests provide benefits such as clean air and water, wildlife habitat, and sometimes recreation opportunities.

Our businesses are dependent on these and many more raw materials. The simple reality is that supplies are dwindling or getting harder to extract or grow. To deal with these decreasing supplies, organizations need to preserve and closely manage their full value and supply chains. Organizational supply chains are complex, and many organizations do not look further than their direct suppliers. However, a full supply chain is a complex system of organizations, people, technology, activities, information, and resources. All players in this chain should work together to ensure sustainability.

Organizations are in the best position to drive the necessary change, since they have the financial leverage and reach as well as the need to secure their own sustainability and survival. In the process, organizations will also guarantee the sustainability of our planet.

THE PATH TO CHANGE

As we have seen, a paradigm shift is needed. Organizations must be responsible for managing their full value and supply chains, from the very first ingredient necessary to create the product until after the product is discarded. They need to manage and ensure their supply chains are sustainable. It is not just a matter of being eco-friendly; it will be a matter of long-term financial viability and, for some companies, of survival. If you are not convinced by now of the need to change, maybe you will be convinced by the benefits.

The *Supply Chain Report 2012* by the Carbon Disclosure Project (CDP) has identified four key benefits of managing the full supply chain to become more sustainable (Figure 2.2):[24]

- Reduced risks from minimizing the supply chain disruptions
- Lower costs due to energy efficiencies and collaborative activities
- New revenue opportunities because of innovations or finding new markets
- Better brand positioning, since today's customers are prepared to pay a premium for sustainable products

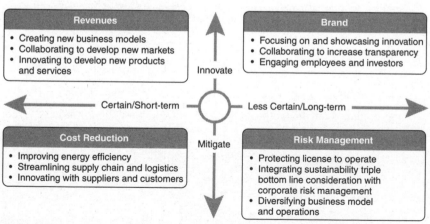

FIGURE 2.2 Active supply chain management not only reduces organizational risks and costs, it also improves revenue opportunities and brand positioning.

Source: Carbon Disclosure Project with Accenture, *CDP Supply Chain Report 2012*, 5.

Companies that have already made this paradigm shift have changed their business models to incorporate sustainability into their strategy, thus driving innovation and long-term change along the entire value chain. We will look at two examples in more detail: the cocoa industry and the retail industry.

Cocoa: Feeding the Sweet Tooth

NATHALIE—I love chocolate. Real chocolate, that is—the kind with at least 70 percent cocoa. Cocoa originates from the river valleys of the Amazon and the Orinoco in South America. Today, West Africa is the largest supplier of cocoa, accounting for 70 percent of global cultivation.[25] About 60 percent of the world's cocoa is used in chocolate products, with the remaining 40 percent used for a range of bakery, confectionery, and beverage products.[26]

Cocoa production is plagued with issues touching all four axes of the SEEE model, including poor health and safety measures (social), poor payment of the farmers and uncertain property rights (economic), and depleted soils because of bad agriculture techniques (environmental), not to mention child labor and poor safety measures (ethical).[27] The cocoa supply chain is complex. Before I can enjoy that lovely chocolate bar, families on mainly small farms grow the cocoa beans in faraway tropical countries, often in bad labor situations. Intermediaries buy the cocoa beans from the farmers, and sometimes after many intermediaries, the cocoa arrives at the cocoa processors who process the beans into cocoa powder or butter, which is then sold to the chocolate manufacturers. The final product then finds its way through distributors and wholesalers to retailers where we, the consumers, buy it. The cocoa supply chain involves anybody who plays a role in producing chocolate. There are many more links in the supply chain than I just described (see Figure 2.3).

Due to increasing demand—especially in markets where there is an emerging middle class, like China—and constrained supply caused by political unrest, unsustainable agriculture practices, and low income for

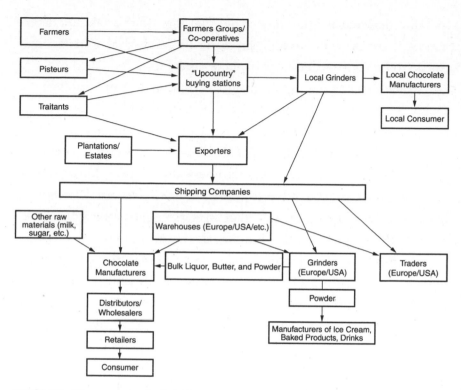

FIGURE 2.3 The cocoa supply chain is extremely complex. Before the cocoa reaches the end consumer, it travels through many hands in many different countries.

Source: Information from a variety of cocoa industry sources, esp. Federation of Cocoa Commerce.

farmers who cannot invest in long-term improvements or convince their children to enter the business, cocoa prices have been rising steadily over the last decade. Some of this money finds its way back to the farmer, but not enough to provide a solid living.

In the last several years a paradigm shift has taken place within the cocoa industry. Several cocoa and chocolate companies, including Mars and Unilever, which manufactures Magnum and Ben & Jerry's ice creams, have started to manage their full supply chain. They recognized the extreme risk their supply chain is under and the potential impact on their business if the children of cocoa farmers pursue a living in the city and refuse to take over the business because the families are so poor, or if the soil is so depleted and the trees so old that they don't produce a decent harvest.[28] And of course no company wants illegal child labor in its supply chain. Today's consumers simply will not accept it.

To make the cocoa supply chain sustainable, all participants in the supply chain have to collaborate. It starts with the supply chain companies and manufacturers that have the financial strength to make a real difference. In the cocoa industry, cooperation began in the cocoa trade associations, especially the World Cocoa Foundation, where decisions were made to invest in ways to increase farm productivity, reduce the incidence of cocoa pests and diseases, and train farmers in good agricultural practices. Everything starts with educating the farmers to provide them the tools and skills they need to make their farms more sustainable and their businesses more financially viable. This improves not only the cocoa bean quality but also the quality of life in the local communities and the prosperity of local farmers because yield is increased. One key technique used is certification of cocoa producers. Certification ensures that farmers do not use child labor, do use sustainable farming methods, and receive a fair price for their produce. A 2012 research report showed that certified farmers in Côte d'Ivoire were receiving higher yields and higher revenue from their cocoa crops compared to similar noncertified small-scale farmers.[29]

Unilever set itself a goal to source cocoa sustainably for its Magnum ice cream by 2015 and for all other products by 2020. Unilever works with the Rainforest Alliance, Fairtrade International, and Unilever suppliers to help certify new farmers. Let's take the Rainforest Alliance relationship as an example. The Rainforest Alliance certifies cocoa according to the Sustainable Agriculture Network (SAN) standards. These standards cover ecosystem conservation, worker rights and safety (including the prohibition of child labor), wildlife protection, water and soil conservation, agrochemical reduction, decent housing, and legal wages and contracts for workers. Unilever pays the farmers a premium for cocoa beans that are certified sustainable.[30]

The cocoa industry is also attacking social and ethical problems. In 2002, the International Cocoa Initiative (ICI) charitable foundation was established through a partnership between nongovernmental organizations (NGOs), trade unions, and the chocolate industry. ICI works toward eliminating the worst forms of child labor and forced labor on cocoa farms and for chocolate production. The foundation was the result of active campaigns by concerned consumers and NGOs targeting the chocolate industry to eliminate child and forced labor from its supply chains. This activism led to the Harkin-Engel Protocol, an industry-wide agreement signed in 2001 with the goal of putting an end to forced child labor in chocolate by 2005, which in turn led to the founding of the ICI.[31] Some of the largest players in the cocoa industry are founding members, including Archer Daniels Midland, Cargill, Ferrero, Hershey Foods, Mars Incorporated, and Nestlé. The ICI has lowered the percentage of child labor in the Côte d'Ivoire and Ghana, increased awareness, improved access to education for children, and provided access to basic services like healthcare, water, and sanitation.

The results of this paradigm shift in the cocoa industry have been significant. The education and certification of the farmers brings economic, social, and environmental benefits. It starts with the farmers getting a premium price for their products, but more important, their new knowledge allows them to improve the quality and yield of their products, providing long-term economic benefits. Social and ethical benefits include prohibition of child labor, better labor situations, and health benefits. The environment benefits from sustainable agriculture practices that result in healthy soil, clean water, and no deforestation. Companies minimize the risks to their supply chain since they are actively managing it from the first ingredient to the last, guaranteeing quality and future supplies. In addition, they are able to receive premium prices for certified sustainable products.

The key lessons from the success of the cocoa industry are:

- *It is a joint effort* by everyone involved in the value chain. Key players in improving the sustainability of the cocoa supply chain include the cocoa suppliers, manufacturers, nonprofit conservation certification organizations, local farmers, local traders, local governments, local NGOs, trainers, auditors, and many more.

- *Companies drive the change* by committing to source only sustainable resources and realize this commitment by (1) providing and financing education and tools and (2) tracking local community impacts on all four SEEE axes (Social, Economic, Environmental, Ethical), including health, education, women's empowerment, family welfare, farm performance, and protection of the environment.

Of course there are still many challenges. One is diversification. The Côte d'Ivoire is the world largest cocoa producer, producing approximately 40 percent of the world's supply of cocoa, but the country is extremely unstable and faces many social issues such as child labor and unequal rights for women. World supplies of cocoa were disrupted in 2011 when a civil war broke out in Côte d'Ivoire, and at the end of 2012, the Côte d'Ivoire government was dissolved. So there is definitely a need for diversification.

Retail: Darth Vader Goes Green

Even if you are not a manufacturer but a reseller, there is a lot your organization can do. Walmart has a lot of critics, and it definitely has a lot of room to improve on the Social and Ethical axes of our SEEE model; however, the company has been revolutionary on the Environmental axis within the retail sector. In 2005, Walmart set goals to be supplied 100 percent by renewable energy, to create zero waste, and to sell products that sustain the world's resources and environment. As in the other industry examples, the key to success was cooperating with all stakeholders in the supply chain, including NGOs, regulators, and supplier firms. Walmart quickly realized that it had no way to measure if it was on track to meet its goal, so in 2009 Walmart introduced the concept of its Supplier Sustainability Assessment (SSA), which is a scorecard used by buyers to assess a product's or supplier's carbon footprint. This assessment set a trend in the retail business.

At the same time, Walmart provided funding to create The Sustainability Consortium (TSC), a consortium of universities, suppliers, retailers, NGOs, and governments that aims to develop a global retail standard for assessing product sustainability. Using the research done by this consortium, Walmart released new sustainability requirements in 2012. The objective is to work with suppliers to identify opportunities within the supply chain so Walmart can eliminate 20 million metric tons of greenhouse gas emissions from its supply chain by the end of 2015. One of its apparel suppliers was able to save 71 percent in annual energy costs by implementing energy efficiency practices identified in the assessment.[32] (For more about Walmart's sustainability journey, see Chapter 6.)

Walmart has used its size and market position to revolutionize the retail industry's approach to sustainability. There are roughly 100,000 companies—from giants like P&G to small suppliers—that now need to make their own processes and products more sustainable if they want to continue to sell to Walmart. Of course the upside is that by doing so, they will eliminate inefficiencies from their own supply chains and lower their production costs.

> *We can't solve problems by using the same kind of thinking*
> *we used when we created them.*
> —ALBERT EINSTEIN

CHAPTER SUMMARY

No matter what industry you are in, you will be impacted by the changes that are already in motion, which include:

- Global climate change impacting supply chains by affecting (to name a few) agriculture, water supplies, ocean acid levels, and extreme weather events.
- Availability of freshwater because of the growing world population and a growing consumer demand for products.

- Scarcity of raw materials driven by growing demand and by limited supplies and reduction in supplies due to changing weather patterns or polluted soils or oceans.

As the examples in this chapter show, within the reality of dwindling supplies and growing demands, organizations that work toward a sustainable value and supply chain reap profound benefits. They lower the risk of supply chain disruptions, identify new revenue opportunities, improve their market position by improving their brand image with customers, and lower their overall costs through supply chain efficiencies. As Chapter 8 will show, it pays to be a value-based company.

Several things are required to successfully make the supply chain sustainable:

- Clear, measurable sustainability goals
- Cooperation between all stakeholders involved in the supply chain
- Protection of scarce and fragile resources
- A standardized system to measure progress and sustainability
- Local resolution of issues in partnership with NGOs, local governments, communities, and local businesses

Sustainable supply chain management is not an option. Rather, it is necessary for business continuation and growth. As the list above indicates, there are many actions that companies can take to minimize the risks to their supply chains and improve the sustainability of the planet at the same time. Recognize that you cannot do it alone no matter how large or small you are. Sustainability is a team sport involving companies, local communities, NGOs, government, and even competitors. No company can do it alone, but one person can initiate the change.

Companies have the ability to change the path we are on and create a sustainable planet. As Chapter 3 will show, your customers, communities, and society at large are expecting it.

RELUCTANT CARETAKERS OF PUBLIC TRUST

How can the people trust the harvest, unless they see it sown?
—AUTHOR MARY RENAULT (1905–1983), IN *THE KING MUST DIE*

GREG—On a recent trip to New York City, I decided to make the trek to the Apple retail store at the southeast corner of Central Park. I wanted to see what the Midtown Manhattan store looked like and compare it to other stores I had seen around the country.

The store swelled with people viewing and handling every conceivable Apple product. Literally hundreds of people were streaming in and out or looking at products, especially the latest iPad. I have to admit, as an engineer, I considered the iPad a work of art. The entire experience was amazing. I own four Apple products, so it was very interesting to see how the world continued to react to the release of this new device.

But in spite of Apple's wow factor, the company tested my loyalty once again. In Chapter 1, we discussed the challenge that Apple faced with one of its suppliers (Foxconn) in China. Apple responded quickly, hiring the

Fair Labor Association to do an independent investigation, and revised the contract with Foxconn based on the results of the investigation to ensure that future work conditions and labor practices in Chengdu would be better. Apple also published its list of suppliers and made available its supply chain code of conduct. Tim Cook, CEO of Apple, personally visited two of the China-based Foxconn facilities in one year to show his commitment to addressing the problem. Apple proved that it was listening.

However, within three months, Apple faced another challenge. Newer Apple computer designs did not fit neatly into the Electronic Product Environmental Assessment Tool (EPEAT) standards. After a series of disagreements stemming from a dispute over the manner in which the battery in certain Apple computers was recycled, Apple dropped its products from the voluntary certification.[1]

Customer response was swift. In a press release, Bob Mansfield, Apple's senior vice president of hardware engineering, stated that the company "heard from many loyal Apple customers who were disappointed" in the change.[2] Probably the most significant customer complaints came from municipal and state governments, whose acquisition specifications sometimes require EPEAT certification. The City of San Francisco, for example, said it would drop Apple from its preferred supplier list since the city can buy only EPEAT certified equipment.[3] Although Apple computers represented only about 1 percent of the computers purchased by the city, San Francisco's policy was a harbinger of other possible boycotts. Universities across the country also began to consider dropping Apple computers. Since nearly 15 percent of Apple's sales are to educational institutions, this could have hurt the company financially. Just days later, Apple reversed its decision.

Even though Apple responded promptly, the company's reputation may have been harmed by the incident. In November 2011, Greenpeace ranked Apple fourth in its Guide to Greener Electronics, up from ninth the previous year. In November 2012, it slipped to sixth.[4] Will these events continue to slowly erode Apple's reputation? Was Apple's temporary rejection of EPEAT a knee-jerk reaction based on political disagreements, or was it merely an uninformed decision?

I believed at the time—and I continue to believe—that Apple is a great company that, like many others, is finding that the path to becoming a sustainable global company may get tougher in the future. But Apple's recent behavior made me think about the relationship between ethics, trust, and company values. Luckily, shortly after Apple's EPEAT controversy, I had the opportunity to spend time with Dr. Harold Kerzner, senior executive director at International Institute for Learning and a personal mentor, as well as a well-respected author and consultant on strategy deployment and business execution. Our conversation focused on the subject of ethics and trust. We discussed issues related to public trust of companies and how far down (or up) the executive chain of command decisions should be made regarding a breach of public trust or ethics. We discussed many scenarios and personal experiences. Surprisingly, our mutual conclusion was that there isn't a right or wrong answer but rather that what is most important is the conversation about public trust, values, and ethics, which should be conducted with executives in every company and deployed throughout organizations. In the unlikely event a breach of public trust occurs, a company should be ready to act, and act quickly, to repair the damage. Call it "exercising the ethics muscle."

As I said, I believe Apple is a great company with a remarkable product line and a great service model. But like thousands of other companies, Apple is still finding its way in this very transparent and open global marketplace. Here's the question: is there a direct relationship between public trust and the value of a company as well as the sale of its products and services?

THE SHAPING OF PUBLIC TRUST

The last several years have seen many significant errors in business judgment and ethics, some of them far more damaging than those faced by Apple. The millennium began with the bursting of the dot-com bubble followed quickly by the Enron scandal and the resulting Sarbanes-Oxley Act, the 2008 collapse of the global financial sector and the housing bubble, the post-tsunami Fukushima Daiichi nuclear disaster, repeated controversies involving conflict minerals and materials, and a lack of sufficient consideration for the value of humanity in global supply chains. All of these problems have led to a gradual erosion of trust in business and government.

Some leaders are optimistic that they will get over these problems like they've gotten over other problems in the past. But things may have changed. It appears that, especially in business, a lack of trust leads to buyer rejection, or buyers deciding to boycott a product or to opt for a competitor's product. Product quality and performance alone no longer determine a buyer's decision. Never before has there been clearer evidence that consumers and stakeholders around the globe expect companies to "do the right thing." And doing the right thing seems to include the way companies treat and build relationships with employees, the environment, society, and communities. Whether organizations realize this fact yet or even appreciate its importance, they have become the reluctant caretakers of public trust.

Trust and Buyer Decisions

The 2012 Edelman Trust Barometer provided great insight into one of the most important drivers of strategic change. Since 2000, Edelman Communications has been assessing and analyzing the perceptions of intelligent, global consumers and business professionals regarding trust in business, government, and other institutions. The 2012 study led Richard Edelman to clarify a growing trend. He concluded from the survey results that businesses can no longer act solely in their own self-interest but must execute on both profit and societal good.[5] His conclusion was based on the observation that half of the 25,000 respondents (49 percent) felt that government doesn't regulate business enough. But, surprisingly, what stakeholders wanted was more consumer protection and responsible corporate behavior, actions that can be provided by businesses without any government regulation. In short, the public was wary and mistrustful of business and believed that government intervention was necessary to ensure the "right thing" was done.

The 2013 results released in conjunction with the World Economic Forum confirmed this impression. In his executive summary, Edeleman wrote:

> Business must embrace a new mantra: move beyond earning the License to Operate—the minimum required standard—toward earning a License to Lead—in which business serves the needs of shareholders and broader stakeholders by being profitable and acting as a positive force in society.[6]

Edelman further concludes that in order to earn the "License to Lead," an organization must:

- Establish a vision and transparently share reasoning, purpose, and results
- Enlist a broader range of advocates, including employees, action consumers, social activists, academics, and think tanks, seeking their input and reaction
- Embrace all channels of communications, actively listening to new voices of influence, and adapting
- Shift from vision to implementation with transparent measures guided by continual engagement

Edelman's findings tell us that our future leadership must be different in order for the public to trust business. For both publicly traded and privately held companies, public trust is critical to survival. Transparency, broad stakeholder engagement, and accountability are hallmarks of those companies that will be able to sustain themselves in the future. Clearly, gaining public trust in the future is going to require a different approach than it has in the past.

The Critical Importance of Trust

Reading Edelman's summary, we wanted to know which characteristics or attributes matter most. Digging deeper into the survey, we found a list of 16 attributes most important to building trust (Table 3.1).

As in 2012, there has been a shift in what the respondents considered most important. The 16 attributes fall into five categories:

- Engagement
- Integrity
- Products and services
- Purpose
- Operations

TABLE 3.1   Edelman Trust Barometer Attributes for Building Trust

16 Attributes for Building Trust
• Listens to customer needs and feedback
• Treats employees well
• Places customers ahead of profits
• Communicates frequently and honestly on the state of its business
• Has ethical business practices
• Takes responsible actions to address an issue or crisis
• Has transparent and open business practices
• Offers high-quality products or services
• Innovator of new products, services, or ideas
• Works to protect and improve the environment
• Addresses society's needs in its everyday business
• Creates programs that positively impact the local community
• Partners with NGOs, governments, and third parties to address societal needs
• Has highly regarded and widely admired top leadership
• Ranks on a global list of top companies
• Delivers consistent financial returns to investors

The 2013 Edelman Trust Barometer highlights "16 specific attributes which build trust" in a business. The attributes are organized into five "performance clusters" (not indicated here).

Source: 2013 Edelman Trust Barometer Executive Summary, 9.

Most important, three of the categories—engagement, integrity, and purpose—represent more than half of the characteristics. The results are even more startling when assessed using the question, "How important are each of the following actions to building trust?" The difference between what is most important and the performance of organizations against these attributes is striking. There is no doubt that product and service quality are still most important, particularly in the buyer's mind. However, fair treatment of employees and customers; quick and responsible actions in a crisis; ethical business practices; and protection of the environment, society, and local communities are all ranked far higher than consistent financial returns and global corporate listings. This is not a unique response for 2013. On the contrary, a growing trend indicates a far more concerned and informed consumer.

Building Trust and Reputation Globally—A Difficult Challenge

Building trust is not simple, nor is it possible without significant effort. Chapter 1 delved into the growing global population and the significant growth of an emerging middle class. Remember, this emerging middle class will not be in the developed world; the greatest growth will be in Asia, Africa, and Latin America. The Edelman Trust Barometer in 2013, as in years past, shows that trust varies considerably from one country to the next. Companies headquartered in developing nations face a significant "trust discount," according the survey summary, while trust in companies headquartered in Canada, Germany, and Sweden has remained steady since 2008.[7] Clearly there are considerable differences in the way that companies and their leaders are perceived across the globe.

This difference translates to company reputations as well. The Reputation Institute's 2012 RepTrak 100 represents the opinions of nearly 50,000 professionals from 15 countries, who contributed almost 150,000 ratings of companies throughout the world. The findings also reflect the variation in trust and reputation across borders. Even the companies with the best-surveyed reputations failed to maintain that lead across the 15 market countries surveyed. As the survey reports, "Only 11 out of the 100 companies made the Top 10 in five or more of the 15 markets underlining the challenge of building a strong global reputation."[8] Sixty-four of the companies in the top 100 suffered significant decreases in reputation outside their home country, and only 11 had reputations that were greater than in their home country. It seems that maintaining a reputation that's as strong globally as it is locally is quite difficult.

And yet the most significant conclusions in the RepTrak 100 Survey involved buying decisions. The survey concludes that consumers will buy from companies with the best reputations, whether by industry or globally across the board. Figure 3.1 demonstrates that word-of-mouth advertising works in your favor when you have a great reputation. These findings probably won't surprise anyone. The real issue is whether or not companies are changing to ensure that their reputations—and more important

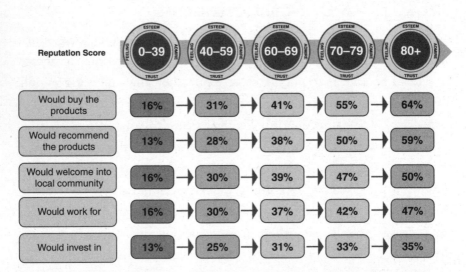

FIGURE 3.1 In its 2012 RepTrak 100 report, the Reputation Institute concludes that "Reputation is your #1 driver of support." This chart shows reputation score and its effect on buyer decisions and word of mouth, using percentage of respondents. "If a company improves its reputation by 5 points, the number of people who would definitely recommend the company goes up by 7.1 percent."

Source: Reputation Institute, 2012 Global RepTrak 100: *The World's Most Reputable Companies*, 19–21.

the public trust placed in the companies—are based on the attributes that will make a difference in the future.

THE FUTURE IS HERE—BUT IT IS UNEVENLY DISTRIBUTED

This phrase (usually attributed to science fiction writer William Gibson, who also popularized the term *cyberspace*[9]) reminds us that the goal is always deliberate progress, not necessarily perfection. So even after reading these fascinating surveys and acknowledging their startling results and trends, we still have to ask the question, "Are organizations reacting in a way to become better caretakers of public trust, and if so, what are they doing?" Or, more simply put: "Are we really making progress?"

Let's start with the size of the marketplace. It is difficult to fix a truly accurate count of the total number of government-registered companies in the world due to the variation in the manner and process for registering companies; however, estimates today put the number between 75 and 100 million.[10] Of that number, less than 50,000 are filing or publishing any sort of sustainability or social responsibility reports and attempting to share their targets publicly in a standardized fashion.[11] However, a growing number of firms are evolving into more socially and environmentally responsible organizations but have yet to publicize their efforts. On the other hand, companies such as Whole Foods, IKEA, and Patagonia were founded with principles centered on social and environmental responsibility. Their founders recognized that sustainable companies should concern themselves from the beginning with contributing to sustainable communities and a sustainable planet.

Balancing Risk Mitigation with Accelerated Change

For the vast majority of firms, however, change has been evolutionary rather than revolutionary. There are several reasons for the slow transition. For larger companies, it takes time to develop and integrate a feasible plan while mitigating the risks of failure.

The Coca-Cola Company, for example, had a lot at stake when it began contemplating a net zero water strategy. Coca-Cola has more than 145,000 employees worldwide, over US$47 billion in annual revenues, more than 3,500 individual product lines, over 25 percent of the market share in soft drinks, and one of the most recognizable brands in the world.[12] The company has 1,110 manufacturing sites and operates in virtually every country in the world. It uses over 10,000 suppliers to provide over 20 million customers 1.8 million servings of Coca-Cola products every day. Coca-Cola also remains the world's largest juice producer. "Big" may be an understatement in this case!

To mitigate the risk of the change, Coca-Cola had to educate and bring along its franchised global bottling plants, since only 30 percent of Coca-Cola bottling plants are company owned. Education was critical before the company could implement a deployable strategy to move toward net zero water usage (i.e., to return all water to the communities in which Coca-Cola operates as clean, safe drinking water). It took Coca-Cola nearly 15 years to conduct internal and external studies, to collaborate with the World Wildlife Federation (WWF), to engage and educate a wide array of internal and external stakeholders, and to establish realistic goals. However, once the effort was completed, then chairman and CEO E. Neville Isdell made it clear that The Coca-Cola Company was implementing a net zero water strategy worldwide.[13] In a recent discussion, Jeff Seabright, vice president of environment and water resources, explained that Coca-Cola utilizes about 320 billion liters (84.5 billion gallons) of water per year. To become water neutral in its bottling operations, Coca-Cola would need to return one liter for every liter used—no small task.

To meet this ambitious goal, an entire engine of change was developed. It has been integrated into the current 2020 Vision, Coca-Cola's strategic plan. Accountability is assured through a clear objective-setting process, which assigns tasks to individuals like Seabright who are deploying this program. A Source Water Protection Plan was developed and implemented that included a rigid accountability process for local bottlers and suppliers.[14] Specific processes, directions, and commitments were required in order to establish the necessary infrastructure and ensure deployment.

This type of change is not only profound and long lasting, it is also costly. But Coca-Cola recognizes that water is a critical resource for corporate sustainability, one the company must cherish and carefully manage. Coca-Cola also recognizes that it is in its best interest to embrace and work with the local communities to contribute to their own sustainability.

Clearly, this effort would not be possible without investment and commitment. And to maintain the effort, continuity in leadership must be at the top of the list in ensuring that 2020 Vision is achieved. A breach of vision by one leader could destroy the ability of the company to deliver. In a recent interview with *Harvard Business Review*, Coca-Cola CEO and chairman of the board Muhtar Kent was asked how the company plans to stay ahead as a good corporate citizen when the ground is shifting, and consumers are demanding more and more out of companies. Kent replied:

> You stay ahead by being absolutely truthful to yourself about the fact that you are doing these things not because they sound good, but because they are part of your business philosophy. And the beauty of some of these things is that they're actually very good for business, too.[15]

Without a doubt, Isdell and Kent share the same belief, the same passion, and Kent recognizes that it is up to him to make sure Coca-Cola succeeds in this important initiative. (Chapter 6 will address some of the significant changes under way at The Coca-Cola Company, where the engine of change runs at high speed.)

THE CARROT AND THE STICK

One of the most glaring reasons that sufficient and rapid change has not been undertaken is that executive leaders today are rarely rewarded for being socially and environmentally responsible, either by their boards, management committees, or shareholders. An example of this phenomenon is shown in the 2013 "Best Performing CEO Study" conducted for the *Harvard Business Review*. Over 3,000 CEOs and their companies were analyzed and assessed on their long-term financial and corporate social performance. Financial performance was tracked along six different indices, while MSCI ESG IVA (MCSI Environmental, Social, and Governance Intangible Value Assessment) was used to analyze their social and environmental performance.

The study demonstrated that there is a great opportunity for CEOs to focus more on sustainability than they do at this time. The reason? *Performance objectives and associated incentives.* The study authors stated:

> Everyone in the business world seems to agree that executives should be less obsessed with quarterly earnings and more focused on the long term—everyone, that is, except the decision makers who hire and fire executives and the people who buy and sell company stock. The short-term emphasis won't change until a new paradigm for evaluating performance emerges.[16]

This is a fact of life that leaders and others in decision-making positions have to deal with. Leaders today, *not* tomorrow, must bring to the table a stronger long-term vision of company sustainability, whether they have incentives to do so or not. They need to recognize that sustainability *pays*, not *costs* the company. In some cases, this type of vision has led to the creation of an entirely new organization. In others, however, the change has been slow and evolutionary. In either case, when such vision leads to a corporate awakening, a strategy can be developed to prepare the company for the future. Even reluctance can be overcome by risk assessment, mitigation and growth strategies, and strategic evolution. For most, this is the path to take.

Whether companies, businesses, and enterprises realize it or not, the stakeholders place their trust in them to act in an ethical fashion and expect the company to do the right thing. Companies have found that "spinning" communications about breaches of trust is no longer manageable or acceptable. Readily available Internet tools, pervasive social media, and mission-driven NGOs have created an unlimited number of channels to expose and attack such behavior and, ultimately, the value of the organization. And the understanding of *stakeholder* (the "who and where") has broadened well beyond stockholders and direct consumers. To provide more clarity, let's look at two companies and their reactions to ethical, social, and environmental challenges.

Johnson & Johnson: A Principle-Based Decision Pays Off

It wouldn't be fair to talk about trust and ethics without first reviewing the classic case of Johnson & Johnson and Extra Strength Tylenol. Anyone who has pursued an MBA or participated in a leadership forum in the last 20 years has most likely reviewed the case study. It was one of the most profound examples of how a company can demonstrate its care of public trust.

To recap: In 1982 several bottles of Extra Strength Tylenol capsules, manufactured and distributed by Johnson & Johnson, were apparently tampered with and contaminated with cyanide. Before the crisis was over, seven people had died.[17] Overnight, Tylenol became a dreaded product. James E. Burke, then CEO of Johnson & Johnson, immediately recalled all bottles of Extra Strength Tylenol capsules from shelves and inventories worldwide, at a cost of more than US$100 million.[18] Johnson & Johnson also ceased production of all Extra-Strength Tylenol capsules, switching to caplets, until the source of the cyanide could be identified and further contamination prevented. Burke's justification was simple—the credo written by Robert Johnson in 1943: "We believe our first responsibility is to doctors, nurses, and patients, to mothers and fathers and all others who use our products and services."[19]

It was painful. Johnson & Johnson went from 35 percent market share in the nonprescription pain reliever market to 8 percent before the year was over.[20] Still, the company continued to communicate with the public and to have regular press conferences. By spring 1983, Johnson &

Johnson released a new safety bottle—a market standard since then—that had a triple seal. The company regained the public trust and completely recaptured its market share while revolutionizing safety in handling over-the-counter medications. Furthermore, the company's stock price exceeded its precrisis mark. Johnson & Johnson demonstrated true leadership in the industry and to stakeholders around the world. It was a brilliant example of a company adhering to its founding principles in assuring stakeholder safety.

Less than four years later, there was another contamination crisis. Johnson & Johnson knew what to do, and the public knew the company would act appropriately and quickly. Johnson & Johnson removed Tylenol capsules from the market permanently to demonstrate its commitment to public safety.[21] Public trust was maintained, and Johnson & Johnson didn't lose market share or even experience a significant loss of value. People believed that Johnson & Johnson would do the right thing. The public *knew* that Johnson & Johnson would be trustworthy. In short, Johnson & Johnson acted as a caretaker of the public trust, and repeatedly demonstrated an awareness of this role.

It's impossible to prepare for every event that might endanger the various stakeholders in an organization. But taking responsible and immediate action, prompted by strategy, is often the way to establish public trust. Looking back at Table 3.1, we can see that Johnson & Johnson excelled at the following attributes of public trust:

- Placed customers and stakeholders above profits
- Took quick, responsible action to address a crisis
- Demonstrated ethical business practices
- Addressed society's needs in its everyday business
- Had transparent and open communications about its solution to the problem
- Communicated frequently throughout the entire crisis
- Demonstrated innovation by creating a new safety standard for the industry

Johnson & Johnson recovered from the crisis and grew in reputation and stature as a result of this incident. To maintain the public's trust, the company had to be decisive and deliberate, relying on its founding principles rather than a rulebook of do's and don'ts.

BMW: Embracing Society's Issues and Building a Sustainable Workforce

GREG—In 2006, I attended a CEO forum in New York City conducted by Forbes Group. About a hundred CEOs were in attendance, from nearly every sector of the economy. The forum focused on organizational success, and the speakers were some of the most successful individuals in the world, including Helmut Panke, then chairman of the board of BMW AG.

Panke is an extraordinary leader. He has a PhD in nuclear engineering, taught at the University of Munich, consulted with McKinsey and Company, and has held several leadership positions with BMW. In particular, he was CEO of BMW USA, where he opened the Spartanburg, South Carolina, plant and brought it to full production of the Z3 and X5 models. As CFO of BMW AG, he was instrumental in divesting Land Rover, restructuring corporate finances, and bringing the company back to financial health. He was also the corporate leader of the group that revolutionized the manufacturing software process, allowing customers to select and customize their vehicles from the showroom, and preparing the manufacturing process for significant transformation. Once he was promoted to chairman in May 2002, Panke led BMW through one of the most remarkable transformations in the history of automotive manufacturing. Under his leadership, the company revamped all existing models and introduced several new ones in both the automotive and motorcycle divisions. In short, he worked miracles at BMW, and I couldn't wait to hear his story.

Panke's presentation centered on the transformation of BMW from a German manufacturer to a global car company. His style was smooth and engaging, and when he finished, he took questions from the audience. Panke's answer to the last one caught my attention: "What issue about the company keeps you awake worrying at night?" Panke paused, looking out at the audience, and finally said, "I guess it is whether, as a global manufacturer, we can still deliver on the brand promise of BMW." Anyone who has seen BMW ads knows the phrase "The Ultimate Driving Machine." Panke felt that every BMW owner should be able to identify a BMW, blindfolded, only by touch and smell, regardless of where it was manufactured and assembled. However, he was still worried about his elite company's brand promise.

He had reason to be concerned. While serving as CEO of BMW USA, Panke managed the division's recovery from a disastrous Z3 launch. He knew that transferring manufacturing and assembly across the globe to serve new markets required careful planning. He also knew that he needed a motivated, well-trained workforce, regardless of its location. Intrigued by the presentation and by this exchange, I began detailed research.

The BMW brand has become a global icon of high performance vehicles. In addition, BMW is one of the most sustainable car companies in the world, recognized globally for its work in sustainability and, just as important, in helping to build sustainable communities.

One of the most remarkable examples of BMW's contributions to building sustainable communities involves the BMW manufacturing facility in Rosslyn, South Africa.[22] Launched in 1975, it was the first BMW manufacturing and assembly facility built outside of Germany. Over the years, the Rosslyn facility became one of the best in the BMW family. Throughout the 1980s, the facility drew accolades from the auto industry, both in South Africa and around the world. It was a great example of globalization.

Then the HIV/AIDS epidemic struck at the heart of the employee community. By the late 1990s, a significant percentage of Rosslyn's 3,000 employees and their families were impacted in some way, either by HIV infection or by experiencing personal losses from AIDS. In response, BMW SA implemented a special employee treatment program that went well beyond a typical employee healthcare program. It included education and awareness programs, a voluntary counseling and testing program, and

comprehensive care including access to highly active antiretroviral ther-
apy (HAART). The program was successful in helping BMW associates
diagnose and treat HIV/AIDS victims.

BMW chose to support the local community as well, investing in its
source of future staff and employees. One of the most significant examples
of this effort was the ambitious private-public partnership that created
the Soshanguve Health and Wellness Centre in April 2008—a joint venture between the BMW Group (now under the leadership of Norbert
Reithofer), SEQUA (an agency of the German Federal Ministry for
Economic Cooperation and Development), the Karl-Monz Stiftung,
3M South Africa, the Gauteng Education Department, Tshwane Local
Council, and the Ikhwezi Group. The Soshanguve Health and Wellness
Centre forms an integral part of the BMW Group's ongoing HIV/AIDS
campaign and demonstrates BMW's recognition of the fact that the
problems associated with HIV and AIDS extend beyond the workplace.
Considering that Soshanguve is home to a community of approximately
700,000, the support extends well beyond the fewer than 5,000 direct
BMW employees and associates. The center was sited in Soshanguve
because it is the home to many of BMW South Africa's employees, but it
provides counseling and treatment, training on in-home services, and primary healthcare to the entire community. In time, this program became
part of a global strategy to reduce and eliminate AIDS that extended to
Thailand and Southern India.

Over the last 15 years, BMW has continued to expand its HIV/AIDS
program to include:

- A youth center in an underprivileged community in Knysna, South
  Africa, with a program that includes special education for youth in
  AIDS prevention
- Global fund-raising for the Nelson Mandela Children's Fund, which
  directs support to children with AIDS
- The Schools Environment Education Development (SEED)
  Project, designed to develop a stronger sense of the environment

among South African children and to teach them about growing vegetables, health education, and hygiene standards

This BMW program, and the company's global program against AIDS, exemplifies Edelman's conclusions about what it means to be licensed to lead in the future. BMW demonstrated its license to lead by tackling a critical social issue threatening not only its employees but also communities in which BMW operates around the globe. As a result, BMW has not suffered but in fact has thrived, becoming the automotive industry's 2013 Super Sector Leader of the Dow Jones Sustainability Index, which recognizes BMW as the most sustainable car company in the world.[23] In addition, BMW was recognized in the RepTrak 100 as the most reputable company in the world in both 2012 and 2013.[24]

Are the challenges faced by BMW to remain a technological leader in automotive design and technology getting easier? On the contrary, it has never been more challenging, and in the future (2020–2025), governments throughout the world will be regulating emissions to ensure that BMW and other car makers deliver emission-free, sustainable mobility. BMW must focus on remaining the leader in sustainable mobility design as well as building both direct and indirect supply chains that are ethically, environmentally, and socially sustainable. It will also take a healthy and competent workforce, with investments such as those made by BMW in combating HIV/AIDS. This effort is an absolute necessity for BMW to remain a market leader throughout the twenty-first century.

CHAPTER SUMMARY

Chapter 3, and the entire first section, has provided a look at the challenges ahead, explained why significant change is necessary, and described how some companies are changing to be worthy caretakers of public trust. Among the conclusions in Chapter 3 are:

- Richard Edelman's clarification of the importance of change: "Business must embrace a new mantra: move beyond earning the License to Operate—the minimum required standard—toward earning a License to Lead—in which business serves the needs of shareholders and broader stakeholders by being profitable and acting as a positive force in society."
- Engagement, integrity, and purpose compose the majority of the attributes influencing public trust in organizations. In fact, the attributes included in these three groupings are rated far higher than consistent financial returns and global listings.
- Both the Edelman Trust Barometer and the 2012 RepTrak 100 Survey confirmed that trust and reputation vary worldwide, while RepTrak confirmed that few companies can maintain the same reputation they enjoy at home in other countries.
- Few if any incentives are provided to top executives to implement strategic change embracing social and environmental responsibility.
- Companies like Coca-Cola, Johnson & Johnson, and BMW have demonstrated the attributes that help shape public trust.

Part 2

The Awakening of Organizational Leadership

Chapter 4

SUSTAINABILITY AS A CORE VALUE

We must be the change we want to see in the world.
—MAHATMA GANDHI

NATHALIE—Near the end of 2007, my dear friend Kimberly Wiefling introduced me to ALC Education, a Japanese education company. Through ALC, I started working with Japanese companies to develop leadership skills among their managers so their companies can continue to thrive in the global marketplace. This experience was an eye-opener for me. Many of these corporations have long-term visions, a hallmark of Japanese culture. Because of that, these Japanese corporations are concerned not only with the sustainability of their organizations but also with that of the societies in which they operate. You could say that sustainability is part of their DNA. Seeing them put their values into action was a true awakening for me.

The quotation from Gandhi at the beginning of this chapter is one of my favorites. When there's a problem, it is so easy to blame others or the situation and think that we cannot make a difference. If everyone thought that way, nothing would change. We probably would still be eking out a scant existence as hunters and gatherers, isolated from other communities and at the mercy of disease, disasters, and the elements.

In my workshops with Japanese corporations, I often hold an object at shoulder height above the ground and let it drop to the floor. I then ask the participants, "What caused it to drop?" The overwhelming response is always "gravity," which of course is one answer. But after some encouragement, someone will softly say, "you." Gravity is a force we have to live with and cannot change, but the real reason the object drops is because I let it go. Only after I let go can gravity do its work.

It's a lot easier to think that something is out of our control. It means we don't have to take action or responsibility. We can keep sitting on the sidelines and complain about everything that is wrong in the world, blaming "them": politicians, capitalists, investment bankers, you name it. Accepting the viewpoint that we are in control suddenly implies that something is within our power to change. Instead of seeing ourselves as a victim of circumstances, we are compelled to act to improve the situation.

It takes courage to step up and be different. This chapter will highlight some companies that decided to be different from the outset or that decided to change their business model decades before corporate social responsibility (CSR) became fashionable. These owners founded their companies—or drastically changed their business models—believing they should do good for their employees, their communities, the environment, and society at large. More important, they followed through and did not give up when they were challenged. They believed they could run a successful, profitable business without causing unnecessary harm to the communities they touch, while implementing strategies to improve existing environmental stresses.

Patagonia: Do Things Right and Profits Will Follow

NATHALIE—Like many who have experienced a personal awakening regarding the planetary situation we are in, I'm looking at what I personally can do to improve it. One personal goal is to buy only organic food, preferably locally grown. However, while conducting research for this book, I realized I have not extended the same discipline to my clothing closet. My best friend tells me that I am her example on how to declutter. I go through all my closets almost every year and give away anything I don't use or wear. But I've never deeply thought about the environmental and social impact involved in the creation of my clothes and shoes. If I had, I would have shopped a lot more often at Patagonia.

Yvon Chouinard, Patagonia's founder, has been in business for over 50 years. He started out selling climbing equipment out of the back of his truck before founding Chouinard Equipment in the 1960s. In 1972, he founded Patagonia, a manufacturer of high-end outdoor clothing and equipment. He is an eclectic executive, as a 2007 *Fortune* profile illustrates:

> Scaling the likes of Yosemite's El Capitan, Chouinard had learned big lessons. The biggest was that reaching the summit had nothing to do with where you arrived and everything to do with how you got there. Likewise, he thought, with business: The point was not to focus on making money; focus on doing things right, and the profits would come. And they did.[1]

Chouinard has always put the environment at the core of his business ventures. An avid rock climber, he designed pitons that would not permanently damage the rock. This new style of climbing equipment became a huge success, and Chouinard became a reluctant businessman. His distaste for business stems from his conviction that most companies focus on their short-term returns rather than on their long-term liabilities.

The fact that analysts focus only on quarterly returns and do not care at all about sustainability reinforces this short-term view. Patagonia takes a different approach. The company mission statement is, "Build the best product, cause no unnecessary harm, use business to inspire and implement solutions to the environmental crisis."[2] Patagonia makes clothing for climbing, skiing, snowboarding, surfing, fly fishing, paddling, and trail running—all sports that are closely connected to the very nature they are looking to protect.

Building your company around sustainability means you have to ride it out when your business hits rough waters. It means being prepared to go out of business rather than compromise your values. It means you never concede to a way of business that is not sustainable simply to stay in business. This is how Patagonia makes decisions.

In the mid-1990s, Patagonia's rapid growth was followed by financial distress. Chouinard first made the necessary changes, including the first ever layoffs at the company, and focused on eliminating the company debt. Then he evaluated how well the operations and supply chain were living up to the company's values and made changes accordingly. For example, after finding out that toxic chemicals were used in farming Patagonia's cotton, he insisted on sourcing 100 percent organic cotton. Insufficient supply at that time meant sharply increased supply costs.[3] Chouinard didn't care:

> Even organic cotton is bad. It's better to make clothes out of polyester if you can recycle them into more clothes, and keep doing it—like we do with aluminum cans—instead of growing more organic cotton and selling cheap clothes that people just throw away.[4]

Organic cotton is significantly better for the environment than conventional cotton, which uses toxic chemicals that poison the soil, air, and groundwater. However, organic cotton still uses an inordinate amount of water, and cotton cultivation depletes the soil, so it cannot be grown year after year on the same piece of land. Being true to your values also means you need to think outside of the box. What innovative ways of doing business will help you optimize running a profitable, sustainable business? With that philosophy in mind, and understanding the drawbacks of organic cotton, Patagonia introduced the very first fleece jackets with polyester from recycled plastic bottles in 1993,[5] and partnered with a Japanese fabric company to create polyester clothing that can be recycled almost indefinitely.

A commitment to true sustainability implies that, as a company, you have nothing to hide and are fully accountable when things go wrong. Full disclosure should be provided about the company processes, supply chain, and ecological footprints, as well as any mishaps that might affect the environment or local communities. Patagonia provides this full transparency on its website through "The Footprint Chronicles," which details the company's supply chain.[6] In the quest to find environmental solutions, its latest campaign employs large advertisements discouraging customers from buying new Patagonia jackets. The Common Threads Partnership between the company and its customers promotes this mindset with the slogan "Reduce, Repair, Reuse, Recycle, Reimagine."[7] For example, Patagonia creates long-lasting, high quality products in a sustainable way, and as customers, we promise not to buy anything we don't need. Together, these choices and actions reduce the overall impact of our transactions. Patagonia also offers to repair its products and provides a way for customers to reuse products by selling secondhand Patagonia clothes and gear on the company's website. Patagonia will even take back worn-out Patagonia products for recycling.

Many companies still believe they have to choose between making profits and implementing sustainable practices. On the contrary, making your business more sustainable maximizes efficiencies on all operational levels while reducing costs. It also opens new market opportunities and expands your customer base while increasing brand loyalty. Profits will follow if you do things right. Patagonia is a great example. The company is able to demand premium prices for its products because of its brand image and environmentally friendly reputation.

We can hear the skeptics now: "Patagonia has it easy. It's just a small company. It's privately held, so it doesn't have to deal with shareholders who are looking for a quarterly return." However, this small, rebellious company has influenced thousands of companies worldwide, including some of the world's largest.

We Are in This Together

Sustainability is a team sport. No company can do it alone, and Chouinard recognized that early on. It takes a different kind of leader to be able to stick to your values, recognize that you need others to succeed, and make yourself vulnerable so people can trust you and are willing to create important partnerships with you.

Patagonia also believes in philanthropy and has donated 1 percent of its sales to domestic and international grassroots environmental groups since 1985. Chouinard recognized a kindred spirit in Craig Mathews of Blue Ribbon Flies, a retail fly-fishing store in West Yellowstone, Montana. In 2002, Chouinard and Mathews realized they could have a larger impact by partnering and created the "1% for the Planet" movement: an alliance of businesses that promise to donate 1 percent of their sales (*not* profits) to approved environmental organizations worldwide.[8] Over 1,300 businesses in 38 countries have joined so far.

Size doesn't matter for partnerships. In 2008, Chouinard received a phone call from Lee Scott, then CEO of Walmart, asking the Patagonia founder to help him create a sustainability index and criteria for apparel products.[9] Patagonia taught Walmart's internal buyers how to do a social and environmental assessment of everyone they do business with. Even though the companies' core values are different, Walmart's leaders had gone through a gradual environmental awakening and realized that if they did things right for the planet, profits would follow. In their case, sustainability meant a lower cost of doing business and higher revenues because of a better brand image.[10] This unlikely partnership eventually led Walmart to create the supplier sustainability assessment tool mentioned in Chapter 2 (and discussed in detail in Chapter 6), for which Walmart is now exemplary in the retail business.

This partnership between Patagonia and Walmart also contributed to the creation of the Sustainable Apparel Coalition (SAC). Chouinard and John Fleming, then Walmart's chief merchandising officer, sent a letter inviting competitors to join them in creating a sustainability standard for the industry. The letter's last paragraph said it all:

Creating a sustainability standard will improve the welfare of our workers, communities, consumers, and environment far more effectively than the fragmented, incremental approaches that characterize existing efforts. Together we are better. We hope you will join us.[11]

The moving appeal struck a chord, and some of the world's largest apparel companies—including Levi Strauss, C&A, Nike, Adidas, H&M, and Target—joined the effort. Almost three years after its initial formation, the SAC now includes NGOs, universities, and government agencies as well as dozens of corporate manufacturers. This innovative coalition is focused on reducing the impact to society and to the environment of apparel and footwear production. The core of SAC's work is the Higg Index, "an indicator based tool for apparel (and footwear products) that enables companies to evaluate material types, products, facilities, and processes based on a range of environmental and product design choices."[12] The Higg Index gauges sustainability performance and drives improvements through a series of "practice-based, qualitative questions" clothing and footwear manufacturers can use to evaluate and select designs, materials, and manufacturing processes. Instead of starting from scratch, the SAC used existing indexes as input. One of the major ones was Nike's Materials Sustainability Index (MSI) database. After the public condemnation Nike received in the 1990s regarding child labor in its suppliers' factories, the company developed and has been using an index to improve the sustainability of its products.

The SAC coalition might not bring immediate change, but it will bring transparency. The apparel supply chain is marred with labor issues, from child labor to dangerous work environments, and it significantly pollutes the environment, sometimes beyond repair. Shockingly, many apparel companies do not know exactly where their products are made or under what conditions.[13] Even Walmart, with its vast reach, has been caught unaware. The company discovered that one of its suppliers had illegally subcontracted to an unsafe Bangladeshi factory when clothing with Walmart labels was found after a terrible fire that killed more than 100 workers.[14] The SAC's vision is to create a database scoring every player in an apparel item's value chain on various social and environmental metrics like water use, pollution, waste, energy efficiency, and labor practices, thus allowing apparel companies to select suppliers based on their own sustainability goals. Hopefully, in the future, customers will be able to check the label of a piece of clothing to see its sustainability rating.

The Patagonia example shows that no matter the size of your company, if you truly believe you can make a difference, you can, sometimes simply by inspiring others to act. Chouinard is a collaborative, purpose-driven leader, but he does not have to be an exceptional example. All companies can follow in Patagonia's footsteps. It starts with taking action and sticking to your values no matter what. The next step is to find partners. You cannot do this alone.

NATURA: CHANGING THE FACE OF THE BEAUTY INDUSTRY

Since the time of Cleopatra (and probably before) people have used cosmetics. The global market in personal products, including cosmetics and fragrances, was $308 billion in 2012.[15] Most of us use skin products, soap up in the shower, wash our hair, brush our teeth, put on sunscreen, use deodorants, and apply fragrances from time to time.

The cosmetics industry is not known for sustainable practices. The industry's use of animal testing has been widely publicized. Less well known might be the fact that some of the ingredients used are toxic for both humans and the environment. Two examples are parabens—widely used synthetic preservatives that have been linked to breast cancer and lower sperm count[16]—and 1,4-Dioxane, a carcinogen that forms as a by-product during the cosmetic manufacturing process. Dioxane has been banned in Europe since 1976 and is also banned Japan, but it is only monitored in the United States.[17] Another looming issue is that many cosmetic ingredients are sourced from the lush rainforests of the Amazon. Increased demand for cosmetics means more demand for these ingredients. Sourcing them in a nonsustainable way leads to Amazonian deforestation and a loss of biodiversity.

Unlike the food and beverage industry, the cosmetics industry is largely unregulated, and government regulations are not expected any time soon. In the United States, the natural regulator would be the federal Food and Drug Administration (FDA). Instead, the FDA website states, "The Federal Food, Drug, and Cosmetic Act (FD&C Act) does not authorize the FDA to approve cosmetic ingredients. In general, cosmetic manufacturers may use any ingredient they choose, except for a few ingredients that are prohibited by regulation."[18] There are some standards, but these vary from country to country and sometimes even within a country. When you see the label "organic" on a cosmetic product, you can't know what standards were applied. We are dependent on self-regulation within the cosmetics industry.

One cosmetics, fragrance, and personal hygiene company that is striving to meet this goal is Brazil's Natura Cosméticos. In 1969, Antônio Luiz Seabra founded Natura with the goal of building a better world by creating harmony with oneself, with others, and with nature. Well ahead of its time, Natura has used environmentally sustainable practices to develop its products since 1970. Five years after its founding, Natura changed to a direct sales model, economically empowering thousands of mostly poor women. In 2012, Natura had 1.2 million resellers worldwide. Training and other incentives are offered to develop the direct sales force, provide social independence, and limit attrition.

In the 1990s, when inflation was driving prices sky high in Latin America and most of Natura's international competitors decided to leave Brazil or halt investments, Natura stayed true to its direct sales model and lower prices, which helped spur the company's growth. Natura is now the number one beauty company in Brazil, surpassing Unilever (manufacturer of Dove and St. Ives products, along with many, many others) and even Avon.[19] Natura has remained true to its environmental and social values as well. In the company's 2006 annual report, Natura's "Reason for Being and Beliefs" are described as follows:

> Commitment to the truth is the route to perfecting the quality of relationships. The greater the diversity, the greater the wealth and vitality of the whole system . . . The company, a living organism, is a dynamic set of relationships. Its value and longevity are connected to its ability to contribute to the evolution of society and its sustainable development.[20]

Like Patagonia, Natura realized conducting business with sustainability as a core value involves doing business in the best interest of the environment, providing full transparency, and working toward zero impact on the planet. To minimize its footprint on this world, Natura uses sustainable sourcing techniques for its core ingredients, especially since many come from the Amazon rainforest. To reach this goal, Natura works closely with cooperatives, scientists, NGOs, and farmers, and the company supports Brazilian governmental efforts to eliminate illegal logging. The company promotes conservation by partnering with certification organizations and even helps communities find alternative sources of income so they are not economically dependent on Natura.

As early as 1992, Natura started to focus on limiting waste by providing refills for high-volume products, which reduces packaging waste and keeps prices lower for its consumers. An environmental label was introduced on all Natura products in 2007 to increase transparency and counteract the uncertainty regarding cosmetic ingredients due to the lack of industry standards and regulation. Similar to food nutritional labels, it displays the origin of raw materials in both the product and package. The label also indicates whether the package can be reused or recycled.[21] In addition to informing consumers of the product's origins, the voluntary label highlights Natura's commitment to sustainability.

Sometimes sticking to your values means that you need to make business decisions that seem like bad business at first. The payoff is in brand value, customer trust, and the ability to ask premium prices in certain markets. For example, Natura decided against a presence in China because local regulations require cosmetics to be tested on animals. Natura has also decided against acquisitions that would have significantly increased market share because those companies did not live up to Natura's sustainability and ethical standards.[22] This commitment to principles paid off in 2012, when "clean capitalism" magazine *Corporate Knights* listed Natura as the second most sustainable corporation in the world in its yearly ranking.[23]

Natura's model is not without flaws. Its products contained parabens before anybody knew they were harmful, and Natura used animal testing until 2006. The company held itself accountable to its values and principles and started the process to replace all animal, mineral, and synthetic raw materials with vegetable-based materials.

One of the key lessons of Natura's growth is to put partnerships at the center of one's business model. Natura lowers the risk to its supply chain by partnering with the communities sourcing its ingredients. This ensures the sustainability of the environment as well as of the communities. Natura partners closely with its direct sales force, providing empowerment and creating brand loyalty. The company even partners with universities and research centers for its product research and development (R&D) in order to help innovate new sustainable product ideas. This allows Natura to employ just about 150 R&D staff—a fraction of the staff other large cosmetic firms retain—while 70 percent of Natura's sales each year come from either new products or improvements to existing products.[24]

SUNTORY: WATER FOR LIFE

NATHALIE—One company that inspired me to write this book is Suntory, the Japanese food and beverage company featured in the movie *Lost in Translation*. Suntory founder Shinjiro Torii strongly believed in social responsibility. "We are able to earn profits from our business thanks to people and society," he said. "I want those profits to be useful not only for reinvesting in business and providing services to our customers and business partners, but also for making a contribution to society."[25] Based on that belief, over 110 years ago, he put into practice the idea of "sharing the profit with society." This spirit is still alive today within the company. Suntory's mission statement is "In Harmony with People and Nature," and every employee is aware of and lives by this motto. The current chairman of the board, Nobutada Saji, has extended Torii-san's vision to include environmental management practices that show respect and gratitude for the natural resources Suntory uses and that help create a sustainable society. In Saji-san's words, "Many of our businesses rely on such indispensable natural bounties as water and agricultural crops, and we believe that one of our most important duties is to pass on a healthy global environment to coming generations."[26]

Suntory's core business is whisky, beer, and soft drinks. Realizing its tremendous responsibility for the indispensable resource of water, Suntory chose "Bringing Water to Life" as its corporate social responsibility slogan and has positioned water sustainability—which aims to ensure subsequent generations still have access to good quality drinking water—at the core of its business. Programs include ensuring water safety through quality control, water conservation in its plants, strict drainage controls, and water education projects aimed at teaching the younger generation about the importance of water. One specific program goes back to the very first ingredient of Suntory's core products: water. The program focuses on protecting freshwater sources and the environment that produces water by creating sanctuaries around Suntory plants. By conserving forests, Suntory hopes to cultivate groundwater in amounts greater than the company uses in its plants. Since 2003, Suntory has created more than 7,000 hectares (17,000 acres) of natural water sanctuaries to meet its goal of achieving water sustainability. As with the cocoa supply chain, all members in the value chain need to collaborate in order to be successful. Suntory works together with local governments, local communities, and experts to achieve its objectives to develop forests that have a great capacity for cultivating water resources, are rich in biodiversity, are able to withstand flooding and landslides, have great carbon dioxide absorptions capabilities, and are a pleasure to visitors.[27]

Suntory's program focuses on safeguarding the future supply of freshwater. Initiatives like this need to be combined with other sustainability initiatives along the full supply chain, like zero waste, energy efficiency, water efficiency in production of raw materials and in operations, and recycling in both factories and consumer packaging.

There's no such thing as sustainability. It's just kind of a path
you get on and try—each day try to make it better.[28]
—YVON CHOUINARD

CHAPTER SUMMARY

The common threads of the companies highlighted in this chapter are continuous innovation, staying true to core values, willpower, and passion. The companies are closely connected to their customers. They care about the communities they operate in and look for ways to give back socially and economically. They understand that driving change takes commitment—a lot of it.

We have an immense task ahead of us to deal with climate change, dwindling supplies, and growing demands, but that's no excuse to remain paralyzed and continue business as usual. As the examples in this chapter show, staying true to your values and acting accordingly will make a difference, and you might inspire others to follow your example. It will take determination, persistence, and patience, but results will follow.

To remain sustainable and profitable in the future, companies need to focus on long-term value, not just short-term returns. Organizations are responsible not just for competitive returns but also for improving the social, environmental, and economic conditions of the communities they touch throughout their entire value chain. These responsibilities are two sides of the same coin. To survive in the long run, organizations need to manage their products and services from cradle-to-cradle: from the raw materials they use to manufacture their products all the way to encouraging changed customer behaviors like Natura's refill options or Patagonia's "Reduce, Repair, Reuse, Recycle, Reimagine" initiative.

Successful sustainability efforts depend on business models and product innovation as well as real partnerships with communities, governments, international governmental bodies, NGOs, and sometimes competitors. The problem is already here. Something must be done. Instead of waiting for others to act, be the change you want to see in this world.

Chapter 5

SOCIAL INNOVATION FOR SUSTAINABILITY

Innovation is anything but business as usual.
—ANONYMOUS

We have an unprecedented opportunity to reshape our world. We have accumulated more knowledge than ever before. The last 100 years have yielded astounding advances in engineering and technology. We have put men on the moon, put satellites in the sky, created worldwide communication networks, and explored the ocean to record depths. Through satellite photography, we can see the world in a way that none of our ancestors could. In the words of National Geographic explorer-in-residence Sylvia Earle, "Now we *know*."

We are starting to understand our impact on Earth. With that knowledge, we can take action to change things for the better. We are at a crossroads: continue business as usual and deplete the Earth, or take action to preserve it. The good news is this: now we *know*—while we still have choices available. The crises affecting our planet require fundamental and innovative changes to every aspect of our lives. We need to change our mindset and create a bold new future. Business as usual will not get us there. We need innovations that focus on solving real problems without creating new ones. We're not talking about incremental changes in products or services, though they do play a part. We need revolutionary innovations: sidewalks that power streetlights, buildings that eat smog, nuclear plants that run on radioactive waste.[1] This is not science fiction. These are real innovations people are either working on or have already created and implemented.

This chapter is about **social innovations** rather than pure technology or product innovations. There are many definitions of social innovation, but we like the one used by the Canadian Centre for Social Innovation:

> Social Innovation refers to new ideas that resolve existing social, cultural, economic and environmental challenges for the benefit of people and planet. A true social innovation is systems-changing—it permanently alters the perceptions, behaviors and structures that previously gave rise to these challenges.[2]

To deal with the problems of dwindling supplies, climate change, population increases, and consumption growth, we need new innovation technologies or business models that have a real, positive impact on society and the planet. Global commitments from governments are desirable but are unlikely to occur. As we have seen over the last two decades, getting all two hundred or so governments[3] to commit to the same objectives is not realistic.

Innovation is crucial for the long-term survival of any company. Social innovation takes different forms: process innovation (like the open source movement), business model innovation, or innovation with a social purpose. Innovations can come from business, government, not-for-profit organizations, individuals, or communities. Increasingly, they arise from partnerships between several of these groups.

WHY OWN WHEN YOU CAN SHARE?

NATHALIE—Look around your home. Do you really need everything? I know I don't. From personal experience, I know we tend to fill the space we have. When I lived in Amsterdam in the 1990s, I lived mainly in sublet apartments that I rented from people while they were traveling, and I moved seven times in six years. (I guess I was an early adopter of the collaborative consumption economy.) During that time, I learned to live as a minimalist. If I hadn't used an item since my last move, I decided it was not needed and either gave it away or threw it away. But after living in the same apartment for 10 years now (a record for me), I have somehow accumulated far more "stuff" than I could ever need.

One innovation trend gathering speed worldwide is variously referred to as **"collaborative consumption,"** "the sharing economy," or "peer-to-peer economy." Whatever one chooses to call it, we're excited about this trend. Collaborative consumption is a process and business model innovation. It is driven by a shift in consumer values from product *ownership* to product *access*. Collaborative consumption is based on the growing realization that we own too much stuff and that by continuing to consume as we do, we accelerate the planetary problems of exhausting our resources and increasing our waste.

The collaborative consumption philosophy holds that instead of buying more stuff, we should rent, lend, swap, barter, gift, and share products with each other. This will reduce the number of new products bought and thus the number of products manufactured. It will also reduce waste, because if fewer products are purchased, fewer will be discarded. Product life spans may extend as well, since even though we have no use for a product anymore, someone else may still have a use for it. Overall, this philosophy will reduce the pressure on our natural resources and improve the sustainability of our lifestyles.

In the sharing economy, you can share anything you can think of, from office space to unoccupied seats in your car (hitchhiking in the Internet world) to clothing. What percentage of your clothes and shoes have you not worn in the last six months? How about instead of throwing those out and buying new ones, you swap them with someone else? More and more people are getting comfortable with the idea of paying for use instead for ownership.

So how does the collaborative consumption model work in reality? We rent out our stuff to perfect strangers: our car, guitar, empty spare room, surfboard, motorcycle, or anything else that's collecting dust in our homes. Sharing is as old as humankind. Forty years ago, you would walk over to your neighbor's house to borrow the lawn mower, pin a note on the announcement board of your local grocery market, or put a classified ad in the newspaper. Now that we have moved from the Industrial Age to the Internet Age, we can use online services that serve as virtual marketplaces.

Craigslist and eBay were some of the earliest online markets in the United States, both of which started in Silicon Valley. They took the concept of the newspaper classified ad and created an online marketplace with a significantly larger reach. They also changed the cost structure. Where normally you paid up front to publish a classified ad, with eBay you pay only after a successful sale (plus a nominal listing fee), and you don't pay at all with Craigslist. Instead of creating a sales platform, the collaborative consumption model focuses on sharing things. Instead of buying a product from a store or an individual, you can pay a small fee for the use of the product without ever owning it.

Many of these peer-to-peer sharing companies—companies that enable individuals to share directly with other individuals—were founded during the financial crisis of 2008 as an innovative way to deal with hard economic times. It's a win-win business model. As the owner of the asset, you get to make some money for something you already own but aren't using; as the renter you pay for access, which is significantly cheaper than ownership. The companies providing the sharing platform collect a fee for their infrastructure and in many instances for insurance and background checks. Society wins too: since consumption is reduced, fewer products are made, fewer resources are depleted, and less waste is generated.

The wide availability of smartphones is one of the key enablers of the sharing economy model. At the end of 2012, there were six billion active mobile phones worldwide, of which more than one billion were smartphones. Smartphones are the fastest increasing segment in mobile phone sales.[4] The Internet and smartphones have drastically reduced the transaction cost of renting assets and have made the transaction itself significantly easier, enabling millions, if not billions, of people to participate.

Do you get goose bumps at the thought of renting your car, spare room, surfboard, or drill to a complete stranger? It sounds risky, but the approximately five-year track record of most sharing economy companies like Airbnb, Fon, and TaskRabbit has shown that these exchanges seldom go wrong.[5] Most peer-to-peer companies also provide insurance, but in the end transactions are all based on trust. Here again, technology is the enabler. All sharing companies allow you to leave reviews about your experience and about the person you rented from or rented to. Reviews build trust. In addition, getting bad reviews means you will get less business or will be less able to rent things, creating peer pressure to provide a certain level of quality. When did you last buy something online that didn't have several good reviews? We don't stay in hotels or rental vacation homes without checking the reviews first. A nonscientific survey of colleagues and friends reveals that we are clearly not alone in this.

Current fears and concerns about the sharing economy are similar to the fears people had about e-commerce in the 1990s. People were very worried about privacy and security at first, but once they had several good experiences and companies like Amazon and eBay provided a sense of security, people adopted e-commerce wholeheartedly. Today, most people buy products and services online without reservation. eBay is an interesting case: it started out as individuals selling to other individuals, but these days many established companies, including Barnes & Noble and United

Kingdom's Tesco, use eBay as a sales and distribution channel.[6] The sharing economy might move in the same direction, with established companies stepping into the space.

Mobility over Ownership

Let's look at one specific example. On average, a car in the United States, Canada, or Western Europe sits idle for 22 hours a day.[7] What if we put these idle assets to use? There are three mobility models that replace the need for car ownership:

1. *Car sharing*. Self-serve access to cars that are parked at designated spots in the city and are owned by the car sharing company. In general, you must return the vehicle to its initial location. You can reserve the car by the hour or day via smartphone app or Internet. In most cases you pay a membership fee instead of a rental fee, and you unlock the car with your membership card.
2. *Peer-to-peer car sharing*. Existing car owners make their vehicles available for you to rent for short periods of time. The peer-to-peer car sharing company provides the technical capabilities (e.g., a mobile app or website) for the transaction and takes a transaction fee. You get the keys from the owner of the car.
3. *Ride sharing*. Individuals pick you up in their own cars, in general for very short shared rides and on very short notice. The ride sharing company provides the technical capabilities for the transaction.

Car sharing has been around for decades. One of the first large-scale initiatives was Witkar (Figure 5.1), which shared one- to two-person electric cars in Amsterdam in the 1970s, following in the footsteps of the citywide Witte Fietsenplan (White Bike Plan) started in 1968. Sadly, the Witkar project died in the mid-1980s due to lack of funding and government support, which goes to show that being profitable is crucial to survival. It seems the original social inventor of the project is looking to revive the Witkar in 2013.[8]

FIGURE 5.1   A Dutch Witkar (White Car) from the 1970s. The all-electric vehicles featured a 24-volt motor, three wheels, two seats, and a maximum speed of 30 km/h (about 18 mph). *Photo credit:* Amsterdam Museum / CC-BY-SA-3.0.

Throughout the 1980s and 1990s, Europe was at the forefront of car sharing with projects like the Dutch Greenwheels (1995) and German StattAuto (1990), most of them small initiatives. Inspired by these European projects, U.S.-based companies like Zipcar and nonprofits like City CarShare in San Francisco were founded in the early 2000s.

Of course, with car sharing you still have to get to the car sharing parking spot, which is what got RelayRides founder Shelby Clark thinking. While biking through Boston in some very nasty winter weather to get to the nearest car sharing parking spot, he passed thousands of parked cars that were not being used. Inspired, he founded RelayRides, a peer-to-peer car sharing company, in 2010. Peer-to-peer car sharing takes the concept a step further. Companies like RelayRides do not own any cars.

Instead, they serve as a matchmaker between people looking to use a car and people looking to rent one out. As the owner, you set the rental rate for your vehicle and decide when it's available. The renter picks up the car from you and delivers it back to you. RelayRides provides the online and mobile interfaces to locate a car for rent close to you and enables the transaction. The company takes a 40 percent commission on the transaction amount, mostly to cover the US$1 million insurance offered. In a way, it's a no-brainer. So many cars sit unused, sometimes for days or even weeks. Why not use them? Peer-to-peer car sharing delivers several economic benefits: Car owners make some money. Renters save money by renting instead of owning. The environment benefits from the reduction in car ownership, which means that fewer cars need to be manufactured, which in turn means that fewer raw materials are extracted. Social benefits include possible reductions in air pollution and fewer required parking spaces, which could mean more green space for leisure time.

Especially in the United States, the car has long been the ultimate status symbol. Where would James Dean have been without his car in the movie *Rebel Without a Cause*? But this status symbol isn't inevitable or unchangeable. These days, people are shifting their mindset from needing a car to simply wanting mobility. In San Francisco, not owning a car probably gives you more status than owning one. Social media has altered the way we express ourselves. Instead of projecting our identity with the stuff we own, we use our social networks. This is especially true for the generations that have grown up as digital natives.

Established car companies have taken notice of this phenomenon and are moving into the field. General Motors (GM) was one of the first on board. In 2010, GM partnered with RelayRides to make the OnStar navigation and roadside assistance system, automatically installed in all GM vehicles, available to RelayRides customers using GM cars. The OnStar system allows RelayRides' mobile application to lock and unlock the car without having to get the keys from the owner. In addition, OnStar provides security against theft or unauthorized use of the car, because the system can slow or stop the car remotely.

You might wonder about the benefit to GM. Stephen Girsky, GM vice chairman, put it this way: "Our goal is to find ways to broaden our customer reach, reduce traffic congestion in America's largest cities, and address urban mobility concerns."[9] GM realizes that more and more people are looking for mobility, and not necessarily to own a vehicle. Of course, personal car ownership for everyone is not even a sustainable model in a future with more than nine billion people. GM recognizes this reality, and is looking for innovative ways to deal with it. Instead of just selling cars, the company is starting to look at part of its core business as being a mobility service provider. It aims to make the driving experiences people have in GM cars, though any venue, as pleasant as possible. As a result, people will hopefully favor GM in any mobility solution they adopt. And if someone does decide to buy a car, it might be one of GM's.

GM is not the only company that recognizes the need to prepare for a world with fewer resources and more environmentally conscious customers. Overall, the majority of the major players in the automotive industry understand they have to find other ways to make money. As early as 1997, Volkswagen pioneered car sharing with very localized programs[10] and in 2011 launched Quicar, a service similar to Zipcar. In the same year, Daimler launched an all-electric Car2Go car share service in several large cities around the world, allowing customers to drop off the car at any Car2Go charging area—not necessarily the one where they picked up the car.[11] (Today Car2Go also provides conventional gas cars in certain cities, which you can park in any parking spot.) In 2012, Zipcar invested US$14 million in Wheelz, a peer-to-peer car sharing firm,[12] and in January 2013 Zipcar itself got snapped up by the Avis Budget Group for US$500 million cash—a 49 percent premium over Zipcar's stock value.[13] The hope is that both car sharing models—commercial and peer-to-peer—will reduce the number of cars on the road, along with the pollution and waste they create. In addition to providing an alternative to car ownership, these models provide an alternative to public transport in areas where public services do not provide good coverage. Ideally, car sharing would also provide transportation options to less privileged segments of the population.

HERE TO STAY

It is tempting to dismiss the sharing economy and collaborative consumption as a fad, but this social innovation is disrupting established businesses and industries right now. *Forbes* estimates that the peer-to-peer sharing economy will gross more than US$3.5 billion in 2013,[14] and some advocates believe it could be a US$25 billion industry by 2016.[15] This model is redefining consumption patterns and businesses operations.

Current laws, regulations, and policies are based on the consumption model of ownership. Warranties and insurances are linked to the owner, and sometimes the product itself, but rarely to the user of the product. Most of these laws and regulations were written well before the invention of the Internet. As a result, regulators are struggling to understand how to manage the sharing economy. Take as an example services like Lyft, a ride sharing company that enables individuals to offer rides in their own personal cars in exchange for donations. Are these collaborative consumers taxi drivers or not? In Amsterdam, regulators have used Airbnb to track down people who rent out their spare bedrooms and crack down on them for not having a permit or satisfying lodging requirements.[16] Clearly some rules and regulations are needed; however, if individuals have to live up to the stringent standards that apply to conventional brick-and-mortar businesses, the peer-to-peer economy most likely will not survive.

Some regulators are realizing that existing rules need to be adapted to the new reality of a networked world. The city of San Francisco is currently reviewing existing regulations and tax systems—most created between 40 and 50 years ago—and updating them to fit the Social Era.[17] As more and more established businesses step into the sharing economy or partner with peer-to-peer companies, legal and policy aspects will have to adjust accordingly.

Constrained by circumstances and lack of resources, citizens of developing countries are very familiar with the concept of sharing products. Still, the emerging middle classes might want to adopt the unsustainable mass consumption model of the developed world as a symbol of success and prosperity. April Rinne, chief strategy officer of the World Economic Forum's Collaborative Lab, described a conversation she had with a middle-class friend from India. When Rinne shared her enthusiasm for the peer-to-peer car sharing industry, her friend told her that the previous genera-tions of his family had worked very hard so he could own a car. He could not imagine a better use for his car than to sit in front of his house for all his neighbors to see, honoring the hard work of his parents and grandparents.

We hope developing economies will leapfrog the developed world in methods of consumption, just as they did by skipping fixed telephone lines and jumping immediately to mobile networks. If the value proposition of sharing is large enough, we believe the developing world could skip the mass consumption ownership economy entirely. The question is what can prompt the developed world to make that leap.

The sharing economy will not replace traditional industries; rather, both models will coexist and provide consumers with more options. This social innovation also provides a potential source of income for owners. When most of these companies began during the Great Recession of 2008, unemployment rates were up around the world. Unemployment is still at an all-time high in Europe at the time of this writing. Even well-educated people with extensive résumés struggle to find jobs. According to the Edelman Trust Barometer, trust in traditional businesses and government dipped to a low point in 2012. In the 2013 Edelman report, experts and peers top the scale of trusted sources, with CEOs and government leaders at the bottom of that same scale (Figure 5.2).[18]

The sharing economy model works only because of the self-created community where peer reviews create or corrode trust. Thanks to the online world, it has never been easier to create a livelihood. Technology has enabled the sharing economy, and this in turn has created microentre-preneurship: people monetizing their assets, skills, and knowledge directly through the Internet. Technology has empowered people to decide when and how much they work, for what reward, and which skills or assets they will share. This allows people who might otherwise find themselves on the margins of the economy to thrive and support their communities.

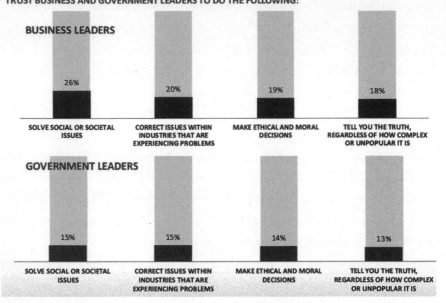

FIGURE 5.2 The 2013 Edelman Trust Barometer surveyed 26,000 people in 26 countries and found that their trust in business and government leaders was extraordinarily low. These graphs show positive responses ("Trust a Great Deal") to the question "How much do you trust business leaders (or government leaders) to do the following?"

Source: Edelman Insights, Global Deck: 2013 Edelman Trust Barometer.

When innovation threatens your business, you have a choice: you can embrace it and ask what this change makes possible, you can do nothing, or you can fight it. History has shown that fighting innovation might slow the process but has seldom, if ever, stopped it. Instead, the businesses that fight change are, in general, the ones that end up on the margins of the economy or simply obsolete (think of Kodak and Blockbuster).

From Producer to Service Provider

Another social innovation that goes even further than the sharing economy is the **circular economy** model, which is based on the natural world. In nature, things live, grow, die, and are reused by other organisms. There is no real waste. In contrast, our current economic model is based on cheap, easy access to available resources. We use those resources to make products, which are then used and discarded in ever-growing mountains of garbage. This toss-and-replace attitude causes many of the problems we have been discussing. Forty percent of the food produced in the United States ends up in the trash![19] This is a shocking and inexcusable waste.

The circular economy combats this waste with a performance-based system. As with the sharing economy, customers in this model are looking for access to products and services rather than ownership: they shift from being consumers to being users. Companies keep ownership of their products and license them for a small monthly subscription fee, providing services when needed, sort of like a car lease service. Maintenance and repairs are part of the service, and potentially even operational costs like electricity. Companies retain ownership of the precious materials used to make their products, and it is in their best interest to design for high quality. Product design in the circular economy focuses on quality so the product will last for a long time. Reusability must be part of the design as well. It's important to incorporate the ability to disassemble and reuse the components at the end of the product's life—a world apart from today's "throwaway" products.

Not many companies have tried this model yet, but Japan's Ricoh Group has implemented it for its copiers and printers. In 1994, Ricoh introduced the Ricoh Comet Circle initiative. The Ricoh website describes it this way:

> The Comet Circle expresses the greater picture of our environmental impact reduction scheme, which includes not only the scope of the Ricoh Group as a manufacturer and sales company but also the entire lifecycle of our products, including upstream and downstream of our business activities.[20]

Ricoh copiers and printers that return from a lease are inspected, dismantled, and "renewed" by installing new components and updating software. After going through the renewal process, the "old" copiers and printers are reintroduced in the market under Ricoh's GreenLine label, with the same warranty provided on brand-new products. This emphasis on recycling extends to individual product parts as well. When parts and products can no longer be recycled in the "inner loop" of the Comet Circle, a variety of recovery technologies are used to reclaim components and materials for use in another generation of long-use primary products.[21] This innovative focus makes the Comet Circle a central component of portfolio planning for Ricoh management.

Customers in the circular economy model would care most about access and quality of performance, not ownership. Car sharing initiatives from the major manufacturers could fit into this model if the cars were designed to be dismantled and the parts reused. Nonownership systems are on the rise, displacing the producer-consumer relationship. Nobody knows how large this movement will be, or how disruptive, but it will inevitably have an impact. Every company should join the emerging market and find a role in it.

Instead of mass-producing, companies in the circular economy would move toward make-to-order models, thus significantly reducing waste from the mass production model. Here again, technology is providing the tools. Current technology enables us to print one book instead of the traditional five thousand or more. 3D printing enables us to make cheap prototypes from virtual blueprints of almost anything, significantly reducing the cost and waste of designing and prototyping products.

The point of the circular economy is not just to reduce our ecological impact but to strive to eliminate it. Michael Braungart and William McDonough championed this worldview in their 2002 book *Cradle to Cradle: Remaking the Way We Make Things*. Braungart and McDonough call for a mindset shift from merely minimizing the harm we do—"reduce, reuse, recycle"—to ecologically intelligent design where we co-create in a way that emulates nature's cycle: create things, use them to their full extent, break them down at the end of their life cycle, and use the components to create new things without ever generating waste. Products will be designed in such a way that after their useful life, they provide nourishment to the Earth or to other products. Repurposed products in a circular economy would not be "downgraded" to a lower-grade use (e.g., office paper becoming newspaper becoming paper towels) but would continue as high-grade ingredients in a closed loop, circular system like the Ricoh copiers and printers. In a way, businesses would "mine" old products to create new ones, cradle-to-cradle. The challenge is yours. How can you transform your products or services so they co-create instead of simply minimizing their damage? In McDonough's words, being less bad is *not* being good.

Using the Power of the People

We have mentioned the critical importance of partnerships several times now. In today's world, it is no longer possible to run a profitable business while single-handedly managing your full value chain and continuing to innovate to stay viable. More and more companies are realizing that they need to reengineer their business models and start using the knowledge of the masses, also called **crowdsourcing**. Wikipedia—itself a great example of the power of crowdsourcing—defines the concept this way: "The practice of obtaining needed services, ideas, or content by soliciting contributions from a large group of people, and especially from an online community, rather than from traditional employees or suppliers." Not that long ago, when we needed to know something, we would ask our elders or flip through the pages of real books, such as encyclopedias. (Remember those?) Today, we use a search engine like Google (*google* has even become an accepted verb in major dictionaries), or we look it up using online encyclopedias like Wikipedia.

Wikipedia owes its very existence to people just like you. Anyone in the world can create a page in the crowdsourced encyclopedia, and almost every page is available for public editing as well. There have been some challenges as to the correctness of the information, and expert validation is important—but with each new innovation there are always new problems to tackle. No single company could have assembled the knowledge base aggregated in Wikipedia. The numbers are staggering: worldwide, 39 million registered users and uncountable anonymous contributors have created over 25 million articles in 285 languages, all accessible to anybody with an Internet connection.[22]

As with the sharing economy, crowdsourcing existed before the Internet. The original *Oxford English Dictionary* was crowdsourced in the 1800s, and the vast genealogical resources of the Mormon Church provide another prominent example. However, modern technology has made the barrier to entry extremely low and extended access to users worldwide. Current generations have grown up using collaboration sites and sharing information. The Information Age has even made the baby boomer generation more familiar with sharing information online. Visionary executives can use the power of the crowd to identify new, innovative products and services to drive future revenue and cost reductions. The collective knowledge of humanity is much more powerful than that of any single executive or even the knowledge of a company's employees, taken together.

This new interconnected and sharing era was named the Social Era by Nilofer Merchant, a columnist for the *Harvard Business Review*. In the Social Era, businesses need to realize that power lies with the community and not the company. The youngest generations especially are loyal to their networks and not necessarily to corporate hierarchies.

Unilever is one example of a company taking advantage of this new era. The Unilever Consumer Creative Challenge used crowdsourcing to create ad content for several Unilever global brands in 2010.[23] In the United Kingdom, Unilever actually dropped the ad agency it had used for 16 years in favor of crowdsourcing ideas from creative individuals.[24] Unilever is even crowdsourcing the solutions to its sustainability challenges. In 2012, the company created a new Open Innovation website to gather ideas for meeting the targets set in the Unilever Sustainability Living Plan.[25] Unilever's leaders realize they need the knowledge and creativity of the crowd to find solutions for the problems we face.

Crowdsourcing also breaks down the barrier between the developed and developing world since the Internet does not have borders. Consider

99designs, which launched in 2008 in Melbourne, Australia, as a market-place for crowdsourced graphic designs, typically a very expensive service. Imagine you need a company logo. You create a "design contest" detailing your needs. Designers all over the world compete. You pick the design you like best, and that designer gets paid; none of the others do. It does not matter where you are or what social class you are from; if you have a com-puter and an Internet connection, you can participate. 99designs has some heartwarming stories of designers in India and Indonesia who have been able to support their families and communities by winning design contests. 99designs' revenues are growing about 120 percent a year, a remarkable figure given that the company doesn't invest in marketing or sales. It grows through word of mouth: more than 90 percent of 99designs' customers come from referrals.[26]

Crowdfunding is another example of crowdsourcing enabling rapid innovation. In this model, individuals pool their money through an Internet platform to fund social initiatives. Kickstarter is a great example. If you have a project idea that falls into one of the many areas supported by Kickstarter, you can list it on the Kickstarter website along with a funding goal and deadline. If the crowd—people like you and me—think it's a good idea, they pledge money to support it. In many instances, supporters get a token of appreciation, like a signed DVD of the movie you funded, but sometimes there is no tangible exchange—your only return is knowing you helped launch the project. Funding and payment take place only when the project hits its funding goal. Kickstarter enables otherwise hard-to-fund projects to find the money needed to realize their potential. For example, SkyLight, which was funded through Kickstarter, is a smartphone acces-sory that can be used with a microscope to make diagnostic images that can be sent to medical experts for potentially life-saving diagnoses. The most famous Kickstarter project to date is the *Veronica Mars* movie, which reached its US$2 million goal less than 11 hours after it was posted.[27]

Even limited funds can make a world of difference. Consider the crowdfunding platform Kiva. Kiva's mission is to connect people through lending to alleviate poverty. Kiva works with microfinance institutions on five continents to provide loans to people without access to traditional banking systems. One hundred percent of your loan is sent to these microfinance institutions, called Field Partners, who administer the loans. Unlike Kickstarter, your Kiva loan is generally repaid, though without any interest.

The world of the near future will increasingly be about the value you are adding to society. Look at how you can engage with new trends and technologies instead of focusing on how to maintain the status quo. The travel agents, bookstores, record stores, and newspapers that tried to fight innovations are no longer around. Those that innovated are. Companies like 99designs level the talent field worldwide. People in the developing world have as much chance of winning a design contest as those in the developed world. The money they earn by doing so may be more than their annual salary at their usual job. These kinds of innovations are helping communities throughout the world!

What will you innovate? Those companies that collaborate with the power of the people instead of trying to resist change or attempting to do everything themselves will excel.

Learning and innovation go hand in hand. The arrogance of success is to think that what you did yesterday will be sufficient for tomorrow.
—WILLIAM POLLARD

CHAPTER SUMMARY

We stand at a unique moment in history. In the Industrial Era, we were focused on producing things and mass consumption. The Social Era is all about networks: connecting people, ideas, and things. The power is with the people, and they are looking for ideas and products that benefit society and the planet. Some of the resulting social innovations are highlighted in this chapter. Customers, employees, and citizens are getting more and more vocal, and they have tools they never had before. Technology in general and social media in particular have changed the business landscape by giving a direct voice to customers and employees, who demand transparency, social innovation, and corporate consciousness. We know the consequences of our current way of doing business—something we didn't really understand before, at least not on this scale. It is inconceivable for us to continue "as is." We have the opportunity and the ability to change our ways. Let's seize this moment:

- Focus on shared value that connects people inside and outside the organization.
- Use the power of the people. It is not the hierarchy that counts but the community.
- Crowdsource innovative ideas.
- Collaborate, collaborate, collaborate—establish co-creative relationships.
- Think circular instead of linear. Design for the circular economy—high quality and fully reusable. Your current products should be the "mines" for your future products.
- However intimidating it may be, embrace the change!

Chapter 6

COMPANIES IN TRANSITION AND THE NEED FOR STRATEGIC CHANGE

No one has to change. Survival is optional.
—DR. W. EDWARDS DEMING

GREG—At a recent luncheon, I got into a great discussion with someone who was, well, a sustainability zealot. I tend to bring that out in people when I speak publicly on the need for the type of organizational change we advocate in this book. This young woman approached me after my presentation. She was enthusiastic, but I was taken aback when she said that the change I described is only just starting today and is guided only by a few leaders who are truly "aware." Corporate leaders in the past and those in large companies today, she maintained, were never committed to sharing values with communities, nor did they realize that the care of society must always be foremost in their minds. She sounded almost cynical, but I sensed she was more of a skeptic. I always say that the world needs skeptics to keep us honest and cynics to keep us laughing. Though

I understood her point of view, I don't agree. To offer her a different perspective, I shared several examples.

In 1990, I was in my second full year as CEO of the Institute of Industrial Engineers (IIE). We were undergoing massive change, and we needed to rethink ourselves as an organization. I felt that I needed help to expand my capabilities as a leader. And so, after much personal research, I settled on an organization in Greensboro, North Carolina, called the Center for Creative Leadership (CCL). CCL had developed a brand and global reputation for advancing the understanding, practice, and development of leadership for the benefit of society worldwide. My attendance at the program shifted my perspective significantly. I found it so valuable that I sent many of our other executives over the next several years. CCL clearly drove home a message about the impact organizations have on society and the important role leaders can play in ensuring that this impact is beneficial.

As I was putting together a report on the program for our HR director, I was surprised to discover that CCL had been created by H. Smith Richardson. The son of the founder of the Vicks Chemical Company, the man who brought Vicks VapoRub into my home, was the founder of one of the most profound leadership programs I had ever experienced. After 60 years in business, he was still a visionary.

After an hour of good dialogue, the skeptic became less skeptical. It's satisfying to bring someone around to your point of view, but I still hope she never abandons her skepticism. A healthy dose of skepticism holds us all accountable for our motives, our beliefs, and our mission. In an age where social, broadcast, and print media are merging, we need engaged skeptics to help us all ask the right questions and seek out the right answers. In this century, the questions skeptics ask are the questions associated with real strategic change.

H. Smith Richardson founded the Center for Creative Leadership (CCL) because he believed certain questions were not being answered correctly. For many years before commissioning the program, he struggled with—and continued to ask critical questions about—the keys to sustainability of companies like his own. In particular, he wanted to know how businesses could "remain vital and continue to provide useful, innovative products and services through economic ups and downs, in the face of changes in the marketplace, and in spite of the inevitable succession of management groups."[1] Simply put, Richardson was suggesting that individual leaders needed to possess the ability to look well into the future and become more adaptive to the changes ahead. He was describing one of the key leadership characteristics needed to transform a company into a sustainability leader.

Richardson eventually concluded that most leaders lose "the ability to recognize and adjust to new and changing conditions," which often led to business failures.[2] He felt that organizations needed innovative leadership with a broader focus and a longer view, not just a view of the present and short-term future. He concluded (over 40 years ago!) that these new leaders needed to be equally concerned with the place of business in society, not just with profits, markets, and business strategies. For long-term sustainability, businesses and leaders needed long-term vision, adaptability to changing conditions, and an understanding of the need to have a beneficial place in society. This perspective raised my awareness of what it would take to remain sustainable in the long run.

It would be wonderful if all organizational transformations were due to the "awakening" of the corporate leaders to the real benefits of a socially and environmentally conscious organization. While this does occur, it is the exception, not the rule. This is neither good nor bad. It is simply reality. Visionaries like Richardson help us raise that awareness, but most organizations will not act until the risks of not changing are seen as a real threat to organizational sustainability.

The risks outlined earlier in this book are neither new nor surprising. And yet there are leaders today who continue to ignore them. Unless these leaders act on them in time, these sustainability-related risks may very well undermine a company's ability to exist in the mid-twenty-first century. The most responsive organizations build the strategic competency to see far enough into the future to realize that if they don't change, a burning platform might take them down. They have the kinds of leaders Richardson described, leaders who possess "the ability to recognize and adjust to new and changing conditions." Then there are those who wait until they feel the heat of the fire on the soles of their shoes. For those who ignore their own burning platform today, we hope that they react in time.

It takes continuity of leadership to sustain real change. Many company leaders around the world recognize the importance of leadership succession and understand the need to have a series of leaders that can bring continuity to massive changes. Take the Coca-Cola Company, for instance. When Asa Griggs Candler bought the formula and rights to Coca-Cola from John Stith Pemberton in 1889, the global population was just over 1.5 billion, and the majority of the world was still uncharted. The industrial revolution had barely started, there was abundant clean water, fresh air was the norm in nearly every corner of the globe, the oceans remained stocked with every conceivable species of fish, and the jungles and forests were barely touched by humans. Widespread water scarcity, overpopulation, epidemic obesity, and climate changes were unimaginable problems.

Over the last 25 years, these issues have become real environmental, societal, and organizational risks. They remain a threat to our planet, our people, and even to Coca-Cola's future survival. To address these risks, the top leadership at Coca-Cola has advanced unprecedented strategic change. Coca-Cola, BMW, Walmart, Patagonia, and the rest of the companies we profile in this book all possess the ability to look ahead, assess risks, and mitigate those risks by making strategic changes.

ADAPTING TO CHANGE BREEDS SUCCESS

To some extent, this book is about being responsive to an onslaught of change beginning now that will have a significant impact in the future. It is about addressing the facts: the growing population, the expanding middle class and its associated consumption, the limited availability of many raw materials, and the need to build sustainable communities. The examples that follow in this chapter demonstrate how large multinational corporations have taken their highly successful models and dramatically altered them to deal with the significant changes looming in the future. The companies in this chapter have a cumulative personnel complement approaching one million employees and cumulative annual sales of nearly US$1 trillion. Their highly visible brands are known globally, and they are recognized as leaders in their industry sectors.

These companies also cut across a wide variety of industry sectors: automotive, consumer beverages, chemistry, communications technology, and pharmaceuticals. Given that diversity, what could these organizations possibly have in common when it comes to sustainability? From a product point of view, the obvious answer might be "nothing." In fact, many of these organizations probably don't even see themselves as competitors. However, from a strategic perspective, they have a great deal in common. These stories illustrate the common elements in each company's strategy and show how these common elements lead to strong and effective transformation.

COCA-COLA: REFRESHING THE WORLD

Of all of the companies investigated in the course of writing this book, Coca-Cola is one of the more interesting ones. It has one of the most visible brands in the world, based on its namesake beverage. It is the largest nonalcoholic beverage producer in the world and surprisingly also the largest juice producer. Coca-Cola has over 500 brands, with more than 3,500 labels in its own product portfolio. Big? Yes. Well known? One of the five most recognized brands in the world. Profitable? The company's impressive annual report speaks for itself. Is Coca-Cola becoming more sustainable for the long haul? In our opinion, yes.

One crucial aspect of Coca-Cola's journey to sustainability is its drive to identify critical risks that may affect its long-term survival. This is one of the most important competencies impacting the company's ability to manage through the uncertainty of the future. Any successful organization must stay focused on the future and navigate around obstacles. It is the strategic radar, if you will, that keeps businesses poised for change.

Coca-Cola's risk identification exercises include evaluating the risks associated with sustainability. Chief sustainability officer Bea Perez told us in an interview that these risks are clearly documented at Coca-Cola and are integrated into the company's sustainability strategy. The approaches selected to deal with these risks aren't shared only with Coca-Cola's internal stakeholders, either. Perez caught our attention by mentioning that Coca-Cola discusses these risks in detail in the annual 10-K reports required by the U.S. Securities and Exchange Commission (SEC) and told us that she wished the analysts on Wall Street would ask how companies deal with these issues. Naturally, we reviewed Coca-Cola's 10-K reports to see how those risks are addressed.[3]

The 10-K report for 2011 lists 34 critical risks that could directly affect the financial performance and survivability of the organization. Obviously, there were specific references to financial and regulatory issues. You would expect that in an SEC filing. Risks like the cost of capital, pension expenses, indebtedness, and uncertainty in the credit market, among others, are included. However, there were many additional risks not directly linked to traditional financial indicators, which Coca-Cola's management believed could have a significant impact on long-term organizational survivability:

- Obesity and health concerns
- Water scarcity, quality, and quantity
- Ability to meet demand in the developing world
- Well-being of the relationship with bottling partners (part of the strategic value chain)
- Escalating energy costs or a disrupted energy supply (part of a critical raw material for operation and distribution)
- Escalating raw material costs or a disrupted raw materials supply (supply chain of such things as sweeteners, fruits, etc.)
- Adverse weather patterns due to climate change affecting supply of raw materials
- Product safety and human rights

The 10-K report is designed to help potential investors understand how an organization is poised for change. What makes this list interesting is the mix of risks focused on social, environmental, and ethical challenges. As a successful organization, Coca-Cola realizes that these factors can undermine its future if the company doesn't prioritize these risks and mitigate the most significant ones through a clear, integrated strategy.

Another aspect of managing through uncertainty is the art and science of understanding the greatest trends and forces shaping consumer interests. Tom LaForge, global director of human and cultural insights, told us about Coca-Cola's approach to identifying and understanding emerging global trends and their impact on the future of the company. This approach translates into a strategic competency through the thorough study of megatrends and macroforces. Furthermore, it is not limited to the traditional spectrum of marketing, branding, and positioning; it is also used to expose factors that could affect the way the company is perceived by existing and emerging customer bases.

According to LaForge, Coca-Cola uses a number of tools to look at these trends and forces. In a presentation at the 2010 Sustainable Brands Conference, he shared several macroforces he believes are shaping the future (see Table 6.1).[4]

TABLE 6.1   Macroforces Coca-Cola Believes Are Shaping Our World

Macroforces Shaping Our World
Growth of populations
Spread of capitalism
Increasing affluence of consumers
Advances in medicine and psychology
Developments in technology and mobility
Environmental changes
The spread of education

At the June 2010 Sustainable Brands Conference, Tom LaForge of The Coca-Cola Company identified and discussed "macroforces" he believes are shaping the world of the future.

Among these macroforces are growth in global populations, environmental changes, and globalization—all of which were discussed earlier in this book. This background makes it obvious that Coca-Cola sees a great potential for growth in the emerging regions of the world. However, these macroforces are interrelated, and one of them will definitely have an effect on customer perceptions of Coca-Cola and other companies: the spread of capitalism, in one form or another.

Over the last 10 years, the "dark side" of capitalism, as LaForge called it (e.g., the collapse of Enron, the banking system, and the housing markets, etc.), has altered current and future perceptions of capitalism.[5] This, in turn, is affecting the future face of capitalism. In fact, LaForge said the two most important macroforces changing business are forces relating to environmental issues and social justice. The environment and social justice are becoming more important to consumers, and these perceptions are forcing a change in business values to embrace environmental sustainability and social responsibility.

One of Muhtar Kent's first tasks when he became CEO of Coca-Cola was an enterprise-wide effort to develop an overall company strategy that would address these issues. Kent described his goals in an interview with *Harvard Business Review*:

> There were two [top priorities]: establishing a long-term vision and restoring growth in North America. I felt that we needed a vision, a shared picture of success—both for us and for our bottling partners . . . It's not for the fainthearted, but it's clearly doable.[6]

When it was announced in 2010, the 2020 Vision strategy was one of the most ambitious plans in Coca-Cola's history. It identifies six critical elements—profit, people, portfolio, partners, planet, and productivity—referred to by company leaders as "the 6 P's."[7] The plan sets company-wide goals as well as specific key objectives (performance indicators) in all areas, along with metrics for measuring movement toward each goal. One of the most ambitious targets is to more than double revenues in 10 years. 2020 Vision calls for doubling the number of servings consumed, as well.

Not for the fainthearted? That may be one of the greatest understatements of Kent's term. These are not subtle or incremental goals. According to Kent, "When we first talked about achieving growth in the U.S., people thought we were trying to go to the moon in a glider."[8]

Though the company is moving noticeably toward meeting that goal, the question that immediately arises is how can you be that aggressive and still be a company focused on sustainability while staring down clearly identified risks such as obesity, water quality and quantity, energy supply, and so on? After interviewing leaders across the organization, we can describe the foundation of Coca-Cola's success in two words: strategy and accountability. Coca-Cola's strategy is robust, and sustainability is integrated throughout. Accountability is open and transparent, with clear measures and metrics, and is pervasive throughout the organization—at the top, in communications to the public, within the objectives of each organizational leader, and in relationships with all bottlers around the globe.

The best way to learn about the depth of change at Coca-Cola is to read the Sustainability Report, published as part of the company's commitment to the Global Reporting Initiative (GRI), which describes the WE–ME–WORLD initiative.[9] Let's look at a few of the accomplishments contributing to Coca-Cola's sustainability and long-term profitability:

- *Energy conservation and climate change.* Approximately 25 percent of all refrigeration equipment has been replaced with hydrofluorocarbon-free equipment, with a goal that all new refrigeration equipment will be HFC-free by 2015.
- *Sustainable packaging and recycling.* Ten billion fully recyclable PlantBottle packages have been distributed across 24 countries, significantly reducing petroleum demand (by over 200,000 barrels since 2009).

- *Water stewardship*. Since 2005, over 382 community water projects have been conducted in 94 countries in cooperation with local governments and nonprofit partners.
- *Product portfolio and well-being*. One of the changes in Coca-Cola has been the deliberate expansion of its product portfolio as a way of addressing such issues as obesity. Coca-Cola currently provides 800 products with low or no calories, including waters, juice drinks, energy drinks, teas, coffees, and milk- and soy-based beverages. Obviously, this is a controversial issue due to the use of artificial sweeteners in some of the beverages. As Coca-Cola moves forward, it must maintain a clear, deliberate focus on its product portfolio in context with its impact on well-being.
- *Diverse and inclusive culture*. Coca-Cola has directly empowered 131,000 female entrepreneurs—with a goal of five million by 2020— through access to "business skills training, financial services, assets, and support networks."

These accomplishments map directly to the strategic risks to Coca-Cola's long-term survivability identified in the 10-K report in 2011. Clearly, Coca-Cola is using critical risks identified by its strategic radar to drive strategy and is using clear accountability to ensure that those strategies drive business and sustainability planning and execution. But how does the company handle a global effort when it has bottlers in every country in the world—nearly a thousand of them being franchised operations? It would take hundreds of pages to answer those questions for every area listed above. Instead, let's take a look at water stewardship and diversity, since without clean water, Coca-Cola could not survive as an organization.

To find out about water stewardship, we talked to Jeff Seabright, vice president of environment and water resources at Coca-Cola. Seabright has been instrumental in achieving the company's targets in this area. He was quick to tell us that of all his work and accomplishments since joining Coca-Cola, this has been the most personally satisfying and rewarding. The two critical areas in water stewardship are the water used in creating products and the water treated in manufacturing (bottling). Clearly, the bottling plants are a critical element of the value and supply chains. Coca-Cola's vision calls for being water-neutral by 2020, meaning that the water used in its bottling plants will be returned to local communities and to nature. This is an immense challenge. According to Seabright, Coca-Cola plants use about 180 billion liters (over 264 million gallons) of water annually and generate 120 billion liters (over 31 billion gallons) of liquid waste. To up the ante further, remember that the revenue and serving goals for 2020 are double the 2010 rates.

Seabright outlined a few critical issues that are moving the company toward these ambitious goals. First, a source water protection plan provides a specific strategy for water stewardship. This plan, mentioned briefly in Chapter 3, governs the design and construction of new plants as well as the retrofit of existing plants. Each bottler is held accountable to a plan requiring it to bottle to a specific quality standard, to treat wastewater to the highest standard possible, and to work with local experts and other important stakeholders to determine its water source and investigate how the plant might create water stress in the area. Essentially, bottlers are asked to learn about, manage, and protect the local water source. Compliance with these goals is checked through an independent audit, which helps Coca-Cola hold the bottlers accountable. If a bottler doesn't comply and refuses to upgrade after receiving below-standard ratings, Coca-Cola will replace it with another franchise bottler.

In addition, the water stewardship platform is tied into production volume. As production grows, more resources are invested in water stewardship and protection. Coca-Cola chose to work in tandem with other organizations to achieve this goal, including manufacturers like Nestlé and NGOs like the World Wildlife Federation.

Along with the governance and planning efforts in its source water protection plan, Coca-Cola is investing heavily in innovative technologies for water usage and treatment, which the company believes can and will contribute greatly to water stewardship. A new water reuse-recycling system called the multibarrier system is being pioneered and tested in

Mexico. Technologies like these could lead to a reduction of 35 percent in water usage for bottling operations—a total of 100 billion liters (26 billion gallons) per year! This reduction would be a breakthrough not just for Coca-Cola but for bottling operations all over the world.

The diversity efforts at Coca-Cola are also significant and show how connected the company's business and sustainability goals are. Charlotte Oades, Coca-Cola's global director of women's economic development, told us that women must be empowered as entrepreneurs to create and maintain thriving communities worldwide. For example, women in the developing world often devote the majority of their daylight hours to hauling drinking water for their families and villages. Worldwide, this represents over 200 million hours of effort every day. If this time could be halved and the women empowered to become entrepreneurs, the global financial impact would be extraordinary.

With that in mind, the 5by20 program aims to provide economic empowerment to 5 million entrepreneurial women by 2020 throughout the entire Coca-Cola value chain, including farmers, shopkeepers, micro-distributors, recycling collectors, artisans, and others. To accomplish this goal, Coca-Cola is helping women build the necessary skills, providing access to financing, and introducing them to mentors who can build and nurture their entrepreneurial spirit, knowledge, and self-confidence. Initially, the program is focused on Brazil, the Philippines, India, and Africa, covering 12 countries in total. As of December 2011, the program had empowered 131,000 women through educational programs, mentoring, and business development opportunities.

Finally, Coca-Cola pursues and embraces partnerships and alliances in the pursuit of sustainability. One recent example is the September 2012 partnership with Dean Kamen and his design team at DEKA (creators of the two-wheeled Segway mobility device). Coca-Cola is supporting distribution and implementation of DEKA's innovative Slingshot, a compact, effective, inexpensive, and highly efficient water purification device.[10] Simple devices like this could put a huge dent in the 200 million hours women spend every day walking to get clean water, and they could dramatically reduce waterborne diseases as well. With Coca-Cola behind Slingshot's distribution, the goal of empowering women worldwide by 2020 is beginning to look realistic.

Another of the more visible partnerships over the last decade is the well documented alliance with the World Wildlife Federation addressing water scarcity, widely acknowledged as a tremendous effort producing great results. And yet another partnership—this one critical to the future of sustainable agriculture—is with Bonsucro, an alliance of producers and manufacturers that depend on sucrose from sugar cane, a natural sweetener used in many Coca-Cola products. Sugar cane is one of the most water-intensive crops in the world, which presents a huge challenge to all beverage producers using it. The Bonsucro alliance is intended to be "precompetitive" by providing standards that help individual farmers improve their yields while embracing human rights and becoming better stewards of the land. It also provides better confidence and visibility in sourcing sugar cane. A quick look at the list of members reveals a who's who of Coca-Cola competitors, yet they work side-by-side to ensure that sugar cane agriculture is sustainable.[11]

The Coca-Cola Company is a world-class example of a company awakening to the risks threatening the twenty-first century and transforming the organization to address these risks. Coca-Cola has undergone a remarkable transformation over the last 15 years, especially considering the way the company was perceived with regard to water stewardship. There is no doubt that Coca-Cola has more work to do; all successful companies recognize that they must continue to evolve, or they will go out of business. Coca-Cola will be challenged in many quarters as it continues on the path to being recognized not only as a great brand but also as a great leader in sustainability. However, Coca-Cola is focusing on the right enterprise competencies that will allow it to be profitable and sustainable, and it continues to evolve through an integrated strategy that embraces the crucial aspects of growth, profitability, and sustainability. Coca-Cola is forging new paths for others in its sector and for business in general.

BMW AG: An Ultimate Driving Experience Through a Global Supply Chain

BMW is a global provider of motorcycles, automobiles, and trucks. The company has manufacturing and assembly operations in Europe, the United States, Egypt, South Africa, Southeast Asia, and China. The supply chain supporting these facilities stretches around the world, with more than 12,500 suppliers in 70 countries. That means at least 70 different cultures, at least 70 different perspectives on business ethics, and 12,500 different approaches to sustainability. Embracing a sustainability strategy that produces real results in this environment is not an easy task; however, it starts with a clear, enterprise-wide commitment.

Earlier in this book, we mentioned BMW AG's commitment to the fight against the HIV/AIDS epidemic. This was a social commitment, rooted in BMW's understanding of the threat the epidemic posed to its future workforces in locations around the world. No doubt, BMW addressed this as a business risk. However, the company chose to move beyond the local communities of its factories and support global efforts. It was a remarkable example of a corporation "fighting the good fight." When BMW signed an agreement to adhere to the UN Millennium Development Goals (MDG), it committed specifically to MDG Goal 6: "Combat HIV/AIDS, malaria, and other diseases." Clearly this is a local community risk in the company's production value chain, but BMW responded with a global commitment to waging war against a crippling disease.

BMW also made a serious commitment to MDG Goal 7: "Ensure environmental sustainability." To appreciate BMW's focus on sustainability, you have to look at everything the company has done since 2001. It made a voluntary commitment to the 10 principles of the UN Global Compact and to the UNEP's International Declaration on Cleaner Production.[12] These commitments were not one-offs but rather the cornerstones of a strategy for success. As the new millennium unfolded, BMW AG began a remarkable internal transformation.

This commitment to sustainability is driven by consumer demand. Consider the words of Dr. Norbert Reithofer, CEO and chairman of the management committee at BMW AG:

> Today, our stakeholders do not just want to know about the efficiency of our vehicles. They are also asking: How environmentally friendly is the production process for the BMW Group's vehicles and motorcycles? What alternative mobility concepts are we developing? And: Do we look for sustainability in the Supply Chain?[13]

In fact, BMW is continuously asking its consumers and other stakeholders about the critical issues they want in the mobility services offered by BMW. Direct stakeholder engagement has helped shape the global growth strategy for BMW as well as the sustainability strategy. Reithofer continues:

> At the BMW Group, we take a long-term approach to our strategy and actions. We see ourselves as part of society and embrace our responsibilities . . . We want to demonstrate that BMW Group is shaping its future. In doing so, our focus is on all three aspects of sustainability— economic, environmental, and social.[14]

In 2007, BMW AG established its 2020 strategy in a program called Strategy Number ONE (Opportunities and New Efficiency). The overall mission was to become the world's leading provider of premium products and mobility services, with a primary goal of becoming the world's most sustainable car company by 2020. The BMW "balanced scorecard" shown in Figure 6.1 illustrates this commitment. As you can see, one critical aspect is the "Environmental Radar," which is embedded in BMW's risk management processes.

Let's look at three key aspects of Strategy Number ONE that are designed to make BMW the most sustainable car company in the world. First is the Environmental Radar and Risk management process. BMW

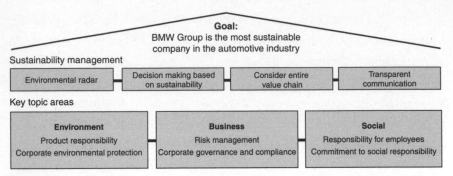

FIGURE 6.1   This diagram, from the 2010 Sustainable Value Report, illustrates the BMW Group's sustainability goal, the strategy for achieving it, and the key topic areas that support the strategy.

Group has a comprehensive risk management system, decentralized and embedded into the entire group. Risk assessment is an ongoing activity, and a key group of executives meets twice each year to review risks and the associated mitigation strategies. In addition, since sustainability is a key strategic principle, every project brought before the board of management is assessed for sustainability and verified with that in mind. The risk management team focuses on a variety of risks but looks carefully at political, social, and economic risks; industry-specific risks; climate risks; supply chain risks; risks rising from dwindling natural resources; and personnel risks. Just as it is at Coca-Cola, risk assessment is embedded in BMW's corporate consciousness in order to achieve long-term strategic goals.

Next, BMW Group focuses on recycling and "cradle to cradle" concepts in all aspects of production and manufacturing. BMW was a European auto industry leader in designing for recycling and was instrumental in rallying European auto manufacturers to collaborate on automobile recycling. Since the early 1980s, the European Economic Community had been considering extended producer responsibility (EPR) legislation that would make a product's manufacturer responsible for taking the product back at the end of its life cycle. This is critical in Europe, where a population of 400 million occupies a landmass only one-third the size of the United States, leaving little room for landfills. EPR legislation was finally passed in 2004 and included phase-out schedules for many toxic materials used in products and manufacturing processes.

BMW did not wait for the legislative mandate, though. In the early 1990s, anticipating EPR regulations, BMW sought out other German auto manufacturers to discuss common recycling approaches and facilities. Together, the group developed a common goal for regulations that provided the right kind of incentives for innovation to eliminate waste and toxic elements. For 10 years, Horst-Henning Wolf, the BMW representative, dedicated his life to making this goal a reality and assisting the EU in passing the 2004 EPR regulations.[15] As a result of this remarkable journey, BMW has had great success in meeting and exceeding the regulations in place in the EU:

- The Steyr plant uses production processes that do not produce wastewater.
- In 2010, producing an average BMW vehicle generated just 10.9 kilograms (24 pounds) of disposable waste. Per-vehicle waste at the Munich and Leipzig plants was down to just 30 grams (1 ounce). Yes, you read it correctly: *grams*!
- The Tiexi/Shenyang joint venture plant opened in China in 2012 is one of the top three sustainable production plants in the BMW family. The breakthrough technologies used at this facility—some of which are world-class benchmarks—yield extremely low energy and water consumption, and reduce wastewater, waste products, and solvent emissions.

As BMW Group looks forward to new products, it addresses new challenges for recycling and life cycle responsibility. Among these is the use and recycling of carbon fiber materials. To date, carbon fiber has been used sparingly in BMW vehicles. One of the most extensive applications is the roof on the 6 series coupe, where it was used to reduce weight and lower the center of gravity. However, beginning in 2013, BMW will release its new "electro mobility" vehicles: the new i3, and soon its sister car, the i8. The i3 uses powerful lithium-ion batteries to provide power to a 125kW (170 hp) electric motor. The passenger cells in these cars are made with lightweight carbon fiber reinforced polymer (CFRP)—50 percent lighter than steel and 30 percent lighter than aluminum.[16]

Unfortunately, recycling processes for CFRP are not mature. In anticipation of future challenges for recycling and compliance with EPR regulations, BMW has recently signed an alliance with Boeing Aircraft Corporation.[17] Boeing is deeply invested in CFRP, since nearly half of the new 787 Dreamliner is made from the material. This is an alliance born of a need for sustainability, though their respective "mobility" industries are very different in nature and customer base. BMW's alliance with Toyota to work on hydrogen and electric propulsion and its participation with competitors in the Auto Aluminum Alliance are additional examples of collaborating to solve common problems associated with sustainability and innovation. Such alliances, even when the partner may be a competitor, are the trademark of a company committed to building a sustainable future.

The last unique aspect of the BMW Group's strategy that we would like to highlight is its sustainability governance model. The governance model is crucial in the deployment and integration of sustainability initiatives. Locate it too far down in the organization, and governance takes on tactical characteristics. Governance at the board level, without a method for strategic alignment, means sustainability initiatives probably will not be implemented, and goals won't be met.

BMW's model is a logical and powerful compromise, with three distinct components (see Figure 6.2). First, there is the Sustainability Board, with responsibility and authority for strategic decision making. This board comprises members of the BMW Board of Management, with Dr. Reithofer serving as chair for both boards. The "board within a board" concept allows for a discussion agenda completely devoted to sustainability and for changes to strategy as necessary.

To deploy sustainability strategy, the Board of Management created a Sustainability Circle with the department heads from all divisions, chaired by the BMW group sustainability and environment representative. The

Responsibility for Sustainability Issues in the BMW Group

Sustainability Board

Comprises the entire Board of Management
Chairman: Chairman of the Board of Management
Responsible for strategic alignment

Sustainability Circle

Comprises heads of department from all divisions
Chairman: BMW Group Sustainability
and Environment Representative
Responsible for preliminary work to support decision making

Specialist Divisions

Implement measures and processes
needed for BMW Group to
achieve its goals

FIGURE 6.2 BMW sustainability governance permeates organizational decision making at every level. The Sustainability Board, which includes all Management Board members, meets twice a year to assess progress, and implementation is guided by the Sustainability Circle, which meets at least twice a year to identify and evaluate risks and opportunities. *Source:* BMW 2010 Sustainable Value Report.

Sustainability Circle is responsible for preliminary support of sustainability strategy implementation. It's an organization dedicated to strategic alignment between strategy and execution. Finally, there are various Specialist Divisions to implement processes and measures that help BMW Group achieve its goals. There is direct line of sight responsibility and accountability from the board down through the organization.

Governance models like this one support quick decision making and deployment. BMW has a Sustainability Board for strategy and strategic designs, a Sustainability Circle for planning the implementation of strategic initiatives, and Specialist Divisions to build the necessary capabilities into the organization. These are the elements of a world-class sustainability governance model.

BASF: INTEGRATED STRATEGIES WITH A PASSION FOR SUSTAINABILITY

GREG—In 1980, in the "dark ages" of recording media, I believed I had assembled a world-class audiophile system. At the time, music was transported primarily on vinyl records or recording tape. Of the tape systems, the reel-to-reel, open spool tape systems provided the highest quality recording, due to the speed of the tape drive and the quality of the recording heads. Coupled with Dolby Noise Reduction Systems, one could get a very high fidelity sound. I was always on the hunt for quality tapes, and my favorite brand was BASF because of the excellent performance of its magnetic coatings. For many years, I believed that BASF stood only for quality tape coatings and quality recordings. I bragged about them, gave them away, and prided myself on my collection of BASF tapes. Little did I know I was talking about one of the largest and most diverse chemical companies in the world, one whose products and services cut across nearly all industry sectors.

From airline fire retardants and interiors, to solutions for renewable energy, to automotive coatings, to sustainable agricultural solutions, to oil and gas exploration, BASF is a leader in chemical research and production worldwide.[18] The chemical giant boasts €72 billion in annual gross revenues, 110,000 employees, and more than 380 production sites around the world, including six Verbund sites (more about this concept a little later).

First and foremost, however, BASF is committed to sustainable production and a sustainable world. Dr. Kurt Bock, chairman of the board of executive directors, is a vocal advocate for sustainability. He speaks often about how important it is to the success of the organization. "For us," Bock says, "sustainability means aligning economic success with environmental and social responsibility. This will ensure our long-term business success."[19] Though it seems like an extraordinary commitment for a company this size, sustainability is achieved through innovation and integration. The effort is based on the philosophy that "in the future, sustainability will increasingly become a starting point for new business opportunities."[20] BASF seems to embrace sustainability as a fundamental element for growing the business and creating value. BASF's mission statement embodies this singular mindset: "We create chemistry for a sustainable world." There is no question as to the company's purpose and no question that sustainability is integrated into its goal and strategy. Even BASF's core strategic principles are expressed with sustainability in mind:

- We add value as one company
- We innovate to make our customers more successful
- We drive sustainable solutions
- We form the best team

BASF is very aggressive about realizing its strategy. The company's goals for 2020 include producing €30 billion in gross sales from products that did not exist in 2010. BASF's sustainability goals for 2020 are equally aggressive, including a 50 percent reduction in the use of freshwater in production processes and a 70 percent reduction in emissions of air pollutants, both over 2002 baselines. These goals were established with full knowledge of the growing challenges we outlined in Part 1 of this book. But BASF leadership clearly believes it is possible to achieve these goals through innovation efforts focused on three key areas: resources, environment, and climate; food and nutrition; and quality of life.

There are many unique aspects of BASF innovation and sustainability, but we found two that set the company apart: The *Verbund* principle and BASF's sustainability governance model.

The unique principle of Verbund is a significant contributor to enterprise-wide innovation at BASF. There is no exact translation to English, but the German word *verbund* means something like "composite" or "to combine"; it could be expressed as "integrated" or "linked." Verbund is a combination of practice and infrastructure.[21] The fundamental principle is focused on intelligent linking of assets to produce value, and it covers production, technology, customers, and employees. The foundation is based on integrated knowledge management with all stakeholders, whether this means linking the R&D departments around the world or linking customer needs to new technologies.

In the case of manufacturing, Verbund is about integrating production processes, energy flows, and infrastructure. BASF has six Verbund sites around the world, which are the most sophisticated production systems in its network. The largest and most sophisticated is in Ludwigshafen, Germany, where the concept was developed and optimized. The integrated systems allow BASF to reduce energy consumption with high-efficiency power plants, reduce raw material usage, and reduce cost. These sites allow the company to produce anything from basic chemicals to high-value-added-products such as coatings for the automotive and aerospace industries. More important, by-products of one production system may be used as the input or raw material for another process.

One of the most visible examples of the Verbund principle is the joint work being done by BASF and Daimler on the Daimler smart car (see Figure 6.3). The concept car, called Smart Forvision, was designed to demonstrate leading-edge technology for electromobility and debuted in 2011 at major automotive shows around the world. Rather than producing a concept car destined for production, the Daimler-BASF team used it as a laboratory and test bed.[22] It was intended to produce a viable concept that not only contributed to climate protection but also demonstrated the economic viability of electric cars. The team pioneered new technologies such as organic light emitting diodes (OLED) and transparent solar cells. New high-performance composite materials, special lightweight seating, infrared-reflective coating on transparent surfaces, and an integrated temperature management system led to better performance while reducing demands on batteries. This was a test bed filled with innovative, breakthrough technologies intended for use in future Daimler models.

FIGURE 6.3 The Daimler Smart Forvision Concept Car is a joint venture between BASF and Daimler intended as a laboratory and test bed for new electric vehicle technology.
Photo courtesy of BASF SE.

The Verbund principle helps to advance BASF's thinking as a unified company. Rapid, knowledge-driven decision making on enterprise-wide sustainability initiatives is also critically important for success. BASF sustainability governance brings this ability to the forefront of its sustainability initiatives. The governance model begins with an enterprise-wide sustainability council that includes the Sustainability Strategy and Relations Group, along with the heads of the operational, functional, and regional divisions of BASF. The council's chair is a member of the board of executive directors. The board has delegated decision-making authority to the council on all issues that are important to sustainability. However, the committee remains the direct responsibility of, and reports directly to, the board of executive directors. This ensures that accountability for sustainability is not lost in a delegation process, and visibility remains at the highest level of the organization. In addition, there are regional councils responsible for deploying enterprise-wise decisions regarding sustainability as well as ideation on regionally focused sustainability issues.

As with BMW Group, BASF sustainability governance employs direct "line of sight" responsibility, accountability, and tracking, from the board's strategy setting to direct implementation of initiatives. The unique composition of the sustainability council, the reporting relationship to the board, and the regional councils all ensure sustainability is integrated into every aspect of BASF initiatives.

WALMART: LEVERAGING THE VALUE CHAIN AS AN AGGREGATOR

The companies discussed so far have provided great examples of, and significant contributions to, organizational sustainability. Their strategy, principles, governance structures, and operating principles all demonstrate leadership in sustainability. However, these companies are all producers and manufacturers and, as such, share the associated characteristics and problems. Retail sales companies, particularly those that aggregate products from multiple suppliers (e.g., department stores, supermarkets, etc.), face different challenges. These companies have a unique opportunity to mobilize a long and complex supply chain as well. One of the largest aggregators in the world, Walmart, has taken on this challenge. In earlier chapters, we mentioned that Walmart set itself some very lofty sustainability goals, and we highlighted the collaborative achievements that resulted. However, Walmart's efforts in rallying its supply chain are among the most remarkable initiatives in the sustainability measurement.

Most people are aware that Walmart is one of the largest companies in the world. Over 100,000 suppliers provide products for Walmart's shelves and web services. In 2012, the three operating segments posted cumulative revenues of approximately US$444 billion. Walmart serves more than 200 million customers each day worldwide through 10,000 stores. Its Arkansas-born founder, Sam Walton, has been hailed as a model of individual entrepreneurship. Over its 50-year history, Walmart has proven to be an innovator and revolutionary in all areas of business. However, the company has also been repeatedly scrutinized for various personnel practices and activities that have not reflected favorably on its brand. In the last seven years, Walmart has begun to significantly alter its image by stepping up its work toward sustainability in an effort that could revolutionize sustainability measurement.

In Chapters 2 and 4, we highlighted Walmart initiatives aimed at making the company a more sustainable organization. As stated in Chapter 2, this began with the 2005 announcement of a three-pronged approach to improvement. A key milestone occurred in February 2007, when then-president and CEO Lee Scott announced the new enterprise-wide sustainability initiative, called Sustainability 360. Essentially, Sustainability 360 looked at all aspects of the Walmart value chain to determine the best opportunities for enhancing sustainability. "Sustainability 360 takes in our entire company—our customer base, our supplier base, our associates, the products on our shelves, the communities we serve," said Scott. "And we believe every business can look at sustainability in this way. In fact, in light of current environmental trends, we believe they will and soon."[23]

This was a bold message. As usual, there were plenty of cynics. Immediately, some observers called it "greenwashing," and many were skeptical. Yet some applauded the initiative. If any company had the wherewithal to launch a globally integrated sustainability program, it was Walmart. As it turned out, Walmart's leadership had done a lot more than draw up targets. Over the next two years, Walmart quickly became the biggest retailer of organic milk and the biggest buyer of organic cotton in the world. Walmart began working with suppliers to find ways to cut down on packaging and energy costs. The company opened two "green," energy-efficient supercenters. As these projects developed, even the harshest critics acknowledged there was more going on than greenwashing. But Walmart wasn't done yet. In his 2007 speech in London, Scott said:

Just think about this: What if we worked with our suppliers to take nonrenewable energy off our shelves and out of the lives of our customers? We could create metrics and share best practices so our suppliers could make products that rely less and less on carbon-based energy.[24]

This was one of the most far-reaching sustainability coalitions announced to date, leveraging Walmart's role as an aggregator and retailer of finished goods to make significant improvements throughout its value chain. Then, in July 2009, Scott announced that Walmart was funding the creation of The Sustainability Consortium (TSC), a new organization that would provide scientific research in support of a new sustainability index, led by the University of Arkansas and Arizona State University.[25]

At the time of the launch, TSC focused on food, beverages, and agriculture. Coca-Cola was one of the first to join. However, the intent was always to include all consumer-goods producers, manufacturers, and other large aggregators. Consumer-goods companies Procter & Gamble, General Mills, Tyson, and Unilever, among others, soon became partners, and competing retailers including Costco, Target, and Kroger were invited to join. Here's how Scott described the sweeping scope of the initiative:

Our first action will apply to all suppliers who work with us through global procurement, who are domestic importers, or who are manufacturers of Sam's Club or Walmart private brands. We will require these suppliers to demonstrate that their factories meet specific environmental, social and quality standards. We have already started doing this, and we hope to extend the requirement to all the suppliers I mentioned within the next three to five years.

Second, we will only work with suppliers who maintain our standards throughout our relationship. So we will make certification and compliance part of our supplier agreements and ask suppliers to report to us regularly. Any supplier that fails to keep its word will be required to take prompt and serious action. If a supplier fails to improve and fix the problem, we will stop working with that supplier.

Third, we will favor—and in some cases even pay more—for suppliers that meet our standards and share our commitment to quality and sustainability. Paying more in the short term for quality will mean paying less in the long term as a company. Higher quality products will mean better value, fewer problems, fewer returns and greater trust with our customers. Saving people money is a commitment to our customers throughout the life of the product.[26]

To some extent, the announcement and creation of TSC set up expectations that all products would have labels indicating their carbon footprint and recycled content by now. Critics have attacked Walmart for not fulfilling that expectation. However, at the Global Milestone meeting in September 2012, Walmart announced that it was ahead of schedule in the pursuit of the sustainability index, now called the Live Better Scorecard. According to the company, buyers for 100 product categories had already received scorecards, while buyers for another 300 categories of products will receive them by the end of 2013.

This is a long and complicated process, one that challenges scientists, business professionals, and suppliers alike. However, it is a breakthrough approach for large-scale aggregators, motivating producers, suppliers, and manufacturers to initiate and invest in the changes necessary to build a sustainable future. Whether or not Walmart has met the original TSC goals, the writing is on the wall for its 100,000 suppliers: get with the environmental program soon, or you won't be on our shelves. It is a sign of the future. When trying to interpret this action, companies must recognize that, no matter how big or small they are, their organizations are in a value chain that may serve a company like Walmart.

CHAPTER SUMMARY

The companies discussed in this chapter represent only a small sample of the thousands of companies that are waking up to the need for change. In the companies we studied and interviewed, we saw groups in many different industry sectors, across many countries, representing small and large organizations alike. However, their strategies and deployments seem to share common characteristics:

1. *Risk "radar."* These organizations possess the ability and corporate competence to identify critical risks that could either damage or enhance their success. This capability goes beyond traditional financial risks and includes risks from social, environmental, and ethical practices.

2. *Clearly defined sustainability strategies, which are integrated into the long-term company strategy.* Usually the long-term organizational strategy embraces sustainability in their values and in their goal setting.

3. *Deliberate deployment of sustainability initiatives.* Most of these companies employ some form of balanced scorecard to ensure that initiatives are driven by the strategy and that progress can be assessed with clear measures and metrics.

4. *Clear accountability and transparency.* Coca-Cola, BMW, and Walmart reported progress against mileposts or goals at all levels in the organization, and most organizations reported them through publicly available annual reports, either through their normal annual report or through guidelines from the GRI.

5. *Assessing the sustainability of the supply and value chains.* The successful transformations occur in companies that recognize their sustainability responsibility throughout their value and supply chains. Accountability in the supply chains, compliance to supplier codes of behavior and conduct, enforcement of all proprietary sustainability requirements, and leveraging the power of being the "owner" of the chain were all approaches used by the companies we studied.

6. *Collaborative approaches to solving industrywide sustainability challenges.* In nearly all cases, the companies were willing to partner with universities, NGOs, and even competitors to solve industrywide sustainability problems. They recognized that there were some

problems that were too large for one company to tackle, no matter how large the company.

7. *Governance models that are responsive, accountable, and informed.* In all cases, the companies recognize that informed decision making regarding sustainability initiatives is critical to success. This meant that decision makers were connected to strategy and responsible for execution. You never have to go looking for a decision in these organizations!

PART 3

PAYBACK
IS REAL

Chapter 7

ARGUMENTS FOR THE RELUCTANT MAJORITY

There is a principle which is a bar against all information,
which is proof against all arguments and which cannot fail to keep a man in
everlasting ignorance—that principle is contempt prior to investigation.
—HERBERT SPENCER, BRITISH SOCIAL PHILOSOPHER (1820–1903)

GREG—"Contempt prior to investigation"—I should have that as a placard above my head to remind me. It is a principle that breeds frustration in any negotiation, a personal characteristic that can stop successful change in its tracks. Contempt for novel ideas arises from a variety of causes: uncertainty, fear of failure, lack of control, and more.

One of my most personal stories about how this affects decision making happened in the mid-1980s. I was considering leaving the Institute of Industrial Engineers for another organization. To a young professional, there is nothing like the seduction of being aggressively pursued by a recruiter because others believe you are somehow special. I was no different. I was excited by another, larger engineering society that offered the lure of a move into a senior vice president's position within a very short period of time. According to the recruiter, I would be "groomed" to take over for a retiring, long-term employee.

I was offered a great package and the opportunity to take over a much larger publishing and education program. After hours of interviews, I was being wined and dined by the long-term employee who supposedly was going to coach me and retire "very soon." During dinner, he asked me what I thought of the offer and in particular the opportunities for growth and change.

The new organization was (and is) great, but its education and publishing programs were outdated and on the decline. In fact, that is why I was asked to come on board. Many changes were needed in these areas if they were to become profitable again. So, believing that he was interested in my opinion, I cautiously told the senior vice president about the changes I thought were necessary to make the operations profitable and vital in the future. I knew he was aware of my previous successes; otherwise, I would not have been at dinner in the first place. We also talked about the trends in both education and publishing, which were already altering the landscape, and how we could keep the organization from falling further behind if we addressed these trends quickly.

Then I got my first dose of reality. He looked me square in the eye and said, "That is all well and good, probably accurate too. But as long as I am the vice president, we will stick to what I know best and what will work."

I was stunned. I asked him if he thought my perspective on the issues was wrong. No, he said, it was just too much change, and there wasn't any urgency. Then he told me I had a lot to learn about organizations like his and that he had a lot to teach me before he retired—sometime in the next five to seven years.

Needless to say, I didn't take the job. Not all leaders are willing to change. Less than three years later, I was CEO at IIE, with more opportunities for growth than I would have ever received if I had accepted that seductive offer. The "retiring" vice president, meanwhile, was still at his post and had pared back his publishing and education group.

A culture that accepts change as necessary and healthy is one in which people and ideas can thrive. If your organization's culture is confined within the static boundaries of a legacy, the limitations can be difficult to overcome. Sometimes it may feel like you're trying to move a brick wall or empty an ocean with a thimble. It is not as impossible as it may feel, but you do need to arm yourself with extensive preparation and the right tools.

Even when you're awake to the reality of our global sustainability situation, it's easy to become overwhelmed by the necessary changes. Internal arguments begin to wear away at good intentions: Why us? Why now? Let "them" handle it. It's too much change too fast. As long as I'm here, we'll stick to what works. You may come up against some of this thinking as you start promoting the changes necessary to ensure your organization's survival and profitability. So in this chapter, we will stop drinking from the fire hose for a few pages and share some assumptions and objections you are likely to hear. Our goal in this chapter is to help you prepare for and overcome the resistance you may encounter.

LEAD, FOLLOW, OR GET OUT OF THE WAY: THE TIPPING POINT IS NEAR

There is good news. Many business leaders believe we are at a tipping point and that it is getting easier to convince others that sustainability is the future of business as well as the business of the future. A 2013 survey of more than 4,000 managers from 113 countries conducted by MIT Sloan Management School and Boston Consulting showed that interest and investment in sustainability has increased steadily for the last three years.[1] In fact, 70 percent said that their companies have placed sustainability on their agenda, and two-thirds said sustainability is necessary to remain competitive in today's environment (up from 50 percent in 2011). Nearly half of all respondents said they had changed their business models to embrace sustainability, and 37 percent are already reporting profits from investments in sustainability. We have to temper this enthusiasm slightly; sustainability still ranks low on the total list of issues. Yet a third of the respondents said they are profitable because they focus on sustainability initiatives. The myriad of other independent surveys and reports we have read all indicate that we are nearing a watershed for sustainable business. The times, they are a-changin'.

Asset management company RobecoSAM conducts the Corporate Sustainability Assessment used by the Dow Jones Sustainability Index (DJSI), which tries to determine the links and relationships between sustainability and financial performance. In the 2013 Yearbook—a joint effort between RobecoSAM and KPMG—Gabriela Grab Hartmann (deputy head of research, RobecoSAM) and Edoardo Gai (head of sustainability services, RobecoSAM) share their thoughts on the progress companies have made investing and innovating in sustainability management over the last decade. What follows is one of their most interesting observations:

> Ten years ago, not much effort was required for a company to portray itself as a sustainable, responsible enterprise. But today that is no longer the case. Many companies are integrating sustainability into their overall strategy. Process and product improvements as well as tangible results are necessary to distinguish the sustainability leaders from the laggards precisely because so many companies have made such big strides.[2]

Both researchers supported the conclusion that differentiation factors were changing dramatically. These are the items that are now mainstream:

- Corporate governance, particularly its relationship to ethical behavior and overall performance
- Environmental policies and procedures
- Tracking total water consumption
- Carbon emissions tracking
- Treating human resources as a critical asset and investing in personnel development

To a certain extent, this list supports the assumption of a tipping point. However, the real differentiation factors have changed considerably. Successful companies are maturing significantly in this area, moving sustainability deeper into the organization and embedding it into corporate strategy. Here are some of the key areas of differentiation for leaders in the 2013 report:

- Management of water-related risks, particularly in regions where water scarcity and quality are an issue
- Enterprise-wide policies focused on climate change
- Supply chain management, with a particular focus on integrating cost and risk management
- Sustainable sourcing, with a particular focus on human rights
- Basing some of the variable compensation of key executives on accomplishments aligned with the corporate sustainability strategy
- Integrated financial reporting that clearly demonstrates the value of sustainability

This final area is probably the one that will challenge most organizations. "Going forward," Gai says, "companies will be expected to actively communicate the financial benefit of their sustainability strategy."[3] As Hartmann succinctly put it, "The real differentiating factor now comes from expressing [sustainability] achievements in financial reports, linking the results . . . to their financial performance."[4]

PUSHBACK: COMMON MYTHS AND CHALLENGES YOU WILL ENCOUNTER

GREG—The path to sustainability will require hard work and focus, and you will encounter resistance along the way. Many of my own discussions have reinforced this. The resistance can be so strong that I sometimes wonder if people have been engaged in any communication about the future and our sustainability.

At the risk of sounding too sarcastic, the response that upsets me the most is the modern equivalent of Herbert Spencer's quote at the beginning of this chapter: "Stop confusing me with the facts! I have my own opinion, and you can't change that!" That kind of resistance can be difficult to overcome. But the fact remains that you must be prepared for scrutiny, both in developing a business plan and in implementing it, particularly as you become more transparent and open about it.

Though it may be frustrating, pushback is good for fine-tuning plans. It creates a tension that breeds creativity and innovation. People may be skeptical, but they are generally reasonable if you can clearly explain the need for change. The good news is that the companies that are already successfully implementing these strategies believe in transparency and accountability to their stakeholders. That means the reports of their work and achievements are public and available as guides and inspiration.

With this in mind, we designed this chapter to address some of the more common myths and challenges you will encounter, based on many interviews and reports and nearly 35 years of combined experience dealing with this subject. Are these arguments all-inclusive? That's unlikely, because reason and facts don't always win out. Are they the most common? Yes, we believe so, and we think you will too, once you begin developing the case for change.

"Only a Few Companies Are Really Investing in Sustainability"

You're likely to encounter this view when you are trying to build a more sustainable organization. In part, this is because most investments in sustainability attract little attention in the general media. Even the business press devotes little coverage to the topic, unless it is surrounded by conflict or drama. Productive research requires a deeper dive into industry-specific news and into reporting networks like the DJSI, DAX, RobecoSAM, and the Carbon Disclosure Project (CDP). After joining and gaining access to these networks, you can see the extensive list of participating organizations. The number of familiar companies may surprise you. You may even recognize some of your competitors. The numbers are growing by double digits every year throughout the world, and a number of publicly displayed reports on accomplishments are readily available.

To deal with the internal pushback that might occur when you're developing a case for change, it is worthwhile to carefully research your industry sector and create a list of participants, paying particular attention to identifying your competitors. Remember, sustainability reporting is not just for publicly traded companies and multinational corporations.

"We're Too Small to Pull It Off"

Companies like Coca-Cola and BMW have vast resources at their disposal. How will a much smaller company be able to implement integrated and far-reaching change? For starters, a small company has a much smaller playing field, fewer people to reach, and hopefully more rapid decision making. Larger companies require more time to change direction, and the legacy of success can be a powerful roadblock to change. Smaller companies can have more fluid lines of communication. Regardless of company size, never forget that developing an integrated sustainability strategy is always about addressing the risks you face in the future.

During our research and interviews, we asked whether company size matters, particularly of the larger companies. The answers were insightful:

- Small organizations have to be creative about finding the resources needed to get the job done. If you are starting this initiative, you are probably the champion and the catalyst. It will be a long process, and patience and persistence rule. However, recognize that you have to convince only one person at a time, not an entire organization.
- Don't underestimate the importance of sustainability to your staff and colleagues. As Coca-Cola's chief sustainability officer Bea Perez told us, strategic change for the purpose of sustainability is "a team sport." Engage your team. You will find that your staff will take pride in this type of work and will want to contribute.

- All of the larger companies have an enterprise-wide sustainability team or a committee. Consider forming a sustainability team to wrestle with ideas and implementation. Although you are the catalyst, you need to expand your circle quickly. Make that the first order of business, and find at least two others to join your effort; in other words, expand your circle to foster debate. Consider at least a team of three, and try to find a good skeptic to join the team. Remember, there is a big difference between a cynic and skeptic. Embrace skeptics; avoid cynics.

- You don't have to do it alone. Partnerships are the rule rather than the exception, even for corporate giants like Mars Candy, Unilever, Coca-Cola, and Walmart. The vast challenges that face businesses in the mid-twenty-first century require collaboration, even with competitors. Look for partnerships and you will find them.

- Unless you are the CEO or founder, you alone cannot change the culture of the organization. For cultural change to occur, you need to work from both the top and the bottom. After forming your team, think about the path to cultural change. Above all, don't create a "bully pulpit" and act like a preacher at a revival. Don't criticize those who don't immediately join up. This is about transforming the culture of a business. Engage people in dialogue, and allow skepticism to come out. A word of caution: Changing culture is not like changing locations or workstations. It requires hard work over a long period of time. In the words of Carol Bartz, former Yahoo CEO, "Changing culture is not a sprint. It's a marathon. It's very, very hard to affect culture."[5]

A big question in smaller companies is, "Where do I start?" To get traction in your company, take the following approach:

- Consider revenue production and cost reduction in everything you do. When you go into a business meeting on sustainability, know

what your initiatives will cost and how they will save money and
produce revenues.

- Look at business processes. You need to understand the implications
  of your decisions in terms of impact on operations and processes.

- Try to identify risks facing your particular core products or services.
  Always remember that inaction can pose a real threat to the survivability of your company. However, to prove that, you need to know
  what the threats or opportunities are. Some call this the "risk card"
  in a game of sales, but it's not a game to the executives. A risk can
  put a company in bankruptcy.

- Finally, be open to scrutiny. No matter how right you feel you are,
  remember the retort of the closed-minded: "Don't confuse me
  with the facts; I have my own opinion and you can't change that!"
  Welcome criticism. Better yet, *ask* for criticism and build your business case around it.

"Where Do We Even Start?"

Developing an integrated sustainability strategy will not be easy and
requires commitment. In later chapters, we will provide guidelines and
approaches for establishing profitable strategies to become more sustainable. However, some of the early resistance you run into while building
internal support will be due to the perceived enormity of the task—what
many describe as decision paralysis, rather than disagreement. So, where
do you start?

The simplest answer is that you start at the beginning. This means
research and education. One of the best ways to determine how to evaluate your own company in terms of sustainability is by looking at specific
assessment and reporting models.

First is the Dow Jones Sustainability Index (DJSI). If you are not a
large-scale or publicly traded company, this may seem like an odd place to
begin. But the DJSI invitations are based on a comprehensive set of criteria
established by RobecoSAM. Thousands of the world's largest companies

are invited to participate in their Corporate Sustainability Assessment each year. This extensive analysis provides a framework for evaluating how effectively an organization integrates its sustainability efforts into all business processes. Even if your business will never be included in the listing, that framework offers a good assessment model. The surveyed companies are highlighted in the annual yearbook mentioned above, which also includes a section identifying the general characteristics used to evaluate sustainability in each of the major industry sectors. By looking at your sector, you can identify the characteristics used to evaluate your competitors, your customers, and your suppliers.

The Global Reporting Initiative (GRI) provides another opportunity for self-evaluation.[6] The GRI is a not-for-profit organization and a collaborating center of the United Nations Environment Program (UNEP) that aims to make sustainability reporting standard practice for all organizations worldwide. GRI accomplishes its mission through two reporting guidelines—G3 and G3.1—with a third under development. It provides a host of excellent publications intended to help individuals prepare accountability reports for public review. As they say, "You manage what you measure, and you measure what you manage." By understanding the reporting guidelines, you will get a sense of areas of interest and focus for organizations trying to become more sustainable.

Another area to review is the family of voluntary sustainability standards facilitated and published by the International Organization for Standardization (ISO).[7] These include:

- ISO 14000—Environmental Management
- ISO 26000—Social Responsibility
- ISO 50001—Energy Management
- ISO 9000—Quality Management

As you research your industry sector, you can find the companies that conform to the relevant ISO standards. Obtaining a copy of the standard will provide great insight into potential areas of investment for becoming more sustainable.

"It's Too Risky, and We Don't Have Time to Understand!"

Another key question that comes up when you're developing an integrated sustainability strategy is how your organization can approach risk management. If you use a business dictionary or a management dictionary, you will probably find a definition of risk management that goes something like this: "The identification, analysis, assessment, control, and avoidance, minimization, or elimination of unacceptable risks." (Don't you just love definitions that use the word they are trying to define in the definition itself?) We warn you now about taking a simplistic approach to this. You may already have a sense of what risk management is, but let's look at a couple of different perspectives before we discuss possible applications.

The most common application of risk management involves financial management and investment—in particular, financial capital investment in the markets, where risk mitigation is a mature and common process. With regard to enterprise performance, risk management also assists companies by identifying the barriers or problems that can impede quarterly and annual financial goals or frustrate medium-term initiatives. These risks address future events or situations that may affect the cost of capital, cash flow, return on investment (ROI), or return on equity (ROE), and quite often live in 6–18 month horizons. This form of risk management will forever remain vital to a successful organization.

We found certain common approaches to risk management in all of the organizations we studied. First, risk management in these organizations typically looked at risks that might affect most or all enterprise activities—beyond short- and medium-term financial events—including innovation, production, manufacturing, communications, and more. Next, these organizations viewed risks as being both positive and negative; in other words, the cost of a missed opportunity might be the difference between keeping ahead of the competition or falling behind. And finally, the most successful organizations used longer horizons than a mere 6–18 months. Most organizations employing scenario planning (a technique we will highlight in more detail in Chapter 11) or rigorous strategic management processes used horizons in the 5- to 15-year time frame. Granted, these horizons are speculative and uncertain at best, but they were typically reinforced by mileposts or measures that helped organizations identify trends that would show the realization of an uncertain risk. Basically, they used risk management as a form of "radar" for managing uncertainty and for developing strong mitigation strategies to cope and survive.

As you work with others to address the risks associated with sustainability, you may very well hear comments like, "It's too complicated, and we don't have time." The risk identification process may be a lot easier than you think. An hour or two with a good search engine will yield a great deal of information. Here are a few ideas to get you started:

- Refer to the national or global trade association that best represents your products and services. Contact that association for industry sector risk assessments. Dozens of trade associations for six industrial sectors were highlighted in one valuable *Inc.* magazine article,[8] but you also can locate associations using the Gale Directory Library, which publishes directories of international, national, state/provincial, and municipal associations.[9] Another excellent source of global trade associations is the Federation of International Trade Associations (www.fita.org).
- The World Economic Forum (WEF) publishes annual global risk assessments that can help identify the potential risk "hot spots" affecting your products, services, communities of operation, and more.[10]
- Contact leading universities collaborating on global risk assessment. The three universities working with the World Economic Forum are:
  - United States: Wharton Center for Risk Management, University of Pennsylvania

- United Kingdom: Oxford Martin School, University of Oxford
- Asia: National University of Singapore

• And then, of course, there is the tougher route of doing a comprehensive risk assessment for your own organization. Risk assessment is a mature process, and resources are readily available. The best route is through local universities. Accredited universities teach risk management at most engineering and management colleges. Professional associations such as the Project Management Institute (PMI) offer education and certification in enterprise project risk management as well. The ISO 31000 standard for risk management may also be helpful.

• Returning again to the DJSI, the RobecoSAM Annual Yearbooks provide a wealth of information. In the 2013 yearbook, available free of charge through the RobecoSAM website, major driving forces are listed for each of the 58 sectors evaluated through the program. These driving forces are the trends and critical factors affecting sustainability in each sector.

The key is to ensure that risk management becomes a strategic competence in your organization. At the very least, you should be able to assess the impact of predetermined risks on your organization. A more comprehensive competency would provide the means to identify, catalog, rate, and address risks in the world at large.

"It's Not Our Responsibility"

This is one of the most common responses in organizations working toward sustainability. When you hear this, just smile and think about Walmart and how its approach will affect the value and supply chains of each of its 100,000 suppliers. Talk about impact! Do you suppose any of the suppliers involved in the Walmart chain looked at the sustainability index and thought, "It's too complicated, and my suppliers are not my responsibility anyway!" That kind of thinking might end participation in a very lucrative market.

That said, the impulse to deny responsibility is understandable, especially if the supplier network has never been evaluated as a chain and the network now has to monitor more than delivery dates and quality. If "sustainable sourcing" is an unknown term in your organization, you will have your work cut out for you. Just as you would when discussing risk management, you must prepare to study and share the work on ethics and sustainability in your supply chain.

Fortunately, this work is maturing quickly, and there are numerous resources to help you establish sustainable sourcing protocols, assessment criteria, assessment tools, and enforcement methods. Again, with a search engine and just a little time, you will find case studies, success stories, and tools to aid you. Coca-Cola, Nike, Nokia, Hewlett Packard, IBM, BASF, BMW, Bayer, Samsung, and thousands of others have successfully developed and deployed sustainable sourcing protocols. The list of successful companies in this area is growing daily. We suspect that representatives from all industry sectors have invested heavily in sustainable outsourcing and supply chains.

However, we don't want to downplay the work you will have to do to build a solid, valuable, sustainable network of suppliers. Sustainable sourcing issues cover a variety of factors:

- The ability to map the supply and value chains for the organization
- Creation of sustainable sourcing guidelines for supplier selection that include social, economic, environmental, and ethical performance
- Protocols and policies for periodically assessing suppliers for conformance and for enforcing these guidelines and policies
- Publicly confirming that your suppliers act responsibly on environmental issues, not only within the environment of the company facilities but also as they affect surrounding communities
- Publicly confirming that your suppliers conform to globally accepted principles and policies of human rights, to avoid human trafficking and slave labor

- Publicly confirming that your suppliers conform to globally accepted principles and policies regarding conflict minerals or materials (e.g., "blood diamonds")
- Continuous ethical behavior, with protocols to enforce company policies and act quickly and fairly on violations
- Willingness and ability to respond quickly and responsibly when there is an exposed "weak link" or failure in your supply chain

The first step is educating yourself and others in the organization. There are several excellent resources that address a variety of models for sustainable sourcing and, in some cases, the cost of nonconformance or inaction. Following are some of the most effective aids in sustainable sourcing protocols:

1. *New Models for Addressing Supply Chain and Transport Risk* is a report by task teams with the World Economic Forum (www.weforum.org), published in May 2011.
2. The Rainforest Alliance (www.rainforest-alliance.org) is an alliance of companies interested in sustainability, particularly as it applies to forest products. In particular, their SmartSource Sustainable Sourcing Program is designed to help companies go beyond compliance when considering sustainable sourcing.
3. The Fair Trade Sustainability Alliance (www.fairtsa.org) is a nonprofit specializing in the development of standards for fair trade and social responsibility, ethical supply chain management, and accountable, sustainable community development.
4. Aside from the companies discussed in this book (see Appendix A for a complete list), review the successes and drivers of other companies noted for building a sustainable and ethical supply chain. The best way is to read about the companies with mature processes, which have been written about often. The Nokia "Responsible Supply Chain" is an example of a strong case study in a mature ethical supply chain. There are many published studies on Unilever and

Hewlett Packard regarding their approach and work in the area of sustainable sourcing and ethical supply chains.

5. Unilever represents another world-class benchmark in establishing sustainable sourcing. In 2007, Unilever came together with several peer companies to establish a global Program for Responsible Sourcing (PROGRESS). The program is now part of the initiatives of the European Brands Association (AIM). Currently, there are more than two dozen members, including Coca-Cola, Nestlé, Danone, Diageo, PepsiCo, Kraft Foods, Colgate-Palmolive, and Procter & Gamble.

6. The Supplier Ethical Data Exchange (SEDEX) is a nonprofit organization founded in the United Kingdom to collaborate on ethical supply chain assessment. Most of the members of AIM have joined SEDEX, and Unilever is now encouraging its suppliers to join the exchange too. SEDEX now has global reach, with more than 400 retailers and branded goods manufacturers using the system. Due to the efforts of these 400 retailers, the websites of at least 22,000 suppliers are registered in the database.

7. The Carbon Disclosure Project (CDP) has a Supply Chain Program that helps organizations implement better supplier engagement strategies. It is a collaborative effort of some 60 companies to reduce supply chain carbon emissions, control water impact, and manage risk in a changing climate. CDP has literature and information that can help you get your arms around the issue and provide clear feedback to your "naysayers."

"Do Investments in Sustainability Pay Off?"

We don't really like this question, though we realize it is one of the most frequently asked and must be answered sensibly. The real questions are: Will investments in sustainability add value to the organization? Will this added value be in the form of measurable financial return? Will it result in a more respectable brand? Or will the organization suffer and fail because investments were made in an area that is unnecessary for the success of the organization?

These are the questions that get at the heart of the matter. Sustainability is about staying in business and doing so as a responsible citizen of the world. That's one of the principal reasons we wrote this book. Part 3 will devote a good bit of analysis to defining and understanding the value added to a company when it becomes more sustainable. The transformation won't be simple, but many companies are demonstrating that it is possible. In fact, the research indicates that a sustainable company will probably be *more* profitable, add value to its brand, and above all, stay in business in the tough times ahead.

CHAPTER SUMMARY

This is the beginning of your journey. We can't stress enough how strongly we believe that a turning point is at hand. The businesses that recognize this and change now will be competitive for a long time to come. Of course there will be resistance, so your greatest assets during this journey are patience, willingness to change, and good listening skills. By way of summary, remember the following:

- *There is abundant proof that the tipping point is at hand.* Changes in the number of positive sustainability survey responses, the growth of participation in the Carbon Disclosure Project (CDP) and the Global Reporting Initiative (GRI), and the recognition of more publicly traded companies through sustainability listings and assessment processes are all indications that change is already under way.
- *The effort is clearly scalable.* All evidence indicates that companies of any size, whether privately held or publicly traded, are capable of navigating the path to sustainability.
- *Start with research and education, and shape a sustainable strategy.* Examine specific assessment and reporting models, then evaluate your own company against those standards. Look at the leaders who have already begun the process of making their organizations sustainable. There are thousands of public resources that will help

you identify the common elements in successful transformations in your industry. Every company is different, but there are common and transferable approaches.

- *Risk management is a critical aspect for success and a cornerstone to strategy formulation.* Risk management will require work, but the process has matured, and there are numerous resources at your disposal. Use them to identify risks and develop plans to mitigate those risks.
- *Comprehensive and focused effort is required* to build the protocols necessary for sustainable sourcing and sustainable supply chains. This task is large but doable, and no matter what anyone says, it is not "too complicated." The processes are mature, and there are many alliances you can join both inside and outside your industry sector.
- *Investments in sustainability will pay off* in financial rewards, brand recognition, and survivability, especially in light of the risks associated with business as usual. The next few chapters will help you see how these investments will pay off, now and in the future.

Chapter 8

Does Corporate Sustainability Create Measurable Value?

Business is all about solving people's problems—at a profit.
—Paul Marsden

Rebecca True has over 15 years of consultative and financial services industry experience. She founded True Capital Advisors, LLC in May 2009 following eight years as a senior financial advisor with Bank of America Merrill Lynch. Rebecca is a certified financial manager (CFM) with a degree in economics from University of South Florida.

REBECCA—Prior to beginning research for this project, I hadn't really considered whether companies that invested in sustainability were more profitable than those going about "business as usual." My initial impression was that sustainability initiatives cost a lot of time and money to implement on a large scale. The payoff seems intuitive, but actually proving it could be extremely challenging. Some may argue that sustainable companies are disadvantaged in financial comparisons for a variety of reasons:

- Up-front costs of implementing more sustainable operational processes
- Costs of implementing sustainability throughout the full value chain
- Ongoing costs associated with more stringent manufacturing and purchasing requirements
- Costs associated with providing more generous employee benefits
- Loss of short-term revenue from passing up business opportunities that do not meet strict social, environmental, or ethical standards

Others may argue that sustainable companies enjoy several advantages:

- Choice of more talented employees
- More reliable supply chains
- Improved community relationships
- Worldwide reduction in environmental or litigation risks
- More competitive product and process innovations

Many aspects of corporate sustainability can be objectively measured—metric tons of waste, percentage of recycled or recyclable material, energy use, and so on. But aspects like improved community engagement and an increased talent selection pool are qualitative and subjective, which makes them difficult to calculate. Also, what value do you put on the mitigation of future risks—for instance, when the sustainability strategy mitigates resource risks by radically changing product design and raw materials? Transformations don't happen overnight, so there's no before-and-after chart showing pre- and post-sustainability profits. Achieving meaningful benefits for stakeholders requires continual evolution and incremental improvement in a variety of sustainability initiatives.

For publicly traded companies, profitability is only one influence on stock price and dividend yield. Future potential and comparisons to industry peers are also important, not to mention the impact of economic and geopolitical factors. Does sustainability translate to increased revenues or business valuation? Does sustainability impact investor returns? What about on a risk-adjusted basis?

I was somewhat skeptical, but I was determined to begin my research with an open mind. My intention was to provide thoughtful, practical analysis that would help global business leaders draw their own conclusions. If corporate leaders and investors can get excited about the benefits of social responsibility including profitability and risk reduction associated with sustainable practices, it will offer far-reaching benefits for everyone.

As an executive building a compelling argument to change your organization's strategy to incorporate a commitment to sustainability, you need to be prepared to answer the questions your traditional stakeholders are certain to ask: Will it be profitable? Will the strategy add value to the organization? We'll take a close look at the data for a number of companies that are identified as leaders in the transition to sustainability. The findings will help you answer these questions so you will be better prepared to implement or refine your organization's strategy.

For sustainability to correlate directly to financial performance, it must have a positive impact on cash flow, credit ratings, financing interest rates, or business valuation. There are four primary theories that suggest sustainability has a positive impact on corporate financial performance:

1. *Managing all stakeholders.* Sustainable companies benefit from "addressing and balancing the claims" of multiple stakeholder groups including their customers, investors, management and employees, suppliers, and communities.[1] For example, through increased transparency and accountability, sustainable companies enjoy fewer disruptions in their supply chains and stronger customer loyalty. Companies that fail to address all stakeholder expectations may lose customers, have disgruntled employees, or inspire less investor confidence, which should eventually lead to reduced profit opportunities and lower corporate credit ratings.[2]

2. *Reputational benefits.* Sustainable companies have a greater potential to attract and retain employee talent.[3] Employees play a significant role in growth potential of a company and directly impact investor returns. Customers sensitive to sustainability issues may increase company sales numbers and may even pay a premium for sustainable products and services.[4] Brand image enhancement can positively impact investors as well as improve supplier and customer relationships. Fair labor practices, along with health and safety standards, reduce a company's exposure to potential litigation and reputational risk.

3. *Enhancing operational efficiency.* Pursuing sustainability principles like environmental best practices, waste reduction, and water and energy conservation typically leads to innovation, offering a competitive advantage over corporate industry peers. The implementation costs of sustainability initiatives are usually outweighed by the profits and efficiencies gained through these innovations.

4. *Long-term perspective.* Companies that emphasize a long-term business perspective should outperform those that do not because prioritizing long-term corporate objectives over short-term profits should contribute to more stable earnings growth and less downside risk.

ARE SUSTAINABLE COMPANIES BECOMING MORE ATTRACTIVE INVESTMENTS?

According to the Forum for Sustainable and Responsible Investment, only 55 investment funds focused on incorporating environmental, social, and corporate governance (ESG) factors in 1995, accounting for a total of $12 billion in U.S. assets. In 2012, that number had increased to 720 investment funds focused on ESG factors, managing over $1 trillion in U.S. assets.[5] As shown in Table 8.1, the vast majority of this rapid growth happened between 2010 and 2012; in two years, the ESG assets in these programs increased by 78 percent! U.S. assets signify only a small portion of the global investment funds that have sustainable and responsible investment strategies. Although North America still has a long way to go

TABLE 8.1   Investment Funds Incorporating ESG Factors 1995–2012

	1995	1997	1999	2001	2003	2005	2007	2010	2012
Number of Funds	55	144	168	181	200	201	260	493	720
Total Net Assets (In Billions)	$12	$96	$154	$136	$151	$179	$202	$569	$1,013

The number of investment funds incorporating environmental, social, and governance (ESG) when deciding where to place managed assets has grown rapidly since 1995. Environmental issues were a factor in 551 investment vehicles, governance was a factor in 346, and social criteria were incorporated in 622 investment vehicles.

Source: US SIF Foundation.

to catch up with Europe, the largest areas of future growth are in developing countries.[6] Since professional investors place funds only where they expect to see profits, the exponential growth of funds incorporating ESG factors indicates anticipated profitability of sustainable companies.

As it turns out, sustainable investing in the United States is outpacing conventional investment assets under professional management.[7] This is an indication that investors expect a better return on their investment from these sustainable investments, since in general investors do not part with their money if they believe the investment to be a loss. Of the US$25.2 trillion in total assets under management tracked by Thomson Reuters, 12.2 percent is attributed to sustainable and responsible investing. In other words, sustainable investing in the United States represents nearly one out of every eight dollars under professional management.

Where is this tremendous growth coming from? Who is driving demand for sustainable investment funds? Are those investors truly energized and passionate about their social, environmental, and ethical views, or is this pure capitalism at work? Or is it both?

A number of benchmarks and methodologies have been developed to attempt to measure the corporate social responsibility (CSR) or environmental/social (corporate) governance (ESG) investing experience. As mentioned in the previous chapter, asset manager RobecoSAM developed one of the most extensive methodologies and offers some of the longest running survey, research, and evaluation tools for benchmarking corporate sustainability. Known as the Dow Jones Sustainability Indexes (DJSI), they are compiled from data resulting from invitations and corporate sustainability assessment surveys to more than 2,500 of the world's largest publicly traded companies. Participating companies are evaluated based on a range of financial sustainability criteria covering social, economic, and environmental aspects. The 73-page questionnaire asks about topics like transparency and governance (codes of conduct, executive remuneration), supply chain management, greenhouse gas emissions, and much more. Participants are scored and ranked against their industry peers. The top 10 percent of globally sustainable assessed companies within each of 58 industries are selected for inclusion in the flagship index, the DJSI World.

Since 1999, RobecoSAM's efforts have identified sustainability leaders across all industries and geographies. Both investors and the companies themselves use the DJSI to better integrate sustainability initiatives and to quantify performance against those objectives. RobecoSAM analysts believe that their sustainability criteria allow a more comprehensive view of potential value creation for global companies, as they note in their white paper "Alpha from Sustainability":

> Sustainability trends such as climate change, resource scarcity or demographic change shape the competitive environment in which companies operate by introducing long-term sustainability opportunities and risks. Our conviction is that companies that can effectively manage risks and seize opportunities related to such trends exhibit a superior capacity to prosper over the long run. A firm's ability to grow earnings increasingly depends on intangible assets such as the quality of management, branding power, human capital development and intellectual capital, to name a few.[8]

Institutional investors would seem to agree with this philosophy, since they have driven most of the recent growth in sustainable investments.

In 2009 alone, institutional investors invested over US$8 billion in financial products specifically associated with DJSI-listed companies. When the DJSI measurements began in 1999, institutional investments in DJSI-listed companies totaled less than US$500 million. One likely conclusion is that institutional investors are expanding their search for suitable investments in companies with attractive long-term potential returns, and they recognize that there are higher risks associated with shorter-term portfolio investments. Clearly, they prefer investments in companies that integrate ESG criteria. It seems investors are increasingly requesting that their investments conform to their personal values. In the most recent US SIF Trends survey, client demand and values were the reasons most cited by investment managers for incorporating ESG factors into financial products.[9] This significant shift in investor interest is more than just a trend and clearly affects how corporations will be valued now and in the future.

How Do Social Factors Affect Corporate Profitability?

When we discuss companies using resources strategically and sustainably to affect their profitability, the impact of employees is one of the most critical components. It's a significant element of CSR and ESG initiatives, just as it plays a vital role in corporate profitability for all types of companies. Let's take a look at a few examples of how companies that pay attention to the role of people in their organizations are improving their profitability.

As discussed previously, good governance is a common characteristic of profitable companies focused on sustainability. Embedded in the concept of "good governance" is diversity of thought, gender, and ethnicity. Many recent empirical studies show a dramatic difference in stock performance for companies that have a diverse leadership or board representation over those that do not. For example, McKinsey showed that companies with a higher proportion of women at board level typically exhibited a higher degree of organization, above-average operating margins, and higher valuations. Credit Suisse Research Institute published its analysis

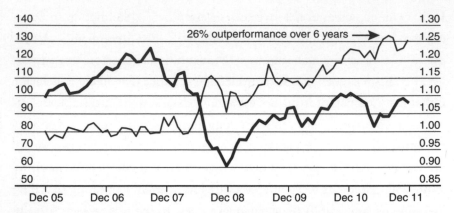

FIGURE 8.1   A six-year comparison of companies (market capitalization of more than $10 billion) with at least one female board member (thin line) versus companies with no female board members (bold line) showed greater than 25 percent outperformance by companies with diverse board representation.

Source: Thomson Reuters, Credit Suisse Research Institute.

of "Gender Diversity and Corporate Performance" in 2012. Looking back six years at relative share price performance for all companies with market caps greater than US$10 billion, they too found that companies with female board representation outperformed those without women on their board by 26 percent (Figure 8.1).

The data across the studies is not entirely consistent, but evidence from many of them does suggest that diverse board representation may be associated with less volatility and greater balance through full business cycles. Minimized volatility tends to signal better profitability for shareholders.[10]

Natura, the Brazilian cosmetics company discussed in Chapter 4, provides a great example of how paying attention to social factors benefits a company. Natura has long been admired for its environmental and social practices. Natura's Ekos product line works with over 2,300 families in 25 communities to grow 31 native species used in Ekos products. Natura paid these communities US$496 million in 2011 for cost of goods, benefit sharing agreements, and use of image, as well as training and advisory services.[11] Natura has also implemented a number of other logistics and recyclable container initiatives that have reduced carbon emissions by 21 percent over the past five years. Prior to the Ekos launch in 2000, Natura suffered from a three-year financial stagnation, with insufficient sales growth and limited distribution channels. Within just two years of the Ekos launch, Natura's net profits jumped from US$15.2 million to US$33.7 million annually.[12] Thanks to the financial recovery, Natura was able to get listed on the Sao Paulo stock exchange in 2004. The subsequent infusion of capital helped Natura open distribution channels for direct sales of its cosmetics throughout Latin America, with a venture into France, which contributed to dramatic revenue growth over the following years. In 2011, revenue jumped by 20 percent in a single year to US$2.9 billion. Natura's commitment to the environment and social innovation with its local communities has certainly paid off, not only for investors but also for local and global stakeholders.

Embracing the Environment Leads to Profitability

There is a lot of data to suggest a correlation between the financial performance of companies pursuing carbon reduction or neutrality and their stocks. Better stock performance is seen from companies that have achieved leadership positions on either the Carbon Performance Leadership Index (CPLI) or the Carbon Disclosure Leadership Index (CDLI). The Carbon Disclosure Project (CDP) and PriceWaterhouseCoopers (PWC) produce an annual study assessing the total return performance for the CDLI and CPLI leaders against the Global 500. (The Global 500 represents 500 of the largest global companies making strides in regulating carbon emissions.) The 2012 report found that since 2006, CDLI companies have delivered total returns of 67.4 percent—more than double the 31.1 percent return of the Global 500. CPLI companies generated average total returns of 15.9 percent since 2010, which also more than doubled the performance of the 6.4 percent return over the same period on the Global 500 index.[13] In just one example, DuPont cut its energy use between 1995 and 2005 by 7 percent below 1990 levels, reduced greenhouse gas emissions by 72 percent (11 million metric tons), and saved more than US$2 billion in the process.[14] This is a significant sum, even for a company of DuPont's size. DuPont shareholders benefitted, with a stock price that doubled over this period, as well as a 57 percent increase in their annual dividend.

Commercial real estate provides a clear glimpse into the beneficial impact of sustainability initiatives for investors. There is strong evidence that environmentally sustainable real estate outperforms properties without an environmental certification throughout various economic cycles. Specifically, several recent studies indicate that Leadership in Energy and Environmental Design (LEED) certified and Energy Star certified buildings provide greater financial return for their owners over nongreen comparable assets.[15]

Investors typically estimate the value of commercial real estate by comparing capitalization rates ("cap rates")—the ratio of a property's net operating income against its estimated value. The higher the cap rate, the higher the annual return on investment. The *Journal of Real Estate Portfolio Management* suggested a direct correlation of significant rental premiums, shorter vacancy periods, lower cap rates, and higher prices per square foot for multitenant Class A properties over the last decade.[16] The performance differences between LEED and Energy Star certified properties in the United States versus conventional properties are astounding. According to a 2012 report, "green" real estate had a 13 percent average higher sales price than less energy efficient competitor properties. These properties also commanded higher effective rents by 7.6 percent annually. The report states, "REIT [Real Estate Investment Trust] portfolios with more efficient properties thus have higher risk-adjusted returns, suggesting that the benefits of investments in 'greening' properties outweigh the costs."[17] In REIT portfolios, a greater percentage of LEED or Energy Star certified properties positively impacts operating performance and reduces the risk of volatility. It also appeared to protect their investors during the most recent downturn in the business cycle. In a paper for the *Journal of International Money and Finance*, researchers Eichholtz, Kok, and Yonder noted that the stock performance for these portfolios fared better than less "green" property portfolios, perhaps because they were less exposed to energy price volatility and to occupancy risk during this period.[18]

Demand for sustainable commercial real estate is escalating globally, which in turn is providing significant financial benefits for investors in these assets. Energy efficient office space provides cost savings benefits for corporations that can translate to improvements in their bottom lines. However, businesses are becoming more interested in additional performance objectives (such as employee productivity) that also have long-term financial benefits. In one 2010 survey, 92 percent of executives considered sustainability a key factor in their location decisions, and a significant number cited employee productivity, health, and satisfaction as their top sustainability concerns. Fifty percent of these executives are willing to pay more for green leased space—a 13 percent jump over the previous year.[19]

For owners of commercial real estate, there are benefits to acquiring or building ecofriendly certified properties that go beyond tenant demand, employee well-being, and competitive advantages with operating efficiencies. In the United States, federal tax incentives—including rebates, credits, and grants—are available for owners that implement green building, and most states (and many local governments) extend additional tax benefits. Financial institutions including banks, mortgage REITs, and private equity firms are also beginning to incorporate preferential financing arrangements for green buildings, since they represent a lower risk proposition. Property insurers offer discounts to owners of green buildings, or to those that upgrade their buildings to obtain certifications, again because of the reduced risk.[20] LEED or Energy Star certified lease tenants benefit through lower operational costs and better working environments, which offers competitive advantages over companies that lease comparable space in nongreen buildings. Companies that invest in developing or upgrading sustainable properties clearly benefit in many ways.

Does Ethical Governance Contribute to Profitability for Businesses?

Organizational ethics is a critical element of long-term sustainability. It affects governance, reporting, auditing, and accountability in both financial and nonfinancial aspects of sustainability. With a portfolio valued at US$230 billion, the California Public Employees' Retirement System (CalPERS) uses its investment heft to influence corporate governance standards. CalPERS's organizational ethics efforts are intended to drive long-term shareholder value and reduce risk to its investment portfolio. Since CalPERS has a fiduciary duty to successfully execute its investment strategy so that it can uphold its large pension obligations over multiple generations, sustainability is very important. CalPERS believes that corporate leaders and investors must have aligned interests on its views about shareholder rights, executive compensation, fund manager terms and conditions, and investor protection.

CalPERS has established a corporate governance strategy called the Focus List program, which works with more than 100 companies in its U.S. portfolio that are financially underperforming on both stock returns and according to its corporate governance standards. CalPERS engages directly and privately with these companies every year and publishes specific guidelines for corporate accounting principles. These principles set the barometer for measuring corporate governance and accounting expectations among institutional investors and many global companies, particularly with respect to monitoring shareholder rights; disclosure of financial and nonfinancial information; and setting expectations on corporate leadership for diversity, corporate responsibility, and market conduct.

Efforts toward corporate governance improvements in the Focus List companies have led this index to consistently outperform its relative benchmark. Performance gains for the companies engaged with CalPERS are significant, and cumulative returns from these companies average more than 15.8 percent above the benchmark after three years.[21] This "CalPERS effect" is well known in the financial services industry and demonstrates that companies with active corporate governance investors can improve shareholder returns.

QUANTIFYING THE BENEFITS OF SUSTAINABILITY

The question still remains: Do sustainable companies outperform less sustainable companies? Let's compare two top indexes, one general, one focused on sustainability. The MSCI World index, comprising over 6,000 global stocks, is the most common benchmark for assessing global stocks in developed countries. It includes companies from all industries and geographies, and most studies measuring the financial returns of sustainability use it as a comparison point. The Dow Jones Sustainability Index (DJSI) World is seen as the benchmark for global sustainable stocks and comprises a smaller group of 700 global companies that have elected to participate and be measured on quantifiable sustainability factors. At first glance, there doesn't seem to be a definite winner. The DJSI World outperforms the MSCI World in some years, and the MSCI World outperforms in others.[22] Without looking further, it would be easy to conclude that the actual data isn't decisive. However, viewed over a longer time horizon, the picture changes significantly:

- From 2003 through 2012, the DJSI World outperformed the MSCI World by 3.66 percent cumulatively.
- The DJSI World and the MSCI World virtually performed identically over the 14 years since the inception of the DJSI World in 1999—a period that included two market downturns and recovery periods. This suggests that sustainable companies stand a good chance to perform as well as their nonsustainable competitors over long time periods.
- In the five-year recovery period following the 2000–2002 global dot-com bubble burst, the DJSI outperformed the MSCI by 7.76 percent cumulatively.

It is important to note that the MSCI World comprises all types of companies, including some that are sustainable or transitioning to improved sustainability over time, as well as others that aren't making the same improvements. As sustainability becomes more prevalent, a greater percentage of the companies within the MSCI World will become sustainable or improve their sustainability in ways that impact business valuation. This will narrow the performance differences between the two benchmarks over time.

A more compelling case for the positive relationship between corporate sustainability and stock performance comes from RobecoSAM's 2011 white paper "Alpha from Sustainability." RobecoSAM sampled companies from developed countries that participated in its annual Corporate Sustainability Assessment between 2001 and 2010 and ranked them after correcting for size, sector, and region. Based on overall sustainability scores, the top 20 percent of companies were named "Sustainability Leaders" and the lowest 20 percent were named "Sustainability Laggards." RobecoSAM's results show that leaders significantly outperformed laggards over the 10-year period and through various market cycles.[23] The study results also included superior performance data during crisis and postcrisis financial periods, suggesting that sustainable portfolios have better risk characteristics, too. The results showed decisively and quantitatively that investing in sustainable companies does pay off for investors:

> The findings of this research provide us with credible evidence that firms that adopt corporate sustainability best practices are not contradicting or neglecting their primary objective, which is to maximize the profits to shareholders. On the contrary, it would appear that the puzzle of corporate financial performance broadly encompasses both financial and extra-financial considerations.[24]

Companies that lead in corporate sustainability as measured by annual assessments tend to obtain financial results that are consistently higher than their average or laggard corporate sustainability peers. Leaders (top

10 percent) have better return on equity, return on assets, shareholder return, and Sharpe ratios (designating higher yields per unit of risk).[25]

Researchers at Harvard Business School have conducted one of the most thorough and long-range empirical studies to date, assessing performance data for sustainability leaders and laggards from 1993 through 2010. By measuring both stock market performance and accounting measure comparisons, their study more confidently suggests that high sustainability leaders significantly outperform their low sustainability counterparts.[26] By measuring stock market performance and accounting performance for groups of high- and low-sustainability companies over an 18-year period (Table 8.2), these findings suggest companies can adopt environmentally and socially responsible policies and simultaneously contribute to shareholder wealth creation.

The Harvard study shows that sustainable firms generate significantly higher profits and stock returns. Since their study researched data over an 18-year period, the authors concluded that developing a corporate culture of sustainability is a source of competitive advantage over the long run:

A more engaged workforce, a more secure license to operate, a more loyal and satisfied customer base, better relationships with

TABLE 8.2 Cumulative Performance of Sustainable Versus Traditional Portfolios

	Sustainable Firms	Traditional Firms
	Value-Weighted Portfolios	
Stock Market Return	$22.6	$15.4
Return-on-Assets (ROA)	$7.1	$4.4
Return-on-Equity (ROE)	$31.7	$25.7
	Equal-Weighted Portfolios	
Stock Market Return	$14.3	$11.7
Return-on-Assets (ROA)	$3.5	$3.3
Return-on-Equity (ROE)	$15.8	$9.3

This table shows the cumulative performance over 18 years (1993–2010) of portfolios composed of "sustainable" or "traditional" firms based on an initial $1 investment.

Source: Eccles et al. HBS working paper 12-035, November 14, 2011.

stakeholders, greater transparency, a more collaborative community, and a better ability to innovate may all be contributing factors to this potentially persistent superior performance in the long-term.[27]

Goldman Sachs has also developed a global equity research methodology for identifying public companies that exhibit superior performance with respect to environmental, social, and governance principles. The ongoing Goldman Sachs SUSTAIN project analyzes approximately 1,400 large companies globally across 27 sectors, with 70,000 data points on ESG performance from publicly available reports. GS SUSTAIN's framework combines analysis of three key drivers of corporate performance:

1. *Cash returns.* Sustained superior cash returns translate to long-term cash flow and earnings growth.
2. *Industry positioning.* Exposure to growth regions, products or assets, and competitive position in markets including market structure, cost of leadership, pricing power, technology, and scale versus peers.
3. *Management quality (ESG).* Assessment of governance structure, stakeholder engagement, and environmental performance as indications of the quality of overall leadership.

From its launch in June 2007 through May 2012, the GS SUSTAIN Focus List has significantly outperformed its corresponding broad global benchmark index, the MSCI All Country World Index (ACWI), by 43 percent![28] The companies that make up this list provided better risk-adjusted returns during the 2008 global market financial crisis and outpaced the absolute performance of the broad global benchmark index in the postcrisis recovery too. The GS SUSTAIN Focus List stocks also outperformed their MSCI ACWI global benchmarks in all sectors over the same time period. Goldman Sachs's analysis suggests that the magnitude of outperformance per sector varies considerably. The greatest magnitude of outperformance occurred in the energy sector, which is generally perceived to be among the least sustainable sectors globally. Smaller outperformance occurred in sectors that already have a larger percentage of transformational benefit associated with sustainability based on their longer-term commitment to ESG principles. Interestingly, one sector in the analysis demonstrated comparable or slight underperformance relative to its MSCI ACWI sector benchmark over the period: technology.[29] Intuitively, as technology companies are by nature on the leading edge of innovation, the slight underperformance of this sector appears reasonably attributable to the shortened product cycles for hardware delivery companies within this sector as compared with other sectors.

Goldman Sachs has been sufficiently impressed with the level of outperformance associated with its GS SUSTAIN methodology that the company is further incorporating this type of analysis across all of its global investment research. Goldman Sachs believes it will lead to identifying better investment opportunities for its clients.

Does Corporate Sustainability Create Measurable Value?

The analysis and examples in this chapter support the conclusions made earlier in the book that sustainability "pays" and demonstrates that organizations, their shareholders, and other stakeholders can benefit financially from the implementation of sustainability practices. An intricate evolutionary path is required to get global companies, investors, and communities to work together to satisfy the longevity concerns of each stakeholder group, and there are many potential outcomes. There are still challenges to overcome with benchmarking sustainability initiatives because of the lack of agreed-upon standards for measuring ESG initiatives across industries and around the globe. Other challenges include:

- There are disclosure level differences among types of corporate entities (public versus private), individual corporations, and geographies that provide some substantial hurdles to forming thorough comparisons. Competitors in different groups may disclose more or less information or may not report on the same sustainability metrics.

- According to the KPMG International Survey of Corporate Responsibility Reporting 2011, only 36 percent of family-owned companies and 46 percent of private equity, investor-owned companies report on corporate responsibility. In contrast, almost double that percentage of publicly owned companies (69 percent) demonstrate sustainability reporting leadership. This explains why most of the research on sustainability and investment returns to date revolves around data gleaned from global public companies.[30]

- KPMG suggests that the low percentage of privately held companies that report on corporate responsibility may be due to a combination of the lack of public investor scrutiny and a tendency on the part of privately held companies to have a preference for action rather than detailed reporting.

Privately held firms can learn a lot from the reported data of publicly traded companies about how to implement sustainability initiatives and the value proposition to their stakeholders. Sustainability performance is clearly an indicator of overall business value. Adherence to sustainability principles can lead to increased brand value, competitive advantages, customer satisfaction and retention, improved employee health and productivity, increased revenues and returns for shareholders, and stronger regulatory compliance, and it offers reductions in operating costs, future global risks, and liability mitigation.

Investors of all types are demanding investment strategies with a longer outlook that integrate social, environmental, and ethical considerations within their portfolios. This trend will continue to grow as more investment dollars reinforce the merits of profitability for organizations. But the growth will be compounded by global demographic changes. A massive societal wealth transfer to members of the Millennial Generation will occur over the next two decades through increased earnings and inheritance. Members of this generation, like none before it, have the opportunity to invest those assets using their conscience as a guide. Millennials in developed nations across the globe grew up in an era when household recycling was the norm from the moment of their birth. They operate and collaborate with their peers as team members, and they see their contributions to the world no differently. In addition, the 2008 financial crisis exposed significant risks to companies that have short-term business strategies. As more investors search for investments with superior business models and better long-term potential, sustainability considerations will exercise more influence over their decisions. The institutional investors won't be the only ones driving demand for these strategy improvements.

When business leaders adopt rigorous metrics to evaluate and scrutinize different aspects of sustainability processes, it indicates that management has a better grasp on the overall details of the company. Corporations and their investors will enjoy much greater financial success over the long run with better sustainability processes and effective implementation and management of these initiatives.

More and more auditing firms, consultancies, academic institutions, pension funds, institutional investors, and investors from Wall Street and Main Street are coming together with organizational stakeholders in agreement about the best financial and nonfinancial performance metrics for judging the long-term benefits of organizational sustainability. As they do, there will be increased pressure on companies that lag in becoming more sustainable.

CHAPTER SUMMARY

Clearly, pursuing sustainability creates measurable value over the long term. Sustainability contributes to positive financial performance for companies through properly managing stakeholders, providing reputational benefits for companies, enhancing operational efficiency, and emphasizing long-term perspectives on business objectives.

Sustainability is not an extraneous pet project. Increasingly, sustainability is valued and even demanded by investors throughout the marketplace and is a benchmark of company leadership indicating long-term vision and viability. Even when initial implementation costs are taken into account, improved sustainability processes and effective implementation results in much greater financial success over the long run:

- A groundswell of support for sustainability has created massive growth in sustainable investments over the last few years. In the United States alone, sustainably focused investing represents nearly one out of every U.S. $8 under professional management. Investors increasingly prefer investments in companies that integrate social, environmental, and ethical corporate governance criteria.
- Diversity profoundly and positively affects company profits. Companies with a diverse board tend to have higher return on equity (ROE), lower net debt to equity ratios, higher price/book value multiples, and better average growth.
- A 10-year analysis conducted by RobecoSAM sampled and ranked companies participating in its Corporate Sustainability Assessment into Sustainability Leaders (the top 20 percent) and Sustainability Laggards (the bottom 20 percent). Leaders significantly outperformed laggards over the 10-year period and through various market cycles, proving decisively and quantitatively that investing in sustainable companies does pay off for investors, and suggesting that sustainability leaders have better risk characteristics as well. The study authors concluded that "the puzzle of corporate financial performance broadly encompasses both financial and extra-financial considerations."
- Researchers at Harvard Business School measured stock market performance and accounting performance for groups of high- and low-sustainability companies over an 18-year period and found that companies can adopt environmentally and socially responsible policies while improving wealth creation.
- Privately held firms can learn a lot from the reported data of publicly traded companies about how to implement sustainability initiatives and the value proposition to their stakeholders. Sustainability performance is clearly an indicator of overall business value.

Chapter 9

BUILDING A STRONG AND LONG-LASTING REPUTATION

Trust is the glue of life. It's the most essential ingredient in effective communication. It's the foundational principle that holds all relationships together. And trust grows out of trustworthiness.
—STEPHEN R. COVEY, *FIRST THINGS FIRST*

At this point in the book, we wish we could say that by focusing on sustainability in your strategy, you will ensure yourself a great reputation and superior brand. Unfortunately, it isn't that simple. An organization's reputation or the value of a brand is based on myriad factors, not the least of which is the perceived value of the product or service. And today more than ever before, perceived value encompasses how the product impacts society and the planet. As previous chapters have shown, the real value of a company's brand or reputation is based on how the company responds over time to all outside forces, and how, not just if, it meets the promises made to its stakeholders.

GREG—The quote at the beginning of this chapter is one of the most sig-nificant guiding principles in my life. I believe it is also the foundation for a positive corporate reputation and a valued brand.

The first time I heard Stephen Covey speak in person was in 1995. I was working in the Washington, D.C., area as the executive director for the Construction Specifications Institute (CSI). Covey was conducting a full-day leadership workshop specifically for leaders of nonprofit organizations, particularly philanthropic, membership, and trade associations. Armed with my laptop, pen, and notepad (tablet computers were still science fic-tion at the time), I settled in to hear him speak about "principle-centered leadership," the core concept of the book of the same name, released just two years earlier.

As is the case for any program promising you will "spend an intimate day with" a celebrity speaker, the room was overflowing. I wondered if we had exceeded the fire safety code for maximum number of occupants and personally expected that intimacy and interaction would be out the window. Covey proved me wrong from the first words he uttered: "Hello everyone. Today, we are going to talk about trust." As they say, he had me at "Hello"!

The discussions that day were focused on the individual leader. Covey spoke of building relationships with individuals and of the fundamental basis for all relationships being trust. What struck me was the simple basis of trust: he said that building a relationship based on trust required each party to be both trusting and trustworthy. In other words, each person in the relationship must keep his or her promises and allow others to do the same (Figure 9.1).

As a leader of an organization, building a strong and lasting relation-ship with and among staff is critical to successfully accomplishing any plan. This means giving staff the resources and support they need and then standing back and allowing them to complete the task. Constantly looking over their shoulders and checking their work, making decisions for them, not delivering the resources promised, or not supporting them in times of crisis can all undermine the element of trust and break down

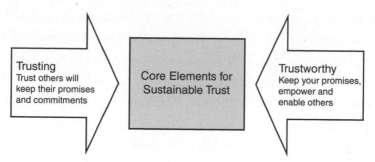

FIGURE 9.1 Building lasting relationships requires sustainable trust.

the relationship. This kind of trust is not easy, especially when a critical initiative is on the line.

At the time, I wondered how trust factored into the organizational framework and what its impact on reputation and brand value were. But before I could ask, Covey explained that this principle applies to organizations as well as to individuals. The key, he said, is to remember that whether we're talking about a one-on-one relationship or a company's relationship with one or more of its stakeholders, trust is always about making and keeping a commitment or promise.

This discussion was profound for me. I began to understand the need to identify the numerous stakeholders of an organization and recognize the needs of each one. It is not enough to consider the shareholder and the customer when implementing a strategic initiative. We must understand how the initiative will impact all stakeholders. Without this understanding, we could easily create a breach in the relationship with a key stakeholder, which might undermine the reputation and success of the company.

TRUST BETWEEN THE COMPANY AND ITS STAKEHOLDERS

Let's put this into perspective by thinking about a product *brand promise*. From the customer's perspective, the brand promise is a commitment to deliver some sort of specific condition, benefit, or experience. Hopefully, it creates a real expectation in the mind of the customer. When BMW chose the slogan "The Ultimate Driving Machine," it immediately created a certain expectation. If a potential customer drove a BMW and found it lacking, the promise would be broken. Failure to deliver what that slogan promised would diminish BMW's reputation and brand. That is why BMW, like other great car companies, goes to such lengths to ensure that the driving experience in its vehicles is unique. "Few crises can wipe billions of dollars off a company's valuation overnight," writes 2degrees CEO Martin Chilcott, "but damage to reputation can."[1]

Let's take it up a notch to the level of *enterprise strategic promises*. BMW stated that it wanted to become "the most sustainable car company" in the world. This is an enormous commitment with no concrete definition. There is no target to point to, no other company to use as a guideline. Very likely, everyone has a unique perspective on what this actually means to a car company. BMW may even be setting the bar for this standard. The company's eventual reputation will be based on BMW's stated intent—to be the most sustainable car company in the world—and will be measured by its ability to carry out that intent. Most important, it is based on the *belief* of all of its stakeholders that the intent has been carried out and that it is of value to the company's mission. A 2005 study by the Economist Intelligence Unit (EIU) put it this way: "Reputation is not just a question of how an organization is perceived, but of how it is perceived relative to peers and competitors."[2]

When determining what this commitment means, a company like BMW would have to consider the myriad stakeholders (Figure 9.2) who will be forming their own interpretations and expectations about what this strategic commitment will mean to them:

- Will local communities benefit from this change?
- Will suppliers need to change their manufacturing methods and sources?
- Will this affect compliance with existing regulations in the EU and around the globe?

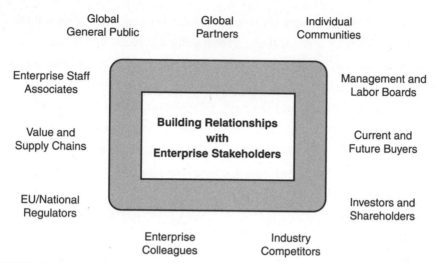

Global
General Public

Global
Partners

Individual
Communities

Enterprise Staff
Associates

**Building Relationships
with
Enterprise Stakeholders**

Management and
Labor Boards

Value and
Supply Chains

Current and
Future Buyers

EU/National
Regulators

Investors and
Shareholders

Enterprise
Colleagues

Industry
Competitors

FIGURE 9.2   BMW's fulfillment of its mission to become "the most sustainable car company in the world" will be judged by a wide variety of stakeholders interested in and affected by the outcome of BMW's transformation.

- Will BMW still be viewed as an attractive investment?
- Will BMW plant managers understand the implications for production schemes and the effect on rate of production?
- Will staff positions be realigned?
- Will staff associates be motivated to follow through on the change?
- Will the fundamental designs of the vehicles need to be changed?
- Will the needs of the local communities surrounding the plants be affected?

The implications are profound and should not be taken lightly. If the company is successful and its reputation is based on its ability to meet this commitment, it will build trust and probably gain a competitive advantage, particularly in a resource-constrained world. This conclusion is also supported in a 2005 report by the Economist Intelligence Unit (EIU), where nearly 60 percent of the risk managers surveyed agreed that "reputation is becoming a key source of competitive advantage as products and services become less differentiated."[3]

But if BMW's actions do not live up to its announced commitment, the trust of one or more stakeholders could be broken, and brand loyalty and reputation will suffer. This could have far-reaching implications for customer buying decisions, employee loyalty, and investor appeal. Doug Gafner, formerly vice president of risk management at Hilton Hotels, places the burden of proof of a good reputation on delivering on your promises. Avoiding a damaged reputation is "more about getting everything else right" than it is about a single issue, he says.[4] In the context of reputations, perception is everything.

DOES SUSTAINABILITY REALLY MATTER IN SHAPING ORGANIZATIONAL REPUTATION TODAY?

When shaping our organizational reputation, we need to examine stakeholder trust and perceptions. Remember that reputation is dynamic and transient, and is always measureable only through the perception of the stakeholders. For 14 years, Harris Interactive has been interviewing stakeholders throughout the United States to determine the reputation of the most visible companies. The methodology used is the Reputation Quotient, an assessment model that considers 20 attributes in six dimensions, highlighting the complexity of reputation today:

1. Social responsibility
2. Emotional appeal
3. Financial performance
4. Workplace environment
5. Products and services
6. Vision and leadership

Harris identifies the most visible companies using online interviews and then assesses their reputations. The nomination and assessment processes engage as many as 20,000 people throughout the United States.

It should be no surprise that the reputation of corporations in America is not as healthy as it could be. In 2011, sixteen corporations enjoyed a reputation considered "great" (rating 80 or higher). In 2013, that number fell (for the third year in a row) to just six.[5] The "great" companies for 2013 were Amazon.com, Apple, Disney, Google, Johnson & Johnson, and Coca-Cola. These six companies have preserved their great reputations for the last three years of overall decline, and Johnson & Johnson has been a perennial "great" company since 2006.[6]

However, what is most interesting is the characteristics separating these "great" companies from others. Table 9.1 compares the top driver characteristics for 2011 and 2013. The perception of corporate trust, ethics, admiration, respect, and the role the company plays in society remain in the mix. These are the elements needed to build a reputation as a company focused on sustainability, and they correlate directly to the social, economic, environmental, and ethical concepts encompassed in the SEEE model.

The concept of trust is based on our personal values and on the culture in which we live and work. Religious affiliations, corporate values, and personal moral convictions are all important in how an individual perceives reputation. The Reputation Institute's Global RepTrak 100 study, discussed in Chapter 3, addresses attributes similar to the ones used in the

TABLE 9.1   Harris Interactive RQ Drivers for "Great" Companies

2011 Drivers	2013 Drivers
Admire and respect	Outperforms competition
Trust the company	Admire and respect
High ethical standards	Trust the company
Outperforms competition	Plays a valuable social role
Good value for the money	Good company to work for
	Good feeling about the company

This table shows how the characteristics distinguishing great companies changed from 2011 to 2013.

From the 2013 *Harris Poll RQ Summary Report*.

Harris Poll. The seven key dimensions in the Reputation Institute's study are:

- Performance
- Products/services
- Innovation
- Workplace
- Governance
- Citizenship
- Leadership

To win the support of stakeholders across the globe, companies have to engage them in all dimensions. The Reputation Quotient, like the Global RepTrak100, shows that corporate citizenship (social impact), workplace quality, and trustworthy behavior and governance are all critical to building a solid reputation. In survey after survey, stakeholders continue to value characteristics that pertain to a company's dedication to a more sustainable presence in the world.

PERCEPTION AND REALITY: BOTH ARE CRITICAL TO SUCCESS

The perceptions of stakeholders determine the real value of reputation. However, it is critical to understand that reputation is not based on image or perception alone; it is also based on real, concrete action. For example, suppose Patagonia built a public image of using sustainable cotton in its shirts through marketing campaigns and extensive public relations but failed to live up to that promise in practice. The disparity would undermine the company's reputation if discovered and would very quickly affect the success of its business. On the other hand, if the company made significant strides in the use of sustainable cotton without making stakeholders aware, it would do little to raise the value of the company's reputation.

In this case, publicizing Patagonia's actions would present a tremendous opportunity to build its brand.

An important study supporting this idea is the annual joint study by Brandlogic and CRD Analytics, which measures perception of and actions toward sustainability leadership.[7] The study poses the question of perception versus reality: Is your reputation built on both action and perception, or just on the promise of sustainability without real progress? Brandlogic measures the "Sustainability IQ" of 100 global companies from nine Global Industry Classifications (GICS). The Sustainability IQ has two components: the Sustainability Perception Score (SPS), a measure of how a company is perceived by key stakeholders, and the Sustainability Reality Score (SRS), which reflects the actual performance of the company against key indicators.

Company SPS scores are determined through virtual interviews of individuals from three stakeholder audiences: purchasing professionals, investment advisors and professionals, and graduating college and university students. The last category is both unique and important to the futures of the companies under scrutiny. These students are the future talent that leading organizations want to attract, and their perception of company reputations is likely to impact their decision about taking a job with an organization.

The SRS score, on the other hand, is an analytical look at key indices and performance indicators. It compiles the performance of 1,200 publicly traded companies that publish reports on environmental performance, corporate social responsibility, or governance behavior containing some of the performance measures provided in the GRI reporting guideline. The study lens focuses on 141 metrics across the three performance areas. From this comprehensive study, Brandlogic produces a rating score for the evaluated companies.

This kind of rigor can be confusing if not placed in the right context, which is exactly what the Sustainability IQ Matrix does (Figure 9.3). This matrix organizes the companies into four categories:

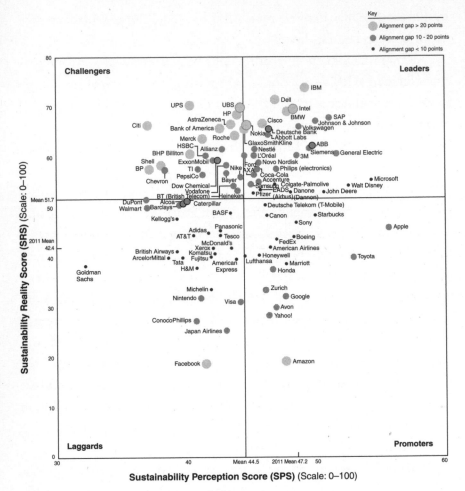

FIGURE 9.3 Brandlogic Sustainability IQ Matrix 2012

Source: *2012 Sustainability Leadership Report*, Brandlogic and CRD Analytics

1. *Leaders.* Companies that have high SRS performance and a strong SPS performance, demonstrating that they are communicating their achievements effectively and building reputations as sustainability leaders.

2. *Challengers.* Companies that are not getting enough public recognition for their achievements in sustainability.

3. *Laggards.* Companies that have demonstrated and are perceived as having a low level of commitment to sustainability.

4. *Promoters.* Firms that receive recognition for becoming more sustainable before they actually get there.

From a general point of view, any organization would love to be placed in the Leaders quadrant, recognized for demonstrating good progress in both achievement and communication. Challengers have an opportunity to improve their reputation as sustainability leaders through careful and effective communication with stakeholders and through implementing a coordinated communication plan at key times during strategic change. L'Oréal made the move from Challenger to Leader between 2011 and 2012. L'Oréal senior vice president of corporate communications Pamela Gill Alabaster told the study organizers, "We understand the value of engaging stakeholders and have increased our efforts to share and communicate our vision for sustainable, responsible, and inclusive growth."[8] Note the emphasis on engaging stakeholders. That means engaging them in solving the problems of sustainability as well. A company that resists stakeholder engagement may surrender the lead—and perhaps market share—to its competition. The competitive edge can be lost quickly.

The Laggards in the Sustainability IQ Matrix are less active and moving much more slowly toward becoming sustainability leaders. These companies have not invested sufficiently in changing their strategy or in implementing a strategy quickly enough. But investing in communications before real action occurs can pose the risk of being categorized as a Promoter. Promoters are not "keeping up with their image." Their publicity and commitment must be matched by visible action. If stakeholders realize that a company's actions and plans differ from what it portrays, the company's reputation will suffer, and there will probably be a breach of trust between the company and one or more stakeholders.

One of the most significant findings of the Brandlogic study is the overwhelming conclusion that good corporate citizenship is a critical consideration in decision making. Whether from the perspective of purchasing professionals in the United States, investment advisors in the United Kingdom or China, or the hearts and minds of graduating students in

Germany, there is a widely held conviction (88 percent) that good corporate citizenship with respect to the performance areas of environmental action, social responsibility, and governance behavior is important.

IMPROVING YOUR REPUTATION WITHOUT LOSING GROUND

Obviously, the next question is how to ensure that you won't devalue your reputation as you begin the transformation to sustainability. Whatever actions you take, you need to address your reputation carefully and treat it with the same degree of caution as you would any critical risk.

There are some important fundamentals to consider when managing and protecting your reputation, particularly during a transformation. First, remember that your reputation and brand have real value. Although it is hard to measure specifically, many companies attribute a value to "goodwill." Publicly traded companies commonly attribute 10 to 15 percent of their market value to goodwill. So your plan should include ways to protect that value while going through the transition. Don't assume that reputation is a "warm and fuzzy" asset. In all of the studies we reviewed, stakeholders indicated they would reconsider personal buying decisions if a company's reputation continued to deteriorate.

Second, remember that word of a damaged reputation will spread like wildfire through dry grass. The 2013 Harris Reputation Quotient poll recognized two types of individual stakeholders when it comes to gaining and using information: seekers and bystanders. Not surprisingly, seekers actively look for signs of goodwill, reputation, and admiration. Bystanders wait to be notified. Over the last two years, the percentage of stakeholders who seek information has grown from 50 percent to 56 percent of those polled.[9] More important, the majority of both seekers and bystanders are willing to share the information they obtain about companies with other stakeholders.[10] You can take advantage of this fact if you engage stakeholders correctly in meaningful conversations about sustainability and use social media tools and other communication channels to assist in spreading the word.

This is a double-edged sword, however. Stakeholders are ready and eager to talk about your company—for good or ill. Show real progress in your plans, work toward achieving your sustainability commitments, and you will have a great volunteer communications department. On the other hand, if you make commitments and then fail, you can bet that the same stakeholders will spread the news rapidly and without mercy, both in personal conversations and through social media. YouTube, Twitter, Gripevine, Mashable, and other online sites present thousands of free portals to help a negative remark go viral. Be sure that perception and reality are the same, or your reputation will suffer.

Third, recognize that your corporate culture is a critical determinant of your reputation. Your company policies, actions, and staff affect stakeholder interaction each and every day. From the EIU study:

> Above all, good companies create a culture where employees take responsibility for enhancing corporate reputation through their everyday activities. Responsibility for corporate reputation, and the threats that can undermine it, extend from top to bottom in today's corporation.[11]

The CEO, in this case, is not the only reputation manager in the company. Every member of the staff team, as well as those in the value and supply chain, shares the responsibility. You must consider training and preparation to shift the enterprise culture in a meaningful way, so that each employee is contributing to the change as well as to the organization's reputation.

Next, reputation has a human component. Figure 9.2 and Table 9.1 show key determinants of reputation leadership, and both have a measure of "feeling." The respect one has for a company or a brand no longer resides on a strict price-value continuum. It is partly technical but often is based on "gut feelings" and on whether or not the values of a company resonate with your values. "Today's brands are in touch with their own humanity and the humanity of others," says Jez Frampton, global CEO of Interbrand, which does the annual "Best Global Brands" study.[12] One prominent example is the "Thank You Mom" campaign Procter & Gamble launched during the 2012 Olympics in London. The ads highlighted the commitments and sacrifices made by the mothers who raised some of the athletes, and they stressed human values, family cohesion, dreams, and mutual love. They were some of the most highly viewed ads in Olympic history. Procter & Gamble's reputation as a sensitive company grew dramatically.

That is not to say that you must create world-class, award-winning ad campaigns announcing your transition to become a sustainable company. Rather, it means that stakeholders need to understand the substance of what you are doing and its impact on society. This information must be communicated with cultural sensitivity. In Japan, for instance, it might be considered inappropriate and arrogant to "brag" or "boast" about special initiatives. In those cases, clear and simple communications would be warranted. In contrast, when the CEOs of Unilever or Coca-Cola or the founder of Patagonia are asked about their sustainability efforts, they describe without hesitation their initiatives and the impact that their sustainability efforts will have on society. In interviews with six different Coca-Cola executives about the content of the ME-WE-WORLD sustainability plan, each one not only knew the material impact of this strategy on his or her own area of responsibility but also how it impacted everyone else's. They spoke of every area of responsibility as if it was their own. In fact, it *is* their own, since they represent Coca-Cola as an enterprise, not just their individual area of responsibility. And they recognize that when they represent Coca-Cola anywhere, they become reputation managers. They believe that it is their responsibility to build a strong and powerful reputation, not only as a beverage producer but also as a sustainability leader.

This transformation will require a deliberate and public commitment to change, demonstrated execution and results, and assurance that stakeholders perceive the change. This approach is called *strategy-based reputation*. When your reputation is based on strategic change, then management decisions and initiatives are driven by a guiding vision or mission. The reputation is built into the organization rather than being part of an "add-on" due to a new product or a unique external incident or crisis. Corporate public relations is not the only group responsible for a company's reputation. Nor is this solely a marketing-led or brand-related approach to reputation management. When building a strategy-based reputation, everyone in the company recognizes that reputation is an imperative pervasive throughout the organization, and it becomes everyone's responsibility to contribute to the value of corporate reputation. Grahame Dowling and Peter Moran, in their paper "Corporate Reputations: Built In or Bolted On," point out the benefits of a strategy-based reputation:

- It reveals the viability and effectiveness of the organization's strategy.
- It forges links to and reinforces other facets of the organization that underpin and support its strategy (such as its culture).
- It makes the organization's future behavior more predictable for stakeholders and competitors.[13]

Dowling and Moran explain that with a reputation based on a clear strategy, all employees become "owners" of the reputation and comprehend the connection between their work and the reputation of the company. The strategy is connected to clear goals, and progress tracking is shared. Each employee can then know his or her role in protecting and enhancing the reputation. If a crisis occurs, the resulting actions will be instinctive rather than knee-jerk; employees will truly understand the importance of their efforts and can help manage the reputation of the company through any crisis.

When reputation is not strategy-driven, reputation management may be assigned to a particular department or group, deliberately or as an afterthought, with the individuals in that group becoming mere "custodians"—just in charge of maintenance—or "visitors" who give only lip service to the entire idea.[14] Visitors may not understand the significance of company efforts toward sustainability, and when pressed, they will fail to deliver a clear description of the drivers and impact of the company's actions. Such behavior can only diminish the company's reputation as a sustainability leader.

CHAPTER SUMMARY

Reputation is not a simple issue. Building a strong reputation takes years, not days or months. As you build a strong case for making your company more sustainable, you need to protect your company's reputation as it exists now and ensure you do not lose ground. Reputation is a valuable asset and as such must be treated with deliberate care. To do so, consider the following:

1. In today's world of diminishing differentiation between competitive products, a strong, positive reputation is a competitive advantage.
2. A strong reputation must be treated like an asset with concrete value.
3. Building a strong reputation requires a bond of trust between the company and its stakeholders. To build long-term trust, the company must keep its strategic promises.
4. The basis for trust is the ability of a company to deliver on its strategic intent—in other words, keeping its enterprise strategic promises. Such "strategy-based" reputations are the most viable, since decisions and resulting action are driven by strategy.
5. The stakeholder list for an enterprise is complex and requires analysis and prioritization to be sure that you are engaging the most important groups. In today's world, the stakeholder list goes well beyond the customer, the board, and the shareholders.
6. Reputation is based on both the company's actions and the perceptions of important stakeholders. If you plan to build a strong reputation, you must engage with your stakeholders to ensure they are aware of the progress you are making on your sustainability

objectives. Those who make significant progress in becoming more sustainable but are not recognized for it have a great opportunity to increase the value of their reputation through improved communication. Companies whose reputation is based more on perception than on real progress risk damaging their reputation.

7. Companies perceived as having a great reputation garner admiration and respect, are trusted by their most important stakeholders, and are expected to play a valuable social role.

8. Your stakeholders will actually seek out information about your company, and the majority will share that information. This can be a key advantage in spreading the word about your successes. Use social media and other communication channels to your benefit, and invest in education and training of key stakeholders.

9. Finally, remember that reputation has a human component. All staff members need to understand the value of becoming more sustainable and the material impact on society. Don't hand your company's reputation over to "caretakers" or "visitors." A strategy-based reputation requires ownership throughout the organization.

Chapter 10

Common Traits of Sustainable Companies

We do not seek to predict; instead we provide a framework
to think about possible futures.
—Christopher A. Kojm

One of the most interesting and common misunderstandings about corporate sustainability is that becoming a better corporate citizen will mean a reduction in profitability. While we were writing this book, one manager told Nathalie, "That is all well and good, but our stockholders are expecting quarterly profits, and thus the main focus of our executives is on profit, not on investing in sustainable practices." Six months after joining the organization, this new manager was convinced his company's primary focus was short-term profits, and he executed accordingly. Yet by its nature, the long-term survival of any organization requires successful execution of long-term strategies focused on traits of sustainability.

In previous chapters, we provided many examples of businesses aligning profitable strategies and a sustainable future for all. Our research

191

revealed examples of impressive transformations by large multinational corporations, midsized companies, and small start-ups making it their mission to perform in a sustainable manner. These companies were willing to put in the effort and found out along the way that being sustainable pays off financially too. Analyzing these cases revealed that the organizations shared several common traits. Cultivating these traits in your own organization will allow you to start or continue the journey to becoming one of the companies that will help create a sustainable future.

CHANGE IS IN THE AIR

Our planet has been changing since long before we set foot on it, but the rate of change in the last 50 years seems exponential. In a 1994 article for the *Atlantic Monthly*, Peter Drucker coined the term "Knowledge Society" to describe a future in which knowledge, not raw materials or capital, would be the driving competitive force.[1] Modern technological advances have made knowledge more available than ever before. We now understand that human beings are altering the fabric of our planet. Something we never thought possible is happening: the very composition of our oceans and the air we breathe is changing.

And people are responding. People are demanding environmental changes; in China, where 700,000 people a year die because of air pollution, intense online social activism in 2012 finally prompted the government to monitor and communicate air quality data.[2] Employees are demanding ethical changes in the way we work and do business; they want to work for socially responsible organizations.[3] And consumers are demanding more sustainable products and practices, though there is still a mismatch between their demands and their buying practices.[4]

Society's paradigm is shifting, albeit slowly. After the Industrial Era, which focused on rebuilding countries and working hard to secure a comfortable living, and the Information Era, which digitalized our lives and enabled us to connect online, a large focus in the Social Era is on life balance and genuine concern with the planetary changes taking place.

Organizations are feeling increasing pressure from markets, consumers, employees, and governments to extend their focus beyond profits. There is new momentum toward acknowledging the long-term societal impacts of business and toward developing strategies, visions, and values that consider all stakeholders.

Previous chapters have described several examples of social pressure forcing companies to change their corporate strategy. One of the first highly public campaigns of this type was launched in the 1990s, after pictures of child labor in Nike factories in developing countries hit the press.[5] Public outrage forced Nike to change the labor practices of its suppliers. "We learned to view transparency as an asset, not a risk," says Nike CEO Mark Parker.[6] Nike created an extensive measurement system to evaluate all of its suppliers worldwide. That system became Nike's Materials Sustainability Index (MSI), which in turn was used to create the Higg Index discussed in Chapter 4.

It's important for companies to respond to social pressure, but it's even better to ensure people have no reason to start a campaign against your company in the first place. Especially in the era of social media, news travels fast. A 2009 research paper of the Stanford Graduate School of Business showed that social pressure could depress a company's financial performance.[7] It's a domino effect: first the company's brand and reputation is weakened, which may lower sales, which demotivates employees. Nobody wants to admit working for that company dominating the news cycle and social media sites because of damaging environmental or labor practices.

As discussed in Chapter 6, leading organizations around the world are redefining themselves to become more socially responsible. Chapter 8 showed that being socially responsible does not mean giving up profit or revenue. But what does it mean to be a socially responsible company? Vigeo, a French sustainability assessment organization regarded as the European leader in this area, has a well-rounded definition:

A "socially responsible company" is one that not only fully complies with the obligations of applicable legislation and conventions, but also one that accounts for how it integrates social and environmental factors into its global strategic decision making, policies and practices.[8]

In other words, sustainability should be integrated into your company's strategic plan, performance systems, and the way you do business. It should be a core business function. When the organizational transformation is complete, you should not be able to distinguish a transformed company from one that was founded on principles of social responsibility. An organization that transforms to become sustainable should have as small an environmental footprint as one that focused on community values and on preserving and renewing resources from the outset.

This takes true commitment and a lot of perseverance. It does not happen overnight. More than 15 years after the original public outcry, Nike still gets media attention for abusive labor practices in its factories.[9] Nike itself admits in its 2010–2011 Sustainable Business Performance Summary Report that labor practices are lacking at some factories.[10] But Nike's strategies and actions show that the company is committed to building a sustainable, socially responsible future.

SUSTAINABILITY LEADERS: WHAT SETS THEM APART?

We define sustainable companies as organizations that incorporate social, economic, environmental, and ethical factors into their strategy and day-to-day management in order to secure a successful business over the long term. Sustainable companies take into account the rights, interests, and expectations of all of their stakeholders, and they are fully transparent regarding their actions and the consequences of those actions. We have observed seven traits shared by all good global corporate citizens in pursuit of a sound social, economic, environmental, and ethical business:

1. Adopting a long-term business view
2. Focusing on results by actively reducing ecological risks and costs
3. Taking responsibility for the complete value chain and supply chain

4. Changing the organizational DNA—an integrated strategy and strategic decision process that embraces and embeds social, environmental, and ethical principles

5. Demonstrating transparency and accountability for results

6. Nurturing innovation

7. Embracing synergetic collaborations

Integrating social responsibility into your organization's strategy should reduce risk, secure long-term profitability, and positively influence your brand. Let's look at each of these traits in more detail.

Adopting a Long-Term Business View

The definition of "long-term" is subjective. In general, if you ask an American manager to define long-term for a business objective, you might get an answer of three to five years. If you ask a Japanese manager, the answer will be more in the range of 50 to100 years, and Europeans will land somewhere in the middle. There are several reasons for this with the main one being historic differences in attitudes toward time horizons.[11] In today's world, every company needs a long-term horizon in order to deal with the diminishing resources, growing demand, and environmental issues threatening supply chains. A longer horizon means a company needs to weigh the interdependence between business and society, paying more attention to the long-term consequences of decisions on society and the environment. It means taking action now for benefits in a distant future.

More and more companies are realizing that long-term thinking is necessary to mitigate risks, to promote development in the communities they touch, to generate wealth, and to reduce environmental harm. To run a profitable business for the long run, it is necessary to incorporate sustainable development into all business strategies. This requires a new mindset. As one example, remember BMW's campaign to fight AIDS in South Africa, discussed in Chapter 3. BMW invests a lot of money in this effort, with no direct profit goal. It is part of the company's long-term vision of ensuring healthy communities in order to ensure a future BMW workforce and customer base and to support the UN Millennium Goals to battle global illness.

Unilever, one of the companies in transition, has extended its horizons too and in 2009 made a statement by discontinuing quarterly profit updates and earnings guidance. Unilever CEO Paul Polman said, "We're not going into the three-month rat races. We're not working for our shareholders. We're working for the consumer; we are focused and the shareholder gets rewarded."[12] Polman believes that shareholder wealth will be a natural by-product of focusing on the long-term sustainable operation of Unilever. In addition, he wants to attract investors who support the long-term value creation approach, not the ones who are looking for short-term profits.

It comes down to full cost accounting over the long run. What are the environmental and social costs of doing business? These costs should be considered so investments to mitigate these long-term costs are seen not as public relations efforts but as real investments delivering long-term efficiencies and benefits for business, society, and the environment.

Focusing on Results by Reducing Ecological Risks and Costs

In today's business climate, companies need to brace themselves for more than just financial risks. Their risk management should also include indirect financial risks brought on by external factors like supply chain disruptions due to extreme weather, social unrest, or water scarcity. For employees to feel secure to take the risk to get involved in specific sustainability initiatives that support the corporate sustainability strategy, they need to feel supported by clear mandates and messaging from top leadership. Clear governance models that are responsive, accountable, and informed should support this. In Chapter 11 we will dive deeper into risk management, which includes creating targets and commitments for social and environmental issues. However, after implementing the internal and direct supply chain risk management plan and learning from the active monitoring and mitigating, the next phase is to extend the focus to the full value chain, again setting clear targets and linking performance to these targets.

The point of this risk management process is to shift from a reactive mindset to a mindset that tries to anticipate future risks and prepare for them before they happen. Every business will be faced with water and resource scarcities. Every business will have to deal with waste management. Proactively dealing with these issues will secure a profitable future business and reduce exposure to sharp environmental and social shocks.

One company that has inspired many others to follow suit is Interface Inc., the modular carpet company founded in 1973. Interface CEO Ray Anderson set out to prove that it is possible to run a profitable business by doing what is right for the planet:

> I wanted Interface, a company so oil-intensive you could think of it as an extension of the petrochemical industry, to be the first enterprise in history to become truly sustainable—to shut down its smokestacks, close off its effluent pipes, to do no harm to the environment, and to take nothing *from* the earth not easily renewed *by* the earth.[13]

Interface decided to drastically alter its business model. The majority of its factories now run on renewable energy, protecting them from the unreliable oil and gas markets. Design and production processes were modified to use recycled materials, especially old carpets, as input for new carpets—a perfect example of a circular economy company! Interface has proven for almost two decades that being a socially responsible company pays off. Between 1996 and 2008, greenhouse gas emissions were cut by 71 percent in absolute terms, and waste going to landfills was reduced by 78 percent. Interface has been producing zero-carbon-footprint carpets since 2003. At the same time, the company has increased sales by 66 percent and has doubled its earnings. Interface's goal is "Mission Zero": by 2020, the company will leave zero footprint in energy, water, and waste, while being a profitable business.

One key to Interface's success is a very thorough measurement system tracking progress toward both ecological goals and social goals. It measures items such as energy use by source, greenhouse gas emissions, recycled material use, waste to landfill, water use per unit, training, safety, and philanthropy. Interface has proven the numerous benefits of being socially responsible: lower costs, higher profits, loyal customers, and brand recognition the most expensive advertisement campaigns couldn't buy. Plus, Interface is a magnet for top talent! What is keeping you from following in Interface's footsteps?

Taking Responsibility for the Complete Value Chain and Supply Chain

One of the most powerful changes an organization can make is to realize it is not alone in the process of delivering a product or service to customers. In the process of creating value for customers, an organization and its suppliers are actually a community. This is the **value chain**: "the successive stages during which value is created when producing, distributing, and servicing a product."[14] What this definition misses is that the value chain encompasses all stakeholders adding value to the product or service. Interestingly enough, there are few definitions of *value chain* that embrace sustainability. Most see the mapping and management of the value chain merely as a way of improving productivity and quality and of increasing profitability. This misses the biggest opportunity: recognizing stakeholders and engaging them in building a community focused on sustainability and long-term profits.

The companies highlighted in this book have taken responsibility for their value chain. BMW engaged its customers not only to get ideas for future design models but also to understand their vision of sustainable mobility. Suntory, which would not be able to exist without clean water, created environmental sanctuaries to protect freshwater sources and the environment that produces water. Chocolate producers have invested in the well-being and development of cocoa growers and their communities to ensure the future supply of high quality cocoa. Coca-Cola realized that its business success depends on thriving, sustainable communities, which depend on empowered women, and thus created the 5by20 program.

Although a company's **supply chain** is part of the full value chain, it presents a unique set of needs and challenges. Essentially, the supply chain is the integrated community of suppliers who provide everything from raw materials to semifinished goods and services for final production. As business people, we often think we have a good picture of a manufacturing company's supply chain: raw materials suppliers, subassembly providers, parts and fastener suppliers, and so on. However, in a sustainable world, we must look also at the companies supplying parts and supplies to these suppliers—for example, all of the suppliers to a company that produces a subassembly for the final product. When you think of supply chain in that light, it becomes a complex, intricate map. Factor in globalization, and the supply chain spans many countries and cultures. Ensuring that your supply chain is sustainable requires a series of critical tasks:

1. Mapping the supply chain
2. Engaging the suppliers in discussions about sustainability and setting goals
3. Developing a code of behavior and a commitment to sustainability to be adopted by all suppliers
4. Finding ways to confirm supplier compliance to the code of behavior
5. Deploying a process to enforce compliance and establishing a set of consequences for noncompliance (which may include replacing the supplier)

Performing all of these tasks would seem quite difficult for a company like Coca-Cola, which has more than a thousand franchised bottlers around the world, or a company as small as Patagonia, which probably lacks the resources necessary for inspection and enforcement. But size does not matter in this case. Both companies found ways to deploy and enforce their supplier codes—Coca-Cola by doing its own inspections, and Patagonia by using third-party certifiers for inspecting organic cotton farms and factories. They are both taking responsibility for their supply chains.

Changing the Organizational DNA

Companies founded on sustainable principles show that social and environmental responsibility can be a key decision driver in the strategic decision-making process. It is embedded in the mission and values of the company; internal and external processes are defined by it; it is part of employee performance appraisals; and it drives the strategic agenda. Sustainability is in their organizational DNA. Companies like Patagonia and Natura have shown that it is also profitable to strive for a sustainable future. Companies in transition—like Coca-Cola, BMW, and Unilever—employ clear messaging and actions from the top down in order to transform their organizations into sustainable businesses. Leadership by example is crucial. These companies treat sustainability as part of their core strategy.

If you see sustainability as a nice-to-have—as "greening" your brand or as a response to outside pressure—you miss the incentive to make the structural changes necessary to deal with the risks facing your company. In addition, you could find yourself facing uncomfortable public scrutiny more often than desired, as numerous stories in this book have shown. Sustainable companies have integrated social, economic, environmental, and ethical criteria into their core business strategy and business model and have changed their decision-making processes to embrace these criteria. The decisions they make take more into account than just efficiency, effectiveness, quality, and profitability. Possible environmental harms, value added to a community, and ethical concerns are all considered. In other words, this is about good business with a sense of purpose, not just about doing good. When sustainability is built into a company's DNA, and thus into the strategies and business model, it is no longer seen as a separate cost factor. Products and services will be designed with mainly renewable resources, taking into account reusability, and with global sustainable supply chains, saving significant costs due to production efficiencies, reduced waste, and improved yields.

Demonstrating Transparency and Accountability

Anyone who was over 18 in 2001 knows about the Enron disaster, a breach of trust and a case of financial fraud that tore down a multibillion-dollar company, destroyed one of the largest audit firms in the world, and penalized innocent employees who lost entire pension funds and gainful employment. Scandals like this weren't limited to the United States. Similar financial fraud was found in Europe, India, and other countries. In the United States, the result was the infamous Sarbanes-Oxley Act (SOX), both loved and hated, which led to a revolution in financial transparency and accountability. SOX was a model for similar regulations in the UK and throughout Europe.

Today SOX is part of the organizational financial process in both for-profit and nonprofit companies, but it is still focused on financial reporting only. In the world of sustainability reporting, voluntary reporting and limited transparency dominate the landscape. The most standardized voluntary reporting mechanism for sustainability initiatives and performance is the Global Reporting Initiative (GRI), explained in Chapter 7. The GRI is not required, and the reports are not always audited to ensure that the progress declared is factual. However, a common trait of socially responsible companies is to become more transparent and accountable. The last few years have seen a dramatic increase in the number of companies submitting GRI reports, and many participants are now seeking independent audits of their results to ensure accuracy. Such accountability builds stakeholder trust and, in turn, strengthens reputation. In the European Union, publicly traded companies are now required to report sustainability efforts and progress as part of their annual reports. This is a step in the right direction and brings us that much closer to showing sustainability performance as an integral part of overall organizational performance in a single annual report. This European legislation will likely affect regulations across the globe.

As privately held companies, Patagonia and IKEA are not required to follow the public financial disclosure and accountability requirements of publicly traded companies or to embrace the public, standardized reporting of the GRI. This could weaken their credibility as transparent and accountable organizations. To mitigate this risk, they created and publish their own sustainability indexes, and they publish extensive accounts of their progress on social responsibility in various areas. This provides some degree of transparency and shows their intent, but without external audits or links to an industry standard, it is difficult to determine if these companies are meeting their commitments and growing in a sustainable fashion. However, as we have shown previously, these privately held companies have the freedom to initiate change quickly and effectively, without worrying about the impact on quarterly reporting requirements.

These and many other organizations participate in coalitions such as the Fair Labor Association, Forest Stewardship Council, and sustainable farming initiatives that lead to certification of growers. These coalitions include nongovernmental organizations and associations that are held accountable for providing the necessary oversight or certification to prevent breaches in supplier codes. Patagonia, for example, has been a part of the Bluesign environmental standards—voluntary guidelines for manufacturers and suppliers considering textiles, chemicals, and related manufacturing products—since 2000. This effort helps to offset the lack of standardized reporting and adds to the measure of transparency critical to an organization's reputation. Public, standardized reporting is the trend and is quickly becoming the rule rather than the exception.

It is important to remember that companies will never be immune to challenges to their commitments to sustainability. One of the toughest challenges of accountability is when a company finds that one of its suppliers fails to meet sustainability standards. For example, a producer who has violated the fair labor principles or a farmer who has failed to comply with required certification might be discovered through an internal audit, or worse, through the press before the company can discover the violations itself. A company's reputation for being socially and environmentally responsible will hang on how well and how quickly the problems are addressed, and on open and transparent communication. This will make or break public trust.

Nurturing Innovation

Innovation is at the core of becoming a sustainable business. First, business model innovation is required to fully integrate sustainability into the business strategy and to provide longevity in business and for the planet. Then product innovation designs sustainability into the product. This is what Interface has done. Interface shifted its business model for one of its product lines—carpet tiles—from selling carpets to leasing them. In 2003, Interface introduced a system allowing consumers to "lease" the carpet tiles while Interface maintains them and replaces them with new ones when they are worn out. The old carpet tiles are recycled and the materials reused to make new tiles.

One of Interface's tools for evaluating the environmental impact of a product or process is life cycle assessment (LCA). Using LCA, Interface assesses in each phase of the product life cycle how a product's creation and eventual disposal uses materials and energy, the type and amount of wastes generated, global warming effects, and other key impacts. A structured assessment process like this would allow you to identify the easiest or most impactful areas for life cycle improvements or to select the supplier products or processes with the lowest environmental impacts when redesigning products.

Royal Philips N.V., another company in transition, is an example of an organization that has put innovation at the heart of the company and of its sustainability efforts. The Dutch company has set a goal to improve the lives of three billion people a year by 2025 (almost half of the world population!) through innovation in healthcare, energy efficiency, and materials.[15] One of the innovations Philips is striving toward is providing a new life for old components in new products. The Senseo Viva Café Eco was one such innovation: the world's first recycled designer coffee machine.[16]

Philips is one of the 29 global companies that make up the World Business Council for Sustainable Development (WBCSD). In *Vision 2050,* the WBCSD describes a path toward a vision of a world where "9 billion people live well and within the limits of the planet."[17] The pathway shows individual paths for nine key elements—including values, economy, agriculture, energy and power, and mobility—and the changes needed over time to reach the overarching goal of a sustainable world for all by 2050. This ambitious vision demands radical change, and two of the key tools for driving that change are behavioral change and disruptive sustainable innovation.[18]

In April 2006, Philips assigned Dorothea Seebode, then senior director of sustainability, to investigate ways to implement sustainability as a business and innovation driver, changing the company's paradigm. After a one-year investigation around the world, both within Philips and in other organizations, Seebode delivered an extensive research report and road map advising the following four steps to any company embarking on this journey:[19]

1. Start the innovation journey with two key questions in the back of your mind: What does your company want to contribute? What strengths does your company bring to the table?

2. Ensure that top management supports the innovation vision and encourages disruptive innovators to explore paths to the future.

3. Incorporate sustainable innovation in your company's DNA. Every department and individual needs to know what innovation means to them and understand the company's message on sustainable innovation.

4. Since people are motivated differently, communicate both the vision and theory behind sustainable innovation, as well as pragmatic approaches on how to realize it.

Nurturing innovation means unleashing the power of sustainability champions within your company. What can you do to ensure that the passion and compassion of social entrepreneurs is allowed to blossom within your business?

Embracing Synergetic Collaborations

Every company highlighted in this book has pointed out that it cannot reach its goals alone. Synergetic partnerships are crucial to success. Coca-Cola CEO Muhtar Kent calls it the Golden Triangle. Nike calls on the organization to "actively collaborate with others, including governments, NGOs, activists and, yes, our long-time competitors."[20] Unilever CEO Paul Polman states that change must happen at a systemic level, which will happen only if all major players in society commit to change and collaborate.[21] Collaborations are happening in all kinds of industries. Coca-Cola partnered with the World Wildlife Federation and the Nature Conservancy. SABMiller has partnered with the World Wildlife Federation. Greenpeace finds itself in more corporate boardrooms than it ever would have been able to imagine in its wildest dreams (or nightmares).

Collaboration is not easy. It takes work. Cultures at partnering organizations can be wildly different, creating potential conflicts. Follow these guidelines to build successful partnerships that add value:

1. Set clear goals for the partnership.
2. Identify clear roles and responsibilities.
3. Prioritize the areas you want to partner on.
4. Involve the right partners with the right expertise and core competencies.
5. Invest time and money to show dedication.
6. Be willing to change your organization based on the outcomes of the partnership.
7. Be transparent.

There are limits to what you can do as one organization. Partnerships in sustainability are crucial to future profitable business.

A new type of thinking is essential if mankind
is to survive and move toward higher levels.
—ALBERT EINSTEIN

Chapter Summary

As you can see, the companies that are striving to be socially responsible exhibit common traits. They continue to surprise us with their innovation, creativity, and commitment to sustainability. One of the most significant characteristics of each of these companies is that none of them views sustainability as an option or as a commitment separate from its day-to-day operations. It is never viewed as extraneous but as an integral part of the organization.

The common traits among companies that took responsibility to transform their organizations to ensure a long-term sustainable future include:

1. Adopting a long-term business view
2. Focusing on results by actively reducing ecological risks and costs
3. Taking responsibility for the complete value chain and supply chain
4. Changing the organizational DNA—an integrated strategy and strategic decision process that embraces and embeds social, environmental, and ethical principles
5. Demonstrating transparency and accountability for results
6. Nurturing innovation
7. Embracing synergetic collaborations

In order to become a successful, profitable, and sustainable company with a solid reputation, sustainability must be woven into business strategy and day-to-day decision making. The next section will explain how to use the SEEE model to start integrating sustainability into your organization.

PART 4

A Road Map for Changing Our Future

11

CREATING THE ROAD MAP TO A SUSTAINABLE FUTURE

I see no other long term choice for industry to survive . . . Each of us has a role in this transformation. We must all learn to make peace with the earth, not to make war on it, or we will lose.
—RAY ANDERSON, INTERFACE, INC.

Every year, we spend more and more money recovering from disasters, both natural and man-made. The year 2011 was the most expensive on record in terms of global insurance losses, in part because of devastating earthquakes in Japan and New Zealand and flooding in Thailand.[1] Even when these events do not touch us personally, they send ripples through our personal and business lives. For example, the 2011 Tohoku earthquake and tsunami caused catastrophic loss of life and property damage in Japan and triggered a disaster at the Fukushima Daiichi nuclear plant that displaced over 100,000 people.[2] However, the impact spread well beyond Japan, spilling over into the global energy industry by putting nuclear power front and center in public debate. Within 48 hours of the disaster, German officials suspended plans to extend the lives of its 17 nuclear power plants,[3] a decision that triggers ripples of its own. Will Germany quickly switch to methane-fired power plants, or will the country move toward renewable energy sources? What will this mean for workers in Germany? How will suppliers of nuclear power technology, such as General Electric, be affected? The Fukushima disaster also had a direct effect on the Japanese auto industry supply chain. Toyota, Honda, and Mitsubishi had to wind back operations, and the effects were felt in other high-tech industries as well.[4]

"Out of sight, out of mind" no longer works in today's interconnected world. To succeed, companies need to take into account the potential impacts of events like climate change, natural disasters, industry slow-downs, and supply chain disruptions. We are living in a transformative era. As the world becomes more volatile, we need to find ways to deal with it.

The businesses that survive and thrive in this new era will plan for significant changes happening now and for changes they envision in the future. Japanese insurance company Tokio Marine & Nichido Fire Insurance Company did this by identifying "climate change and global warming" as a key issue for future generations and a major risk to their business as early as 1999.[5] They responded to this threat by partnering with several nongovernmental organizations (NGOs) to form the Mangrove Planting Project. Since 1999, Tokio Marine Nichido has planted more than 7,500 hectares (18,000 acres) of new mangroves throughout Asia.

Does this sound disconnected? Frivolous? Far from it! The Mangrove Planting Project has numerous benefits from social, economic, and envi-ronmental perspectives. Mangroves serve as natural levees protecting the coastline from tsunamis and surge waves (environmental) and thus pro-tecting the people in coastal communities (social). This in turn reduces insurance claims (economic). Mangroves also provide an ecosystem for wildlife (environmental) and thus provide a livelihood for the local com-munities (social and economic). Like any other forested area, mangroves absorb greenhouse gases and thus lower the rate of climate change (envi-ronmental), which should reduce the frequency and severity of extreme weather events and thus (again) insurance claims (economic).[6] Tokio Marine Nichido has committed to the Mangrove Planting Project for the next 100 years. No, that is not a typo; the company's long-term business view spans generations.

LOOKING INTO THE FUTURE

Absent a crystal ball (we're still hopeful someone will invent a real one), our preferred method for envisioning the future is scenario planning. Scenario planning involves designing several possible futures, visualizing the different paths that could lead to those futures, prioritizing the aspects that are most important to your business, and then creating a strategy to survive and even thrive, no matter which scenario comes true.

History shows that the world does not progress in a linear fashion. Just think back to the 1970s oil shocks or the 2008 collapse of Lehman Brothers. Changes happen in waves and eddies, and the more connected our world becomes, the more unpredictable and complicated these currents will be. So how can we conduct long-term planning in an age of rising uncertainty? This is where scenario planning comes into play.

To be clear, scenario planning is not predicting the future. It is about creating a map of uncertainties around external forces such as political situations, social trends, economic forces, technology innovations, and environmental conditions, with the goal of preparing your company for known and hidden driving forces that are shaping the future.

Effective scenario planning requires creating not one but several different stories about the future. This compensates for the human tendency to oversimplify things. The stories are based on what your organization's leaders, collectively, think the future might hold. What do you think will happen 10 to 25 years out based on what you see today? Will the world have heated up by 4°C with all the associated negative consequences, or will we have found a way to stop the heating trend and maybe even reverse it? Has population growth created increased prosperity or desperate poverty? Scenario planning discussions should be an input for short- and long-term strategic decision making. For example, scenario planning prompted the New York Board of Trade to build a backup trading floor in the 1990s. This contingency probably seemed far-fetched at the time, but it helped minimize the down time after the September 11, 2001, attacks on the World Trade Center.[7]

One of the first large companies to use scenario planning was Royal Dutch Shell, which began scenario planning in the early 1970s. One of its scenarios included a rapid unexpected increase in oil prices. Only a year later, Shell was able to recognize key indicators that projected a dramatic increase in oil prices. Shell changed its strategy to adapt to this scenario and thrived through the 1973 oil shock. Simon Henry, Shell's chief financial officer, said:

> The intelligence and innovation that our Scenarios teams have contributed over many decades has proved hugely beneficial to our business. By providing unique insights and detailed analysis into the ever-changing global landscape, and projecting forward possible outcomes, the Scenarios team helps Shell's senior leadership make better informed decisions about our current and future operations.[8]

While they may sound similar, the difference between scenario planning and forecasting is that forecast planning is typically based on known data. Forecasting frequently involves straight-line extrapolations of past trends. In an uncertain and complex world with unexpected shocks, linear strategic planning is not sufficient to prepare you for the future. Scenario planning weighs the uncertainties and asks leaders to think through what might happen. How would it affect the external business environment, and how would it ultimately affect the day-to-day operations? Scenario planning lets us determine more effectively whether our strategy is robust enough to deal with more than one emergent situation or future scenario, increasing our chance of success. Anticipating multiple scenarios helps your organization become more adaptable, a crucial characteristic in our continuously changing world.

REHEARSING THE FUTURE

For the best results in scenario planning, most companies use an independent facilitator to manage the process. Whether this facilitator is internal, like Shell's separate scenario planning team, or external to the company, the facilitator should be responsible for the full process. Global Business Network (GBN), founded in 1987 and now a part of Deloitte Consulting, is an outstanding resource for scenario planning.

Scenario planning relies on three main principles:

1. *Long-term thinking.* We previously identified this as one of the common traits of organizations that are sustainability leaders. Long-term thinking is also one of the core principles of scenario planning. Viewing a horizon of 10 or 20 years (or longer) enables you to identify and anticipate long-term trends and to examine the long-term effects and consequences of your decisions.

2. *External vision as starting point.* GBN calls this "outside-in" thinking. We tend to think "inside the box," simply because our view of the world is based on our beliefs, values, biases, and perceptions. When we make decisions or set strategy for our business, we tend to think about what we know, which is not enough to prepare us for the future. To prepare for an unknown future, we should first think about what we do *not* know and what might be outside of our belief system. What alternate futures can you imagine? Envision the external aspects of those futures, like political environment, demographics, regional conflicts, social dynamics, technological inventions, or climate. Next, visualize how these aspects impact your company, positively and negatively. Knowing the impacts, what strategic decisions or actions should you take to mitigate the negative outcomes and reinforce the positive outcomes? You have now moved from the future backward to the present and from outside the company to inside the company.

3. *Variety of perspectives.* We need a variety of perspectives when we are envisioning and discussing the future. Homogeneous thinking,

or "groupthink," causes us to miss crucial aspects and will make the scenarios less robust. We can be looking at exactly the same information and see different things. That is why we need a variety of perspectives, to see the things we cannot see—to challenge our assumptions and envision a larger and more complex future than we can envision alone. So make sure your scenario-planning team is multidisciplinary, with people from inside and outside of the company and from different backgrounds, cultures, and age groups.

NATHALIE—In my work, I use many exercises to help people experience the fact that we see the world differently. Geert Hofstede first made me aware of these varying perspectives in a cultural economics lecture at my university. He showed us a picture (Figure 11.1) and asked, "What do you see?" Do you see an old lady? Do you see a young lady? What do your colleagues see? Don't take these varying perspectives for granted.

FIGURE 11.1   The Young Lady and the Old Woman is so familiar that many of us give it little thought; we already know what we see. But do you know what your colleagues see? (Commonly attributed to W. H. Hill in 1915, this illusion is almost certainly based on an image from postcards and ads in the late 1880s.)

SCENARIO PLANNING STEP-BY-STEP

Scenario planning helps create an enterprise competency called "adaptive foresight." Let's clarify this with a simple example. Imagine you are planning a sailing trip across the Pacific Ocean. You would prepare for multiple scenarios that might occur during the trip. You would bring along different navigational tools like GPS, radar, weather pattern charts, and sonar to enable you to pick the route that safely brings you to your destination. Once you start your journey, the route you end up taking will be based on the situations you encounter along the way. The mark of a good sailor is to attempt to foresee these situations and mitigate the potential impact. For example, you might pick up a storm on the radar and be able to navigate around it using the charts and the GPS.

Adaptive foresight is no different. It is the radar system for the organization. You start by selecting the right information, trends, and data to monitor (which is sometimes difficult to do in our world of data overload). Once you know what you're looking for, adaptive foresight watches for patterns and will sound the alarm when emerging global changes that can impact your business are detected. This provides the advance warning your organization needs in order to quickly adapt to these changes.

Scenario planning takes you from an external view of the world to an internal view of the external impacts on your company (see Table 11.1). Let's look at the different phases of scenario planning.

TABLE 11.1   Scenario Planning Phases and Questions

Phase	Question to Ask
	Outside View
1	What possible futures might be reality 10 to 15 years from now?
2	Where is the world today?
3	In which direction is the world moving?
	Inside View
4	What do we need to do to survive in two or more scenarios?
5	How do we foresee the future?

Scenario planning proceeds in phases, beginning outside the organization and progressively moving toward an organization-centric view.

Phase 1: Envision Possible Scenarios

In this phase, we ask the question, "What possible futures might be reality 10 to 15 years from now?" To answer this question, you would go through the following highly interactive facilitated process.

a. *Identify external driving factors* that could shape possible futures. These would include predictable and unpredictable forces, trends, and incidents. Once you have identified the main external driving factors, group them by category (political, social, environmental, technological, economic, etc.) and according to how certain they are to occur (from very certain to uncertain). Then prioritize the factors based on the potential impact your team thinks they might have shaping the future. The result would look something like Table 11.2. There are several studies that you can use as inspiration for identifying potential driving factors (and even scenarios), such as the *Vision 2050* report from the World Business Council for Sustainable Development (WBCSD) or the *Global Environment Outlook* (GEO) reports from the United Nations Environment Program.[9]

TABLE 11.2 Example External Driving Factors

Key Uncertainties	Key Certainties
1. Pace of demand for resources (economic)	1. Increased extreme weather events (environmental)
2. Concentration of power and influence (political)	2. Increased pace of technology changes (technological)
3. Demographic patterns (social)	3. More ecological regulations (political)
4. Political instabilities, war (political)	
5. Global economic state (economic)	
6. Loss of biodiversity (environmental)	
7. Individual empowerment (social)	
8. Millennium Generation as employees and consumers (social)	

An example of potential driving factors for scenario planning, prioritized by certainty level and categorized by type.

b. *Agree on the top two most important **uncertain** driving forces.* There is no "right" answer here. Rather, you should collectively agree on two forces that are the most important to the future of your business and would change the environment in which you operate. Imagine you are a consumer goods company; your leadership might decide that "demand for resources" and "concentration of power and influence" are the two most critical uncertainties in the macro environment likely to impact your industry and business.

c. *Create a future scenarios matrix* using these top two driving forces. One driving force will be on the *x* axis, the other on the *y* axis (see Figure 11.2). Look at each axis as a continuum. Once the two axes are selected, the work begins. Create scenarios that describe the world in each quadrant based on the extremes on the two axes. For example, for the upper right quadrant in Figure 11.2 (Scenario 2) you would ask, "What would life be like if the global demand

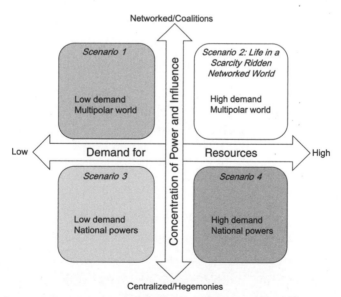

FIGURE 11.2   An example scenario matrix. The axes in this example are taken from the U.S. National Intelligence Council 2012 Global Trends report. The *x* axis tracks relative demand for food, water, and energy. The *y* axis represents global power distribution (i.e., traditional hegemonies vs. multipolar networks and coalitions). Envisioning movement along either axis results in four different scenario stories for use in scenario planning.

for food, water, and energy doubled, and the concentration of power shifted from large hegemonies (e.g., the European Union) toward multifaceted networks without national boundaries (e.g., social networks like the 'Occupy movement' that influence states and nations)?" Obviously, that is not a simple question to answer. An intense strategic conversation should take place looking at as many perspectives as possible. The result of that discussion would be the scenario description for the upper right quadrant in Figure 11.2 (Scenario 2). It should be a vivid story that people can see and understand. Imagine it as a brief, late-breaking news report from the future. For example:

Scenario 2: Life in a Scarcity-Ridden Networked World: Power and influence have shifted from nations to loose networks and coalitions. Resources like water, food, and energy are constrained due to doubling of demand and diminished supplies. The failure to control global climate change has left society and individuals scrambling for resources. People have lost trust in their national governments and connect most strongly with their networks and coalitions.

To complete the task, answer a similar question for each quadrant based on the possible extremes and write comprehensive stories for each one.

d. *Identify the implications of each story.* After you have written the four scenario stories, envision yourself living and working in each one. Write a story for each scenario, describing *what living in this scenario might look like.* What are the implications? Will people relocate because of food and water scarcities? Will megacities emerge, with most people living in urban areas? Will wars break out over energy shortages? The idea is to list the implications of each story and look for common trends. These common trends are the ones you will take into account in your strategic plan later in this process.

Phase 2: Where Are We Today?

Identify where the world is today in comparison to the four scenarios and two continuum axes you have developed. Looking back at Figure 11.2 and knowing the implications identified in Phase 1(d), you would ask, "Is the power and influence in today's world concentrated more on the national level or in multipolar networks?" and "Is the current demand for food, water, and energy low or high, compared to the future scenarios?" Remember, the axes represent continuums. Let's assume your team decides that today's world has similarities to Scenario 3. Mark it for future reference (Figure 11.3).

Phase 3: Where Are We Headed?

Now it is time to identify the trajectory of today's world. In other words, which of the four scenarios does your team think the world is moving toward (the emerging scenario)? Continuing our example from above,

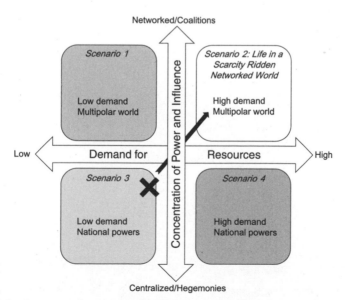

FIGURE 11.3   Once scenarios have been identified and described, the team determines the current state (X) and the current trajectory of world events and driving forces (the arrow). This plot identifies Scenario 3 as the current scenario and Scenario 2 as the emerging scenario.

you would ask, "Is the concentration of power becoming more central-
ized, or more networked?" and "Is the demand for food, water, and energy
decreasing, or increasing?" If the answer is that the world is getting more
networked and demand is increasing, this would mean the emerging scenario would be Scenario 2 (Figure 11.3).

Phase 4: How Do We Survive?

Next, identify what your company needs to do to survive in one or more
scenarios. This is where the SEEE model can be used. The questions
about organizational survival should specifically address the four elements—social, economic, environmental, and ethical—and how they
might affect your industry and your company. Figure 11.4 provides the
underlying framework for each of the four areas. Think of the emerging issues in each area that might impact your company, such as gradu-

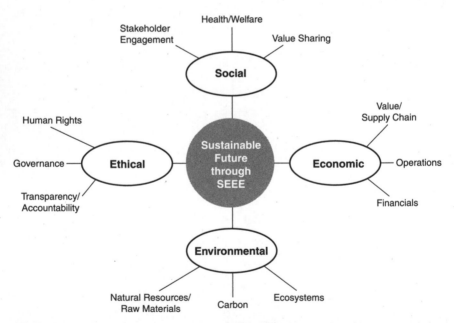

FIGURE 11.4 Potential focus areas using the SEEE model. Your choice of focus areas and
targets will be based on scenario planning outcomes, risk tolerance, and potential investment. Considering your emerging scenario in terms of the four primary SEEE aspects will
help you identify challenges to organizational sustainability and profitability.

© 2013 International Institute for Learning, Inc.

ally depleting raw materials, water scarcity, unethical practices in areas where your company or your suppliers operate, and potential economic issues due to regulations. The objective is to incorporate adaptability into your strategy, especially in the context of the emerging scenario you have selected. Think of this as flight-testing your strategic plan. Consider the company's goals, capabilities, and resources in the context of the emerging future. If your strategic plan appears to falter in this emerging future, your leadership team (and other suitable stakeholders) should determine what is needed to better future-proof the company. This is where you begin to uncover the opportunities for strategic change.

Phase 4 also includes a form of contingency planning. Ask yourself: If a different scenario becomes reality, would our strategic plan prepare us for that future state? If not, what can we do to prepare for alternate scenarios? Asking these questions might expose common strategic implications that must be addressed to prepare your company for more than one future state. This allows you to become far more adaptable.

Phase 5: Adaptive Foresight—Foreseeing the Future

GREG—I owe my passion to write this book, and my sense of urgency about sustainable business strategies, to my personal experiences with scenario planning. For over 12 years I worked as an executive at three different associations using scenario planning. Over time, I became a student of the methodology. For me, the adaptive foresight phase has been the most empowering and enlightening element of scenario planning. Adaptive foresight gave me an uncluttered look at emergent trends that were truly pertinent to the strategies of the organizations I worked with. As an example, during my tenure at PMI we periodically conducted a comprehensive review of the 18 "mileposts" that the PMI board considered critical indicators of movement toward one of the four future scenarios. The board made strategic decisions they believed would better prepare PMI to compete and survive in two or more of the envisioned future scenarios. Interestingly enough, we also saw changes in the critical measures affecting global sustainability. These indicators convinced me that humanity faces immense challenges in the next few decades, and that companies have a remarkable opportunity to make a big difference in our future. That assessment and the subsequent strategic discussions with the board prompted me to begin encouraging companies and other organizations to step forward, change their strategies, and make a difference in the world. Without that foresight, I might never have decided to pursue this work.

In this phase, your organization will create the ongoing "scanning capability" to foresee the future, an enterprise capacity called **adaptive foresight**. So far, the scenarios created and initial decisions made as a result of flight-testing your strategy are based on the perspectives of the scenario planning participants. Now it is time to develop a scanning capability—a set of measures that would identify early indicators—based on hard data. Most companies pick 8 to 10 key measures and associated metrics. These are frequently called *signposts* and are higher-level indicators of global change. Consider signposts that represent the SEEE elements discussed above in Phase 4. For example, tracking the availability of raw materials used in your manufacturing process might flag a situation of diminishing supplies, which could lead to a situation where one of the materials is seen as a "conflict mineral," and continued use might affect the ethics and reputation of your company. Spotting this issue early enables your company to have a strategic discussion and change direction before it becomes an issue. Most companies compile and review signposts every 6 to 12 months. Since these are high-level strategic indicators, more frequent reviews have less value. The enterprise leadership teams revisit where they are, where they are moving to, and their ability to adapt to an emerging future. This is the essence of adaptive foresight.

Scenario planning is not just for large organizations. Our experience has shown that scenario planning can be done even in companies with just a dozen employees. To accomplish this in a small or medium-sized business, you would follow the same process, but the depth would vary. To start, you can obtain published scenarios relevant to your industry by contacting your industry trade association. Many trade associations have already done the work for you. For example, the International Energy Agency (IEA) has published six possible world energy scenarios in the *2011 World Energy Outlook*,[10] and the World Economic Forum (WEF) has published a scenario document that looks at engineering and construction through the year 2020.[11] In fact, the WEF publishes a library of scenario documents available to the public for free. With a small effort, you can find scenarios for virtually every industry in the world. They might not be as perfectly aligned to your company as the ones you would build yourself, but the future is uncertain anyway.

If your company can do only one portion of the full scenario planning process, it should be developing adaptive foresight (the scanning and monitoring capacity). This is the due diligence that you can't afford to ignore. It signals major external changes that might impact your company's survivability. The simplest way to create adaptive foresight is to establish a small, diverse governance team in your company—for instance, a mix of staff from finance, marketing and sales, production, and the executive team. This team would be charged with interpreting and identifying the impact of preexisting scenarios. Select the most likely scenario, and then decide how and when to monitor external changes that have an impact on your future viability.

Zhangzidao Fishery Group, a Chinese aquafarm, is an inspiring example of a medium-sized company that "future-proofed" its business by looking for emerging scenarios. Zhangzidao predicted that optimizing the production of one aqua species (typical in this industry) would raise issues of pollution, disease, and environment depletion. In response, the company decided to aquafarm multiple species simultaneously. This created a balanced ecosystem that needs less additional food, mitigates disease issues, and does not deplete the sea beds. By changing its strategy based on an emerging future, Zhangzidao has grown revenue 40 percent per year from 2005 to 2010, compared to an industry average of 13 percent.[12]

Road to a Sustainable Future

Why are we spending so much time talking about global scenarios in a book about sustainability planning? Scenario thinking sets the stage for making the strategic choices necessary to prepare your organization for an unknown future. Your objective should be surviving that future as a profitable and sustainable company. As Brandlogic points out in *Keys to Sustainability Leadership*, sustainability must be an integral part of an enterprise strategic plan.[13] It is critical that you always consider the constraints and opportunities for the entire company, in an integrated fashion, so that your enterprise survives and thrives well into the future.

The enterprise strategic plan should be translated into a road map to becoming a sustainable company while mitigating critical risks along the way. This starts, of course, with defining your destination: What is the company's overarching goal, and when should that goal be met? With this in mind, set targets for specific focus areas your company wants to tackle in each aspect of the SEEE model in order to reach the goal. As shown earlier, Figure 11.4 provides an overview of potential focus areas. Your choice of focus areas and targets will be based on the outcome of your scenario planning, the level of risk you are willing to tolerate, and the amount you can invest. This model should be used as a catalyst to identify any serious sustainability issues that might affect your company's ability to survive, such as diminishing supply of raw materials used in your products, growing regulations that will affect your production processes, and so forth.

Let's look at the breakdown of the environmental axis. Three potential subareas along this axis are availability of natural resources, greenhouse gas increases in the atmosphere, and stable ecosystems. Table 11.3 shows an example of the situation surrounding a continuing excessive release of carbon dioxide (CO_2) into the atmosphere.

For your company, you would set a target for every area, define a measurement, and identify what needs to change or what actions must be taken. This is a significant undertaking. Analysis and planning are required to

TABLE 11.3   Cause and Effect of Carbon Dioxide (CO_2) Emissions

Environment		
	Result	*Effects or Impacts*
Excess CO_2 release into the atmosphere	Severe climate change	Loss of biodiversity
	Acidification of oceans	Extreme weather
		Reduced agriculture yield
		More regulations

One potential focus area on the environmental axis of the SEEE model is excess carbon dioxide release into the atmosphere. This table shows a simple analysis of potential impacts caused by continued carbon dioxide emissions.

determine whether your organization has the available capacity to change and, if not, what actions are necessary to gain that capacity. It boils down to strategic decision making: if the change is crucial for the survival of the company, tradeoffs must be made by delaying or stopping other key projects in order to build the capacity to succeed in the uncertain future.

For example, most companies are trying to reduce CO_2 emissions in a variety of ways due to its correlation to atmospheric damage and the impact on operations. They typically track progress by measuring their carbon footprint. There is a wide variety of actions you can take to lower your carbon footprint (see Table 11.4). You could reduce energy usage, replace nonrenewable energy with renewable energy, redesign products and services to use less carbon-intensive processes, or invest in carbon sequestration (e.g., replenishing forests).

TABLE 11.4   Target, Measurement, and Actions for CO_2 Emissions

Environment			
	Objective	*Measure*	*Tools/Actions*
Excess CO_2 release into atmosphere	Reduce CO_2 output by 50% by 2020	Carbon footprint	Reduce energy usage in operations by ____%
			Reduce energy usage in supply chain by ____%
			Increase use of renewable energy sources by ____%
			Sequestration of ____ hectares/year

Once SEEE focus areas have been identified, set targets for each area, define a measurement, and identify necessary changes or actions for meeting the target. This table shows potential objectives, measurements, and actions for achieving a 50 percent reduction in CO_2 emissions.

After selecting your strategic sustainability focus areas and setting targets for each subarea (like the CO_2 emission example), it is essential at this point to prioritize and assess the risks and identify those most critical to your future.

MAKING THE JOURNEY LESS RISKY

Based on the adaptive foresight activities, you may have decided on some immediate actions you would like to take. Other potential future implications should feed into your long-term risk management plan so you can recognize triggers indicating that particular possibilities are becoming reality. In a way, scenario planning conditions the brain to be better at spotting indications that a scenario is unfolding.

Our brains are exposed to millions of pieces of data per second. Out of this flood of data, only 40 to 60 bits make it to our conscious mind.[14] If we actively think about something—as we do during scenario planning—we are more likely to spot significant indicators. Have you ever noticed that once you buy a new car, watch, gadget, or piece of clothing, you start seeing it everywhere you look? It's not because all those other cars, watches, or gadgets suddenly sprang into being. Since the information wasn't relevant to you before, your subconscious filtered it out. Once the conscious mind is alerted to the fact that this information is important, these pieces of information get routed to the front of your mind for attention and action. Scenario planning operates on a similar principle.

Your long-term risk plan should incorporate any critical risks that might affect your business and their potential impact. These include preventable risks like equipment breakdown and employee errors, strategic risks incurred by business decisions, and external risks like those identified in scenario planning. Once all the risks are identified, a risk matrix provides a simple way to analyze, prioritize, and manage them.

Risk matrixes are widely used—and also widely criticized for being too simplistic. British statistician George E. P. Box probably said it best: "All models are wrong, but some are useful." The risk matrix is very useful because it is a very interactive tool. Multiple people with sticky notes can plot risks and move them around while discussing impact and probability. The result is a visual representation of abstract issues.

In general, you would start with a risk matrix for each area: social, economic, environmental, and ethical. After finishing each matrix separately, you can overlay them and identify the high impact, high probability risks in all areas at once. The axes of a risk matrix may vary by organization. For example, the WEF *Global Risks 2013* uses "Impact if the risk were to occur" and "Likelihood to occur in the next 10 years." Figure 11.5 shows an example of the WEF's social risk matrix.

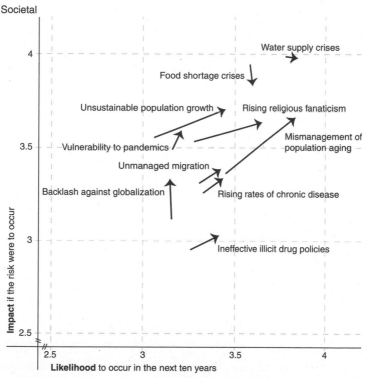

FIGURE 11.5   This example risk matrix plots impacts and likelihood of a variety of societal risks. The arrow origin indicates the current state, while direction and orientation indicate predicted trajectory. For example, pandemics are considered less likely than rising rates of chronic diseases but are predicted to have a greater impact.

Source: Global Risks 2013, World Economic Forum, Switzerland, 2013.

Weighting the different risks based on the descriptions of the risk impact and risk likelihood creates the numbers on the axes. Figure 11.6 shows an example of impact (consequence) and likelihood percentages and how they would map to the risk matrix.

The risk management plan is essentially a way of dealing with and mitigating the impact of a particular risk. Once defined, the risk plan should be communicated widely. Risk management principles and the level of risk accepted by a company should be embedded in everyday business decisions and activities. The biggest risk is going through the full process of scenario planning and risk management planning and then doing *nothing* with the results.

As an example, let's revisit the challenges in cocoa production discussed in Chapter 2. The major chocolate producers looked at the different scenarios for the future and realized one potential and emergent scenario is that cocoa production would flatten—and might even decrease—due to global climate change, ineffective agricultural practices, bad labor practices, and political unrest in the cocoa-producing countries while demand for chocolate is growing approximately 3 percent a year.[16] Their long-term business depends on a sustainable supply of high-quality cocoa, so this scenario presents a grave risk to business continuity for chocolate producers. Thus, the key focus area for chocolate producers is raw materials, with a subarea of unsustainable cocoa agriculture.

In the old paradigm, they might have dealt with scarcity by focusing on waste reduction in the supply chain and government lobbying for incentives to produce more cocoa. In a paradigm where sustainability is fully integrated into the company's strategy, companies instead make fundamental changes by investing in sustainable agriculture and improving labor practices. Sustainable farming requires education, watershed management, better agricultural practices, and quality of life improvements both for workers in the fields and their families in the local communities. Improved labor practices require a focus on, and commitment to, globally acceptable human rights. Mars Inc., Ferrero, and the Hershey Company

		Impact			
	Social				Mass migrations, war, starvation
	Economic				Loss of 30% agriculture land
	Environmental				Sea levels up 6 feet, 4 degree Celcius increase in temperature
	Ethical				50% increase of corruption
Probability		Negligible	Moderate	Serious	Catastrophic
>90%	Almost Certain	2.6	3.2	3.8	4.4
>45%	Highly Likely	2.2	2.8	3.4	4.0
<45%	Likely	1.8	2.4	3.0	3.6
<10%	Unlikely	1.4	2.0	2.6	3.2

Likelihood

Figure 11.6   Plotting the likelihood and potential impacts of various risks on a risk matrix makes it easier to identify just how urgent a particular risk realization is and to prioritize risk management planning accordingly.

This matrix, which is shown partially completed, follows a layout proposed by Julian Talbot.[15]

have all committed themselves to sourcing 100 percent of their cocoa sustainably by 2020.[17] They measure this target using independent certification through partnerships with NGOs like the Rainforest Alliance and the Sustainable Agriculture Network, a coalition of local NGOs. As the major chocolate producers prepare themselves to mitigate the scenario of cocoa scarcity, they are also preparing themselves for the increased pressure of more and more customers who want proof that the chocolate bar they're eating was sourced and manufactured according to specific ethical and sustainability requirements.

More and more companies are using scenario and contingency (S&C) planning tools like adaptive foresight and risk management planning to manage the increasing uncertainty in this world. A 2007 study by Bain & Company found a greater than 50 percent increase in the number of companies using S&C tools after the events of September 11, 2001, and the percentage has increased since then.[18] Scenario planning and enterprise risk management help organizations to avoid disaster and capitalize on opportunities.

THE JOURNEY BEGINS

To put your organization on a path toward sustainability, it's crucial to develop the capability to see change coming early and monitor the dynamics of the world. Evaluate your signposts on a semiannual or annual basis so you can track and react to trends. Adjust your strategy to anticipate the future as it emerges. If done correctly, this approach will open the door to unique opportunities and new strategic decisions. It also leads to a competence in understanding the changes and complexity inherent to the business environment and in responding promptly to these changes.

Your focus at any point along the journey should be on increasing the efficiency of the whole system rather than optimizing individual components. Innovative thinking is a key driver in this transformation process. In a 2012 study by *MIT Sloan Management Review* and the Boston Consulting Group, almost 25 percent of respondents said sustainability yielded real benefits in the form of improved product and service innovation and improved business model and process innovation.[19] But to be innovative, you need to act before your competition does, and that means building effective adaptive foresight in order to spot changes and act on them before your competition.

When this integrated approach is used to build a sustainable strategy for your organization, the resulting strategic matrix looks something like Figure 11.7. Elements of the SEEE model are represented in the row headers at the left side, and the column headers represent the different phases of change your organization will go through during this transformation. (These phases are discussed in detail in the next chapter.)

After reading this chapter you may have a better idea of where you want to go, but before you set out on the journey you need to know where you are right now. What is your current performance in social, environmental, and ethical areas? You have to set a baseline in order to measure progress and make corrective adjustments along the way. Chapter 12 will go into more detail about metrics and scorecards, as well as the development of a strategic change portfolio for execution and tracking. Since change is a given, it is vital to become a learning organization, able to adapt to the changing environment and adjust course and targets if necessary.

> *At every level the greatest obstacle to transforming the world*
> *is that we lack the clarity and imagination*
> *to conceive that it could be different.*
> —Roberto Unger

Chapter Summary

Building a road map to sustainability requires discipline and hard work. This is not a "warm and fuzzy" activity. There are rigorous tools and techniques for navigating the uncertainty of the future and for mitigating the risks your enterprise may face. These tools will help your organization

	Foundation	Incremental	Disruptive	Radical
Social	• Full regulatory and legal compliance, such as Labor Standards • Traditional Quality of Work Life (QWL)	• Analysis and engagement of select stakeholder communities • Assessment of social risks in supply and value chains	• Full stakeholder community analysis • Assume a role in problem solving in local communities	• Global improvements of communities in full value chain
Economic	• Full regulatory and legal compliance, such as Security Exchange rules, Sarbanes-Oxley	• Full assessment of risks of social, environmental, and ethical decisions • Economic value assessment of organization-wide efficiencies • Establish collaboration and partnerships	• Company-wide program for zero waste, including both cost and material efficiencies in company-managed facilities and supply chain	• Increased revenues, market share, recognition due to sustainability practices • Realize savings from cost reductions from zero waste program • Expand zero waste program throughout value chain
Environ-mental	• Full regulatory and legal compliance, such as Euro/ISO Standards, U.S. Environmental Protection Agency (EPA), etc.	• Measure organization's environmental footprint • Find operational efficiencies in water, energy, waste, etc.	• Renewable direct supply chain • Target zero environmental footprint in carbon and water	• Renewable indirect value chain • Carbon "negative" goals • Circular economy process
Ethical	• Full regulatory and legal compliance, such as standards of ethical conduct, Sarbanes-Oxley, etc.	• Evaluate and implement reporting methodologies (e.g., GRI, CPD, etc.) • Provide transparency on progress	• Design and deploy direct supply chain code of conduct with enforcement • Launch selected reporting initiative for full transparency and accountability	• Full value chain code of conduct and assessment model with enforcement • Full value chain transparency and accountability

FIGURE 11.7 This sample strategic matrix shows one possible approach to achieving sustainability using the SEEE model. This is just one example of the foundation of a strategy. You will have to select the time horizon and incremental steps that support and enhance the future of your organization. No two approaches are the same.

become more adaptable and responsive in spite of the uncertainty of the future. Following are the most important elements for you to remember during this journey:

1. Sustainability leaders share the characteristics of long-term vision and vigilance. They continuously scan the horizon to better navigate their organizations through the uncertainty of the future.

2. Scenario planning is one of the most successful methods of visualizing the future, managing through uncertainty, and developing organizational strategy. It is based on the creation of potential future states, which are created through a thorough strategic dialogue. It involves selecting two axes representing two significant implications for the future that are in tension with one another. The result is a matrix of four cells with different potential futures (scenarios).

3. Adaptive foresight is a strategic competency that involves observing trends and measures that might shape the future. Observing these trends helps an organization anticipate changes early and adapt its plans to survive. The trends and measures are driven by, and based on, scenario planning.

4. Risk management allows an organization to identify, assess, and mitigate risks that might affect the future success of a company. Risk management can be used at both the strategic level and the tactical level. It is one of the most constructive approaches to planning for uncertainties.

5. Companies that are successful leaders in sustainability share many things in common. However, one of the most important characteristics is the ability to develop an integrated sustainability strategy.

6. The SEEE model—social, economic, environmental, and ethical commitment—is valuable for sorting through strategic information to become a more sustainable company. When doing scenario planning, SEEE can be used to consider the implications of each future scenario, which will generate a set of potential risks. Then you can

use the model to sort through the risks and begin to establish goals
and objectives for planning.

7. The most dangerous and organizationally fatal risk when building
the capability for adaptive foresight is to do *nothing*—not to react
to the information you have compiled, created, and reviewed. It is
critical that you build the ability to spot and react to indicators that a
potential future is unfolding. This includes a clear system of decision
making for acting on the information.

Chapter 12

ADDING VALUE AND PROFITABILITY

*Growth at any cost is not viable . . . We want to be a sustainable
business in every sense of the word. We do not believe
there is a conflict between sustainability and profitable growth.*
—PAUL POLMAN, UNILEVER CEO[1]

Paul Polman's words are becoming almost a mantra in business. You would expect this sentiment from the CEO of one of the largest consumer goods companies in the world, especially since that company has been trying to become a leader in sustainability. Skeptics might question Unilever's motives, but the skepticism is undeserved. Unilever's actions speak volumes, and the drive toward sustainability is prominent in its annual report and even in its company purpose statement: "Making sustainable living commonplace." Polman is one of many CEOs who are transforming companies by exchanging individual *profitability* for global *prosperity*.

We believe that the world is at a tipping point, with consumers and retailers alike demanding sustainable products that cause no harm to people or communities and are respectful and considerate in their impact on our planet. Yet research tells us that the value of a product or service still tops the list of stakeholder needs. So the key is for companies to invest in sustainable value and *prosperity*, rather than mere shareholder value, or the ability of a company to make money for its investors. A business dedicated to growing sustainably must make money, or the business model will fail. Unilever pursues a path where reporting of quarterly profits is not as important as understanding long-term business growth—and more important, long-term value to humankind and the Earth. This, then, is the mission of business in the future: to grow, prosper, and be a friend to people and the planet.

This transition cannot happen overnight. Personal passion is not enough to fuel the change. In other words, a CEO can't expect much from calling a meeting and simply "declaring" that the company will be sustainable from now on. A meeting like that would probably elicit a round of groans and muttering: "Here we go again. The new business fad of the day is sustainability. Be patient, this too shall pass."

Some may believe sustainability is just another constraint that we have to deal with in business, much like the quality movement, business process reengineering, or the dot-com boom. Many authors view sustainability this way and often suggest that it can be addressed through a separate, parallel strategy.[2] Although the approaches these authors recommend are excellent, we don't believe a separate strategy will maintain growth well into the future. It just won't work. Sustainability must be integrated into an organization's DNA. Nor do we agree that sustainability is yet another "fad" or business stage. Sustainability is a game changer. It will change business models and products, and it will do so quickly. Ignoring sustainability or failing to truly integrate it into the organization will be a death knell to businesses. Simply put, ignoring the need for a sustainable world is a business killer.

GREG—When I first addressed the need to embrace sustainability at PMI in 2007, my executive team reacted with skepticism. Their body language, feedback, and attitude all pointed to the same pushback described in this chapter. Here are just a few of the questions they came up with:

- How will we be able to transform the organization while remaining viable in a highly competitive and sometimes hostile environment?
- What will be in the portfolio of projects needed to accomplish this?
- What do we need to stop doing now to give us the capacity needed to implement change?
- Which group will be responsible for this change?
- Will we have to hire new staff?
- Who will provide oversight and make strategic decisions about this transformation?
- Will our portfolio of products and services change to accommodate some sort of new product line focused on sustainability, offered for those who want sustainable products, or will this completely transform our entire product portfolio?
- Will we be able to maintain our bottom line performance, or will we gradually erode our margins?
- How do we know when we have reached our goal of sustainability, and what will we use to measure the change?
- Will we get incentives for this transformation?

Annoying questions? I didn't think so. In fact, within an hour we had listed literally all of the critical questions we needed to answer. My answers at the time were simple: First we need to uncover as much information as possible and learn as much as we can. Then we need to see how this affects our strategic plan and, more important, our portfolio of new opportunities. And finally, we will develop an action plan to accommodate it. It didn't resolve the tension, but it gave us a path forward.

We believe many questions must be answered to build a successful strategy. More important, these questions need to be addressed through deliberate action so that the company can survive and thrive. In the words of British environmentalist Jonathon Porritt, "There is no way of arriving at a sustainable world that does not involve businesses making money."[3] Profit has always been the motivator for businesses; it has been the stimulus for innovation and the development of new and value-laden products and services. However, going forward, *profit* must be redefined to mean prosperity through sustainability, and *prosperity* must be broadened to include stakeholders in society, not just investors. Unless companies can see the path to accomplishing this end, they will fail as partners in the pursuit of a sustainable world. This chapter will describe the approaches you need to learn in order to become sustainable *and* profitable—but not at the expense of global prosperity.

WHERE DO WE FOCUS?

Achieving complete mastery of each of the target areas we are about to discuss would require years of study and certainly far more than could fit in one chapter, one book, or even a shelf of books. However, you must be able to decide where to focus your time and energy to build the necessary foundation for a successful and profitable transformation. We won't presume to give you a one-chapter, step-by-step approach to completely revamping your company. Instead, we will walk you through the processes that will help you get your arms around the following critical areas:

- *Establish your baseline.* Compile the information you need to determine the baseline of your sustainability. To some extent, this is like doing a sustainability assessment in order to identify the gaps in your sustainability planning.
- *Strategic planning and management.* Strategic management must change to embrace and integrate sustainability into all aspects of the plan. You cannot take a "bolt-on" approach and expect to succeed. So, to build it in, you need to start here.
- *Strategic alignment.* Make sure the strategic objectives you select and the accompanying measures create initiatives that drive significant, measurable change.

- *Product development processes.* Assessing every new opportunity for sustainability using the SEEE model gets to the very root of action. Every new product, service, or project should be judged on its sustainability assessment long before it consumes organizational resources.

In all likelihood, large multinational corporations (MNCs) like Coca-Cola, BMW, and Unilever have previously developed tools such as strategic plans, enterprise scorecards, product development methodologies, and performance evaluation systems as well as supply chain maps and even materiality assessments. These are the products of companies that have the capacity, competencies, and assets to devote to this creative endeavor. If your organization is in this group, this chapter is designed to point out where to penetrate the walls of these systems and begin to change your organization.

Readers working in small- and medium-sized businesses (SMBs) may find that these documents and tools are not available in their organization, and the strategy is "documented" in the mind of the company founder. For example, Yvon Chouinard is the core of Patagonia and provides purpose to the company. He was both the founder and the architect of its strategy. In many people's minds, Chouinard *is* Patagonia. However, he knew how critical it was to ensure his strategy was understood throughout the organization. During the U.S. recession in the late 1980s, at a point when Patagonia was on the brink of disaster, Chouinard began to clarify and communicate his strategy in a way unprecedented in the history of his company:

I took a dozen of our top managers to Argentina, to the windswept mountains of the real Patagonia, for a walkabout. In the course of roaming around those wild lands, we asked ourselves why we were in business and what kind of business we wanted Patagonia to be. A billion-dollar company? Okay, but not if it meant we had to make products we couldn't be proud of. And we discussed what we could do to help stem the environmental harm we caused as a company. . . .

[After the retreat,] while our managers debated what steps to take to address the sales and cash-flow crisis, I began to lead weeklong employee seminars in what we called Philosophies. . . . The goal was to teach every employee in the company our business and environmental ethics and values.[4]

Chouinard took deliberate action to craft a new plan for the company with his team. He also determined that the direct engagement and education of every employee in the company was essential to making Patagonia a prosperous company that respected the planet. He knew that strategic change is a team sport and that change has to start at the top of the strategy pyramid and reach each and every staff member. This type of change is effective and meaningful. That is what this chapter is about: how to deploy change throughout your organization and make sure that it takes hold through deliberate action and engagement.

GREG—Over a period of 30 years, I served as CEO of three nonprofit enterprises that were small in size and revenues compared to BASF and even to Patagonia. As nonprofits, we were primarily mission driven and accountable mainly to our membership constituency. The smallest of these organizations, the Institute of Industrial Engineers (IIE), had a staff of 60 professionals. The largest, the Project Management Institute (PMI), had nearly 300 staff with offices around the world. All three organizations served extensive membership constituencies that affiliated with us so they could maintain vital careers and businesses.

The members and elected board of directors at each of these associations demanded planning processes, but the processes were scaled to capacity. Our process at IIE was far less documented and more iterative. PMI, on the other hand, made more extensive use of scenario planning, the Balanced Scorecard, and gating processes for new projects and products. Though the style and extent of planning and execution were very different in the three organizations, all were effective. Without processes, the organizations would have suffered in the short and long terms. And without staff commitment and literally thousands of dedicated volunteer contributors worldwide, the change in strategy at PMI would never have taken hold.

Regardless of the size and scope of your organization, you have an obligation to develop the tools and the stakeholder engagement that are necessary to accomplish a successful transition. As you read this chapter, consider how you would guide your organization through the transition. There are many good resources in strategic planning, strategic alignment, product development, and personnel evaluation and motivation. Get them, read them, and prepare yourself, as we encouraged in Chapter 7.

ESTABLISH YOUR BASELINE: GETTING TO KNOW YOUR COMPANY

Figure 12.1 represents the journey to your vision, how to think about a strategy that steers you toward profitable sustainability. Without a solid foundation of information, you will not have a baseline to begin the change management process. We call this baseline of information a "compliance" assessment, since it is intended to ensure your organization is in compliance with all legal and regulatory requirements. However, it is also the foundation for decision making. So the first step is to get to know your company's position on sustainability and find the information necessary to begin the change.

In some cases, the first step in your plan will be to build the foundation. In others, you may find that your company is already at the foundation level and ready to begin incremental change. However, if your organization is not in compliance or you are unsure, then your first goal is to bring your organization into compliance and build a library of information that allows you to make decisions regarding incremental, disruptive, and radical change. Figure 12.2 represents the library of information you need to gather.

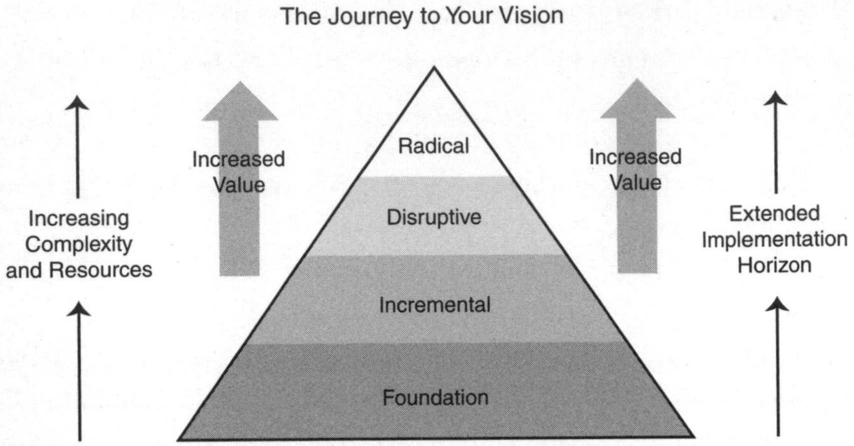

The Journey to Your Vision

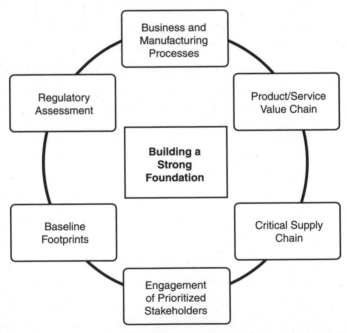

FIGURE 12.1   The change process for integrating sustainability into your company strategy starts from the foundation of "compliance" and moves through increasingly dramatic changes until you reach your desired state.

FIGURE 12.2   To build a strong foundation for your organization's strategic changes, you need a library of information about your current processes, value and supply chains, stakeholder engagement, current organizational footprint, and regulatory requirements.

Business and Manufacturing Processes

MNCs map these processes extensively. SMBs can map them as well, but in the interest of speed and capacity, it will be sufficient to create a simple matrix of the processes, the number of staff involved, raw materials consumed, and the process steps that contribute the most value to the business or manufacturing operation. The important thing at this point is to determine whether actions have already been taken to create sustainable manufacturing and business processes. Don't limit your investigation to the shop floor. Indirect processes like purchasing and customer service are bound by the same principles of sustainability, so examine the entire enterprise.

Product and Service Value Chain

To fully understand your company's impact, you must have a complete map of its value chain. In Chapter 7 we discussed sources you can use for mapping value chains and supply chains. Any company will benefit from this work, regardless of size, particularly when you take the time to map the value chain for the full life cycle of each product or service you provide. This study should encompass the entire life span of a product, from creation through removal from the marketplace and on to eventual destruction or recycling. Some refer to this as studying the value added to a product "from cradle to grave." Value chain mapping will help you identify contributors to the value of the product or service and in turn study the environmental and social impact of those contributors over the life cycle of the product. There are several excellent resources available to help you build a full value chain, including the UNEP Life Cycle Sustainability Assessment (LCSA) and the ISO 14040 series of standards.[5]

Even if it isn't possible to develop a map of your full value chain, **critical supply chain** mapping is essential. Again, Chapter 7 highlights various resources for guidance through this process.

Engagement of Prioritized Stakeholders

There are two key words here: *engagement* and *prioritized*. To build a company focused on sustainability, you need the full list of stakeholders.

Traditional stakeholder lists include investors, shareholders, customers, staff, management, and governance (e.g., the board of executives). In a sustainable company, the stakeholder list will also include regulatory agencies, suppliers, partners, and the communities most closely affected by your products and your operations.

The word *engagement* implies developing a relationship with all of these stakeholders and discussing issues that matter.[6] Supplier discussions should not be limited to things like financial contracts, though obviously those matter a great deal to your suppliers. In this context, the issues that matter relate to sustainability. Further, developing a relationship means sharing your journey with your suppliers (and other stakeholders) and perhaps sharing the tools you will use to assess sustainability.

Finally, remember that *how* you approach your stakeholders is very important. Do you deal with your suppliers as a community, engaging and collaborating with them to solve mutual problems? If suppliers are merely the domain of the purchasing department and engagement is kept to contract requirements only, you are missing out on opportunities. It is also important to assess the competitive landscape (for example, possible replacements for each of the suppliers) and whether or not your suppliers have a sustainability plan.

Baseline Footprints

This is the most time-consuming aspect of building your information library, but it is also the most important. To decide where you are going, you must understand where you are by calculating the social, environmental, and ethical footprints of your business. The SEEE model describes the information you need to compile to measure your "footprint."

Environmental

Water use, greenhouse gas emissions, and consumption of raw materials are the three footprints to calculate here. Each should be calculated for the entire life cycle of each product or service. One or more of these calculations may be available through the trade association(s) representing your industry sector. However, of the three, greenhouse gas calculations may be the most challenging. Whatever the size of your organization, you should consider taking advantage of outside expertise. You can even engage a local university or community college to help. Water use should be calculated throughout the life cycle as well and should include a total-use calculation for operations as well as a net-use calculation of water used but not treated and returned to the community.

Social and Ethical

Just as with your environmental footprint, working with communities and societies throughout the world leaves an impact that goes beyond consumption. This impact, positive or negative, may be affecting your reputation, influencing the value of your brand, or consuming financial or human resources. If you are confronted with a serious public problem, you may need to invest resources to mitigate a negative reaction from key stakeholders—for instance, an ongoing confrontation with local communities. Coca-Cola's long-term difficulties in India (regarding the impact of bottling plants on water scarcity) are one prominent example. This protracted negative engagement has had an impact on Coca-Cola's reputation globally and resulted in high management costs. It also raised awareness of water scarcity as a global issue affecting communities.

Analysis of a company's ethical footprint can yield similar results. Apple's reputation was negatively affected by the problems at Foxconn. The resulting impact required time and money to mitigate risks, not to mention public relations effort, legal negotiations, production cost increases, and travel costs for special staff inspection tours of Foxconn, including three trips in one year for Apple CEO Tim Cook. Taking the time to ascertain your social and ethical footprints allows you to identify baseline economic costs your company can avoid with an effective plan that embraces social, environmental, and ethical aspects of sustainability. Helping your suppliers identify similar impacts from their activities can lower costs in your supply chain as well. These assessments can be part of the justification for launching a sustainability plan and can provide the baseline measurement for analyzing the results of implementing a plan.

Legal and Regulatory Requirements Assessment

This is critical for determining whether you are currently in compliance with all regulations governing your organization. MNCs have periodic internal regulatory assessments, so this information should be readily available. The real issue here is to investigate the legal and regulatory requirements relating to the SEEE model. Your research should include the relevant requirements, the agency overseeing those requirements, the frequency of compliance checks, and penalties for noncompliance. SMBs may benefit from contacting the appropriate industry trade associations for help.

Whether you compile it yourself or utilize outside experts, this matrix of information is critical to change efforts in any organization. Review the elements of the SEEE model and determine what social, economic, environmental, and ethical requirements exist. Then determine whether you are in compliance. You may need to create only a simple list of the regulations, their specific source, and whether you are in compliance.

Strategic Planning and Management

Chapter 11 provided an in-depth discussion of scenario planning and how to build adaptive foresight into your planning process. Scenario planning is just the beginning, though. You still have to establish a strategic plan, whether it's published in a glossy magazine format, presented on a company website, or scribbled on the back of a napkin. The strategic plan is a road map of sorts that helps all stakeholders understand the value your company adds to the world and how that value differentiates you from your competitors. Your strategic plan must also prepare you to be viable and profitable. Finally, probably one of the most important characteristics for a good strategic plan is that it must drive real change. If it doesn't, it is useless.

This is not just an exercise for MNCs. Many small- and medium-sized businesses have written strategic plans. It is time to recognize that such a plan will actually be more critical to your success the more resource-challenged and unpredictable the future becomes. Even small companies with just one or two products in their portfolio will someday consider developing or distributing other product lines. A strategic plan is invaluable for guiding these kinds of decisions. Finally, a strategic plan helps any organization distinguish and maintain market differentiation and keep the organization moving in the correct strategic direction.

Figure 12.3 illustrates the elements of a strategic plan as a road map to success. In order for sustainability to become part of the organizational DNA, it must be woven into this strategy at every level, rather than being a separate, distinct (and easily abandoned) strategy.

Sustainability leaders begin by embracing sustainability at the core of their organization. Their mission, or "reason for existence," defines them

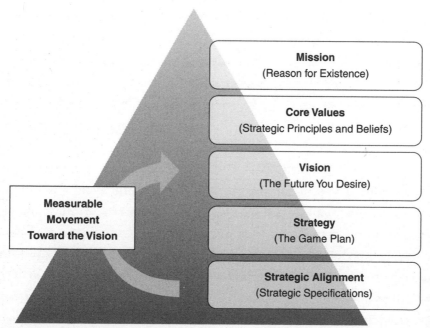

Figure 12.3   Your strategic plan derives from your organization's mission and core values.

from the start. For example, Unilever clearly states its purpose is to "make sustainable living commonplace." This mission statement leaves no doubt that Unilever embraces sustainable living and is dedicated to contributing to that end. BASF's mission statement also refers directly to sustainability: "We create chemistry for a sustainable future." In addition, one of the company's four strategic principles, which describe how BASF will behave or act in support of this mission, is to "drive sustainable solutions." One of Coca-Cola's "6 P's" is *planet*, and the strategic goals for that aspect of the company's mission include "global leadership in sustainable water use" and "industry leadership in packaging, energy, and climate protection."[7] Global healthcare and science giant Bayer, a sustainability leader, uses the acronym LIFE for its enterprise values: leadership, integrity, flexibility, and efficiency. Digging deeper into the values reveals that *integrity* includes full legal and regulatory compliance (part of Bayer's foundation), and that trust with stakeholders is a strategic cornerstone.

Each of the companies on our list of sustainability leaders (Appendix A) has embraced aspects of sustainability in its strategic plan. For these organizations, sustainability is a fundamental element driving change. Yet not one of these pioneers has abandoned profitability or growth. On the contrary, they have ambitious plans, but their economic measures of growth embrace the values associated with social, environmental, and ethical considerations. Value creation in these companies now includes sustainability, not just revenues. They are transforming their organizations through strategic alignment.

If you are in an SMB that doesn't have a strategic plan, at the very least you need to consider how the SEEE model will affect how you do business. For example, if you are a small manufacturer providing a unique product to the marketplace, you need to ensure that you and your staff recognize and understand the significance of the changes you might make to your strategy in order to embrace sustainability. In particular, you need to understand how this will position you relative to your competition. But at least consider developing a simple strategic plan to allow you to focus on longer-term goals, and decide how sustainability can be woven into your plan.

STRATEGIC ALIGNMENT: WHERE THE RUBBER MEETS THE ROAD

Strategic alignment is the part of the strategic management process that creates the means to translate strategy into action. There are many approaches and processes to secure strategic alignment, but one of the most successful and impactful is the Balanced Scorecard.[8] The Balanced Scorecard is the brainchild of Robert Kaplan and David Norton, who teamed up in 1992 for a *Harvard Business Review* article on aligning strategy to execution. The basis for the Balanced Scorecard was a set of pertinent measures tracking the strategic progress of an organization. The analogy they used in the article was that of an airline pilot looking at the instrument panel to gather crucial information regarding the flight. The indicators on the instrument panel are the measures and associated metrics at the pilot's disposal to inform decisions while in flight and tell the pilot if the plane is on course to its intended destination. If the pilot's objective is to arrive at a destination at a specific time, monitoring the instruments helps maintain the appropriate speed, altitude, and fuel consumption rates required to get there. If the flight objectives also include fuel economy, altitude and speed choices might have to be adjusted. Objectives are tracked with measures that drive change and performance—that is what the Balanced Scorecard is about.

The aircraft instrument panel is a simple way of highlighting the concept of a balanced scorecard and its value in steering the company toward a strategic destination. Like the airplane, an organization must first have a strategic destination in mind, such as a clear vision or strategic goal, in order to achieve strategic alignment. The power of the Balanced Scorecard is its ability to align strategy and action by describing the organization's ability to create value, the resources necessary to create that value, and the relationship between them. In other words, it is used to balance the investment of assets toward specific objectives, which will hopefully create meaningful value.

The foundation for the Balanced Scorecard is the creation of a strategy map, which structures the relationships between various objectives by considering four unique perspectives. The map is like an investment ladder, showing management how each perspective is supported by various initiatives as the overall strategy progresses toward the ultimate goal. Each strategy map is designed specifically for a particular organization, but the strategy map is always based on these four perspectives:

1. *Learning and growth perspective.* This perspective views the intangible assets that must be aligned and integrated before they can be transformed into tangible value. Typically, these assets include enterprise capabilities, information, and organizational characteristics such as culture and style of leadership. By themselves, these assets do not produce tangible value. Rather, they are the potential energy of the organization. When properly aligned, these assets will contribute to building value in the organization. If, for example, the company wanted to achieve zero waste in manufacturing operations to reduce overall production costs, they might invest in Six Sigma competency by training all manufacturing supervisors. This would result in a learning and growth objective, which in turn would lead to an organizational initiative.

2. *Internal process perspective.* This perspective is a view of the processes that directly transform intangible assets into stakeholder value and financial outcomes, such as operations and customer service. In the previous example, an objective would be established to create specific processes regarding waste reduction and the application of Six Sigma. The organization might need to foster and develop an innovation process. Either way, an internal process objective would be created, and again, an initiative would be designed to achieve it.

3. *Stakeholder (customer) perspective*. This perspective reveals conditions that the stakeholder considers valuable or beneficial. The stakeholder could be the customer, a regulatory body, or the board of directors of the company. In the case of products and services, the valuable conditions could be things like product quality or product performance. Value can also come from an improvement in reputation, or compliance with a new or complicated regulation. Continuing the example of zero waste, stakeholders may see this as a demonstration of greater respect for the environment, or a probable increase in the perceived value of the brand. As with the other perspectives, an objective relating to this type of improvement would be written, and an initiative developed to achieve or measure movement toward the objective.

4. *Financial perspective*. This perspective is typically the culmination of transforming all intangible assets into tangible value and outcomes. For most organizations, particularly for-profit firms, the end game is a change in financial performance. This could mean reduced production costs or increased revenues. Most company strategies aim for long-term, sustainable financial growth. For example, our zero-waste scenario would lead to a clear objective of reducing costs in all operations, and hopefully of generating higher margins and returns. The investment in training, process improvement, reputation, and brand would transform intangible assets into clear financial returns.

Figure 12.4 demonstrates the integrated relationships between the perspectives. The arrows show the relationships between these perspectives, each one contributing to the next. If the company doesn't invest in learning and growth, all subsequent investments will be hindered. Without investment in Six Sigma training, it would be very difficult to make and measure progress toward zero waste. On the other hand, without implementing the necessary processes in the factory floor, it would be impossible to achieve any consistent reduction in waste.

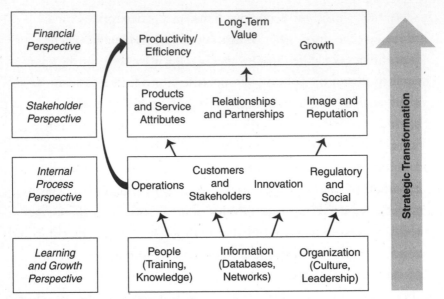

FIGURE 12.4 Balanced Scorecard strategy map.

These maps allow a "balanced" investment in intangible assets, ensuring that a company can implement strategy and achieve its goals. Also, each objective requires action, which prompts creation of an initiative or set of initiatives. If the objective is for all supervisors to be green belt certified in Six Sigma, that establishes a strategic change project for future development of the workforce to achieve zero waste in operations. This objective requires someone to arrange training (learning and growth). Achieving the objective establishes a new company environment that prompts review of internal processes, establishing new initiatives. In this way, workforce development directly supports the eventual goal of zero waste operations.

As another example, let's start from the financial perspective. Imagine a corporation's board and executive management have decided that long-term financial health will now be defined in terms of sustainability. Put another way, the board has decided that the company must create lasting value by being a leader in sustainability while achieving long-term financial health. This one change in strategy will alter the board's entire strategic plan going forward. The executive team now has to define what "being a leader in sustainability" really means, whether it's becoming a supersector leader on the Dow Jones Sustainability Index (DJSI) or achieving specific benchmark indicators associated with their particular industry sector. The balanced scorecard must be updated to accommodate this critical strategic change.

The Balanced Scorecard has been used to assist many companies in their transition to sustainability. For example, Amanco is a producer of plastic pipes and fittings that operates in many Latin American countries. In 2000, Amanco published its first sustainability scorecard. The company had recognized that customers were no longer satisfied with product performance alone. Customers wanted products that "improve the society in which they exist, that protect its environment, and that team up with its people."[9] To ensure effectiveness in meeting this changing customer need, Amanco embraced the Balanced Scorecard framework to revise its own scorecard. This led to a remarkable change in strategy. The first addition was called "the triple bottom line" dimension of value generation, which established three strategic goals:

- Create economic value sustainably in the long run
- Generate value through a system of corporate social responsibility
- Generate value through environmental management

Amanco's traditional financial goals were revised to stress "sustainable profitable growth"—no longer the end goal but rather the means to achieve "the triple bottom line" strategic goals. In addition, Amanco decided that in order to meet those goals, the company needed to add the processes and capabilities internally to alter the way it produced value. Ultimately, Amanco created a new dimension for adding value in the company—the environmental and social dimension—which had three strategic objectives:

- Compliance with social, environmental, and ethical practices and standards

- Incorporation of social impact management systems
- Minimal environmental impact through ecoefficiency concepts

These objectives and the associated measures drove real and immediate change throughout the organization. The Balanced Scorecard helped Amanco to clarify its strategy and to establish scoreboard measures that would drive important strategic changes.

The Balanced Scorecard is a highly effective system and has been used by hundreds of companies to successfully reach their strategic goals. There are many different approaches to building scorecards and other systems for aligning strategy with action. Many companies design their own, extracting some of the principles contained in the Balance Scorecard system. If you are interested in adapting or learning about the Balanced Scorecard, Kaplan and Norton have written five superb books on the subject, which are informative and instructional. Contact the Palladium Group or the Balanced Scorecard Collaborative for more information.

In the context of this chapter, references to some elements of the Balanced Scorecard will demonstrate how strategic alignment is crucial to ensuring that strategy is carried out and strategic change occurs. In particular, it is used to demonstrate some of the techniques for aligning strategy to action through measurable objectives that drive performance (see Figure 12.5).

This process accomplishes several goals:

- *It establishes specific themes or areas of focus.* Focus areas represent a group of critical processes that help create value for the company. The strategic theme in this context is the theme of sustainability, which comprises the collection of processes that assess and evaluate the four areas of the model. The new theme of sustainability will ensure that it is built into the plan. Referring back to Amanco, three new goals related to sustainability drove an entirely new set of processes and activities.

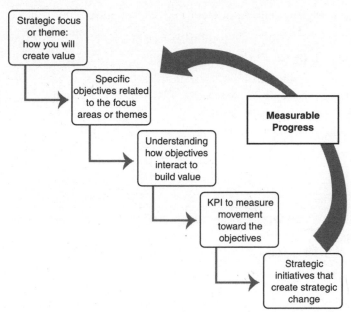

FIGURE 12.5 Measurable progress toward strategic objectives is achieved by aligning strategy to action through measurable objectives that drive performance.

- *It establishes specific objectives aligned with each theme.* In our case, the added strategic theme is sustainability, and the associated objectives are aligned through the matrix to the measure, the target value, the specific initiative, and the level of the SEEE model (e.g., foundation, incremental, etc.). This process helps define a set of appropriate objectives you wish to achieve. Though that sounds quite simplistic, it is the basis for alignment. In Table 12.1 the objectives are in two areas of the SEEE assessment model—"ethical" and "environmental"—based on the scenario planning and risk assessment exercise in Chapter 11. The alignment, along with the granularity in the table, can place it into the ideation process for the new products, services, and projects that will be discussed next.

- *It illustrates the interrelationship between objectives.* This is crucial to understanding how individual objectives lead to a higher level of performance. In the Balanced Scorecard this is done with a strategy map. In this example, the objectives of recognition for supply chain

TABLE 12.1 Aligning Objectives, Measures, and Initiatives

| Alignment to Strategic Theme | | | | | |
SEEE	Objective	Measure	Target	Initiative	Level
Ethical performance disclosure/ accountability	Recognized for ethical supply chain manage- ment	Certification of supply chain by NGO	12 months from launch	Develop and deploy framework based on independent certification through NGO	Disruptive
Environmental performance	Zero net carbon footprint	Tons of CO_2	Net calc. with seq.; year 2000 baseline, achieve by 2020	Full supply chain reduction	Radical

management and zero net carbon footprint are related by green-house gas output throughout the supply chain. A map would show this connection and inform the company team that an ethical and environmentally sound supply chain should contribute to the objective of zero carbon footprint for the company. If a map is not available, use a relationship matrix or a table similar to Table 12.1.

- *It guides the selection of key performance indicators (KPIs).* These are the critical measures established to measure progress toward the objective. Selecting KPIs should be an iterative process to ensure that the specific metrics are actually tracking progress toward the objective. Table 12.1 shows the granularity in the measure by listing the target. Achieving the zero net carbon by 2020 using the footprint from the year 2000 is an aggressive target. It is a net calculation, taking into account investments in carbon sequestration such as sustainable forests. This measure drives a radical change process that will need to be considered in the development of the action plan. Without this level of granularity, the team can become confused and fail to achieve the target. One word of caution: the KPI you select may seem clear from its description. However, once in place and being tracked, it may become evident that the KPI is not correct. This is not unusual, since these KPIs are usually complex and intended to drive strategic change, not just a tactical shift in operations. If a KPI is not driving change—or worse, driving the wrong change or behavior—replace it quickly.

- *It drives creation of strategic initiatives.* The objectives and metrics (KPIs) create a need for action, and the action comes in the form of projects, services, or individual products that will move the organization forward. This is the step that drives performance changes. These initiatives should be vetted through an *initiative or new opportunity development process* (in many organizations called the new product development process)—the last process discussed in this chapter and one of the most important for adding significant value to your organization. Before a new product or initiative is implemented, however, most companies exercise due diligence by moving the project through a "gating" process to ensure that it is thoroughly evaluated. A "gate" is a virtual door to resources that remains closed until the use of the resources is justified. Once the "gatekeepers" (e.g., executive team, portfolio management team, etc.) are satisfied the project is ready to move on to another phase of the product development process, the resources are released, and the next phase begins. Typically, a preliminary scope is drafted for any new ideas, which are then moved into the gating process for review and approval or revision. Many SMBs do not have a formal process for assessing new product development. At first glance it might seem that the absence of a process would streamline work, but it also means that value-producing activities are assessed and prioritized ad hoc. Makeshift or improvised product development processes vastly increase the risk of project failure due to resource inefficiencies, arbitrary priority changes, and more.

DEVELOPMENT PROCESSES: CREATING PRODUCTS AND SERVICES WITH SUSTAINABILITY IN MIND

When integrating sustainability into an organization, the process used to select and develop new ideas for products, services, or enhancement projects deserves careful attention. Most medium- and large-sized companies have some sort of deliberate process for evaluating new ideas and ensuring that sufficient capacity and capability exist to accomplish all of the value-adding work. Companies that thrive on innovation, such as the Dutch company Royal Philips N.V., use these processes to evaluate the numerous product ideas suggested to meet their aggressive innovation goals. This allows the company to deliberately align its initiatives to its strategy and to properly support an enterprise portfolio of products under active development. An effective process will ensure that opportunities are properly funded for development, carefully considered with respect to critical criteria, and perform according to plan.

This process can recover immense value when the evaluation criteria embrace sustainability. Consider the findings of an April 2013 UN-backed report:

> Primary production and processing in such sectors as agriculture, forestry, fisheries, mining, oil and gas exploration and utilities cost the world economy $7.3 trillion a year in damage to the environment, health and other vital benefits for humankind. . . . High impact business sectors in fact make an economic loss when such environmental costs as the negative impact on natural resources, pollution and greenhouse gasses are accounted for.[10]

Integrating the SEEE model into the product selection and development process will yield great dividends for any company. A "gating" or "phase-gating" process is usually used to accomplish this control. The example illustrated in Figure 12.6 uses five gates to evaluate new ideas for viability and to ensure that organizational resources are invested

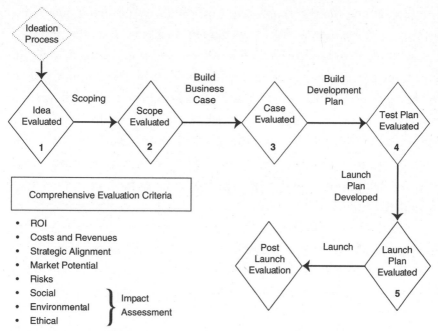

FIGURE 12.6   This example development process uses five "gates" to evaluate new ideas for viability and ensure wise resource investments. Initiatives that do not pass a gate approval are put on hold rather than consume organizational resources for a project that may be unprofitable or even counterproductive. Note that the traditional impact assessments are supplemented with reviews of SEEE factors as well.

wisely to bring approved projects to launch.[11] In most companies today, SEEE criteria are rarely incorporated into screening criteria at the various stages. Including SEEE criteria in the process as early as possible—preferably as early as the idea gate—enables the system to screen out initiatives that would harm environments or communities or pose ethical risks *before* resources are invested. Folding SEEE criteria into later phases as well (e.g., business planning, testing, and validation) encourages additional evaluation of products and services to ensure that actual results and impacts match the concepts approved with the initial project scope. Organizations using SEEE criteria throughout their gating process will be able to mitigate sustainability risks before projects are launched, resulting in significant operational and project cost savings over the long term.

Continuing the earlier example, an initiative to develop and deploy a framework for supply chain management that is both ethical and environmentally sound would have to be scoped to bring it to gate 2. At this point, the gating evaluation team would hold open discussions about the potential impacts of the initiative and provide guidance to the program or project team leader. The project leader would then build a business plan for the initiative, including additional detail on the framework specifications. Evaluating this business plan (gate 3) will reveal enterprise-wide impacts, both positive and negative, that may not have been obvious in the initial review.

This ongoing engagement and dialogue provides a "reality check" on the significance of the proposed change and provides good feedback to the project leader. If the gating evaluation team includes several company executives, this assessment and feedback will be even more valuable.

CHAPTER SUMMARY

Envisioning a new strategy to embrace sustainability is a milestone that should be celebrated and praised. But unless the new strategy causes the desired change, it is just an idea. A Japanese proverb states that "vision without action is a daydream; action without vision is a nightmare." Passion and energy alone will not deploy a new strategy effectively. It takes discipline, planning, alignment, and good execution. Be diligent about planning and execution, no matter what size your company is. Small companies may be quick to act, but they can also be quick to run out of resources when tripped up by poor planning and execution. To be sure you are exercising due diligence when building and exercising a new strategy, remember these key elements:

- *Establish your baseline.* Compile the information you need to determine the baseline of your sustainability. To some extent, this is like doing a sustainability assessment in order to identify the gaps in your sustainability planning.

- *Strategic planning and management.* Strategic management must change to embrace and integrate sustainability into all aspects of the plan. You cannot take a "bolt-on" approach and expect to succeed. So, to build it in, you need to start here.
- *Strategic alignment.* Make sure the strategic objectives you select and the accompanying measures create initiatives that drive significant, measurable change.
- *Product development processes.* Assessing every new opportunity for its sustainability using the SEEE model will get to the very root of action. Every new product, service, or project should be judged on its sustainability assessment long before it consumes organizational resources.

13

THE CONVERSATION CONTINUES

If anybody here has trouble with the concept of design humility,
reflect on this: It took us 5,000 years to put wheels on our luggage.
—WILLIAM MCDONOUGH

By the time this book is released at the end of 2013, even more information will be available about humanity's impact on the Earth and the risks we face in the coming decades. When the groundbreaking book *Limits to Growth* was released in 1972, the scenarios it provided for the mid- to late twenty-first century felt distant and futuristic. In contrast, the projections we've discussed in this book, and the projections that will come to light over the next several months, are much more immediate. These are things that will happen in our lifetime, or if not ours, certainly our children's. At the same time, solutions that would have been considered science fiction in the 1970s today are science-fact and right within our grasp. So, let's have a conversation.

GREG—Nathalie and I have been amazed by the immense global engine of change we have uncovered. Our research has revealed hundreds of organizations that have begun addressing the challenges we face as our planet becomes crowded with a restless, growing population consuming vast amounts of dwindling resources. In the face of that extraordinary effort, how can we close this book neatly? This may be the end of the book, but it is not—it cannot be—the end of the conversation. While it is tempting to stop and think about it for a while—like pressing the pause button on a movie—this story keeps unfolding whether you are watching or not. When you hit the play button again, 2050 will be closer than it was, and you may not like what you see.

Limits to Growth was published less than 50 years ago. The scenarios it contained were imperfect, as all 50-year projections are, but they proved to be surprisingly accurate. In his book *2052*, Jørgen Randers, the last living author of the original study, mused that he believed at that time, perhaps naively, that the initial study would provoke a conversation that would alter the way we lived, produced, and consumed on this planet.[1] Sadly, it did not. Society and industry were not ready. In 1973, President Richard Nixon said he believed the United States could become energy independent by 1980.[2] In fact, by 1980, our consumption of hydrocarbon fuels had grown exponentially, and the United States had doubled its dependence on foreign oil supplies. Despite a dramatic oil embargo and the gas shortages of the mid-70s, once it was over we went on with business as usual. We just weren't listening.

That is one of the principal reasons we wrote yet another book on sustainability. We need to carry on the conversation and to provide a different perspective on how to move forward. If this book prompts even a few companies to step up to the task of strategic change, it will make a difference for all of us.

Fortunately, we have come a long way since the original study was published. The conversation has finally started. More people, governments, NGOs, and companies are listening and talking. Since 2000, hundreds of organizations have signed on to the UN Millennium Declaration, supporting the eight Millennium Development Goals, and thousands of companies have contributed. Many companies today also have a web presence dedicated to their efforts in sustainability, and thousands are publishing standardized sustainability reports according to the Global Reporting Institute (GRI) guidelines.

Companies like the ones we researched have focused their creative talents to alter their own corporate destinies. So we should be pleased and excited, right? You would think so, but in fact, I am not. We have uncovered remarkable progress throughout the world, but it is neither fast enough nor aggressive enough to fully mitigate future risks. For me, the continuing conversation has to be about urgency and action. We get more warning signs almost every day. While we were in the process of writing this book, a building collapsed in Savar, Bangladesh, killing over 1,100 workers and injuring thousands more. This illegally built, eight-story "sweatshop" hosted five different garment factories and was, as a friend remarked to me, "an accident waiting to happen." How can this be? After all of the attention directed at improving poor working conditions around the world, and with the ability to publicize atrocities via social media, how was this "accident waiting to happen" overlooked? Why wasn't it addressed as an issue of social, environmental, and ethical policy?

A report released in early 2013 indicated that the United States had become an "oil and gas surplus-producing" nation.[3] This change in status was attributed to two basic factors: the "shocking realization" that the developing world was out-consuming the developed world, and the use of "fracking" and other new technologies to tap oil trapped in oil sands and under shale. Both of these observations surprise me.

First, projections for nearly 50 years have predicted that the developing world could outpace our consumption, not just in energy but in overall consumer demand. *Limits to Growth*, each of its 10-year updates, the UN Millennium Development Goals, and UN Earthwatch have all pointed this out. In the Interbrand *Best Global Brands* study, Tom Zara wrote that "if China alone were able to achieve First World living standards while everyone else's living standard remained constant, our total human impact on the world would double."[4] Shocking? Hardly. Either people aren't listening, or we aren't having the right conversations.

The second surprise is that our ability to reach ever deeper to tap new oil reserves was presented as good news! There was no mention of the need to move away from hydrocarbon fuels to reduce CO_2 emissions, or the fact that fracking is still controversial due to the possible degradation of groundwater and deep water aquifers, or even that regardless of how large a new oil discovery may be, it is a nonrenewable resource, and our global consumption may very well deplete it in less than 50 years. Avoiding these topics reduces the sense of urgency that is necessary for progress toward sustainability. Again, we need to have the right conversations.

I may sound negative, but my point really isn't about gloom and doom. As we said earlier, it is more about taking action and taking it now. Don't wait, don't delay, don't debate. Be relentless. The projections are real, and we have to deal with them now. We need to continue the conversation and carry the message to others so more companies will take action.

NATHALIE—Certainly, by the end of 2013, more organizations will have taken action to survive and thrive through sustainability, realizing they will have to mitigate the risks they are facing. However, I believe integrated strategic change is needed by *all* organizations to prevent the looming disaster. Actions taken today to cut greenhouse gas emissions, reduce waste, and minimize environmental impacts are admirable and extremely necessary; however, these actions are all focused on doing less harm. Doing "less harm" means harm is still being done, adding to the significant legacy of damage that has already occurred.

For example, when organizations set a goal to reduce greenhouse gasses by 50 percent, they pick a baseline year to measure against. Unilever intends to reduce the greenhouse gas impact of all its products by one-half by 2020 despite higher volumes, but this goal is based on Unilever's 2008 greenhouse gas emissions levels. Unilever was established in 1930 from a merger of the British Lever Brothers and the Dutch Margarine Unie, both companies that trace their roots back to the 1800s. A goal based on

2008 emissions does not take into account the significant damage done in the previous 100 years. To make a real difference, Unilever would have to push the baseline well back into the twentieth century and take an aggressive stance not only to do less harm but to be somehow regenerative. We must completely rethink the solution.

We face a systemic problem in our current world model. Overall consumption is still growing, as is manufacturing output. As Patagonia founder Yvon Chouinard says, "The problem is us. We're no longer called citizens—we're consumers. We're like an alcoholic in denial. Until you get rid of the denial, nothing will happen."[5] More sustainable processes, ecoproduct innovations, and social programs are all crucial, but something has to be done about the underlying system. We must abandon the old patterns of consumption. We need to redefine the problem. We will always consume; we just have to find a better way. Instead of talking about better ecocars, think about the problem as providing mobility. Restating the problem will help us identify disruptive innovations that address the problem from a totally different perspective.

The May 2013 issue of *Harvard Business Review* included a story about Kingfisher, one of Europe's largest home improvement retailers. Kingfisher decided to look at the ecological problems caused by the home improvement industry and asked how it could have a "net positive impact" on the environment by returning more than it uses.[6] The objective here is to invent products, processes, and business models that create a closed loop, so the product parts will be completely reused and recycled without ever entering the waste stream. Kingfisher is revising its business model to include rent or lease of its products. As you might remember from Chapter 5, this is the philosophy behind the circular economy. This is the kind of rethinking I believe is necessary.

In *The Upcycle*, the sequel to *Cradle-to-Cradle*, William McDonough discusses the need to rethink the system and shift our focus from merely protecting the Earth from human impact to improving the planet by redesigning our activities. This would be a co-creative relationship and would leave a beneficial footprint instead of just a less harmful footprint.

When I was in university, I went backpacking through Thailand, Malaysia, and Singapore. I was traveling in a local bus from the Malay East Coast to Kuala Lumpur on the west coast on a road that led straight through the country's heartland. This area had once been a tropical rainforest full of hardwood, but as far as I could see there were nothing but clear-cut hills, brown and desolate. The devastation was almost unimaginable. It looked like a nuclear bomb had gone off. That visual has stayed with me all my life.

Now imagine what the world would be like if we had a positive effect on it. Instead of vanishing, that ancient hardwood forest would continue to exist and even expand. In every footstep we leave behind, life will flourish and biodiversity will thrive. This might sound like tree hugging or flower power, but it is this kind of radically different outlook we need.

In the end, it comes down to completely changing our perspective. We need to look at the problem not from the product side but as responsible citizens of this world. We need to find solutions that benefit both the planet and humans, because those solutions will benefit companies as well. Those are the profitable strategies for a sustainable future.

GREG—Profit is not a dirty word. It is part of being in business. The context in which we create and use profit is what makes the word good or bad. I believe that context will change when trust in business is rebuilt through contributions to social justice and environmental care.

However, the question that most companies still ponder is "Where do we start?" In 2008, I attended a special conference for not-for-profit leaders to rally associations behind the UN Millennium Development Goals and to convince them to sign on. Eight hundred senior executives from about 400 associations attended the event. Noted economist and author Jeffrey D. Sachs delivered the keynote speech, in which he spoke about his new book, *Common Wealth: Economics for a Crowded Planet*. Sachs was articulate and captivating as he explained that we needed a new economic paradigm: global, inclusive, cooperative, environmentally aware, and science based. He said that the seemingly "soft" issues of the environment, public health, population growth, and extreme poverty would become the hard issues of geopolitics in the future. Business must play a role in solving those problems directly, not stand idly by and expect the problems to be solved by others. Businesses must become actively engaged to create this new economic paradigm.

NATHALIE—Looking at where we are in 2013, the biggest roadblock I see is that there are still too many people who either ignore the facts or discount them. As a natural instinct, people are afraid of the unknown and reluctant to change. We would rather stick with what we know than make major changes, especially if there is no immediate payoff. As we have stressed in this book, sustainability pays off not next quarter but next year, or in several years, or in a decade. I also believe that people still need help learning *how* to transform, which has been one of our biggest reasons for writing this book.

Another roadblock I see is that we have altered, and are still altering, the very fabric of the air, land, and oceans and the natural cycles that support those systems—our own life support system. We have put things in motion, and I don't think we fully understand the consequences. The mindset that we have to "save the planet" is wrongheaded and, in a way, arrogant. This is the kind of thinking that leads to inadequate solutions. The planet will survive—maybe highly damaged, but nonetheless intact. It is *we* who might not survive. We need to stop seeing our planet as a provider of unlimited resources and start seeing it as something we depend on for our survival.

Fundamentally, I believe we are at a tipping point. Either we will take into account everything that has happened up until now, realize that there are limits to what we can expect to take from the planet, and take action—or there will be a significant "self-adjustment" to the planet, its resources, and the population. Businesses that do not adapt will not be in business any longer. We absolutely must *act*. The problems we face are global, not confined to a single country or continent. They affect every country and every person on this planet.

Businesses—large, medium, and small—are in the right position to alter the path we are on. It takes dedication and a thorough approach. This is like starting a strenuous workout routine: the hardest part is starting. Once you finally get going, it becomes easier and eventually becomes a habit. Sustainability should be a habit. It needs to be something we don't think twice about, like washing our hands. Of course, investments in sustainable practices are necessary, and some companies might not have the financial means to do this. It is my crazy dream that when we change our perspective toward seeing the planet as our life support system, larger, financially stronger companies will help smaller companies become more sustainable (for example, by providing loans to make the necessary investments). Why wouldn't they, once they realize it will be to everyone's benefit, including theirs?

Leaders should think of this as the most important time in history. What we do, or fail to do, will determine what follows. Of course, every point in history is like that. But never has there been a time like this one. There are cliffs all around us. We can decide to step back or continue forward and fall off the cliff. We have the power. Think about what your business is and how you can use your power not to continue business as usual but to make the planet better.

GREG—I agree that we are at a tipping point. The balance of consumption, need, resources, and personal wealth is quite fragile. Unless we bolster the system, it will tip, and the global economic and social system will go through a dramatic readjustment on its own. Global prosperity requires a global commitment, with businesses coming to the forefront to help achieve it.

The roadblocks are numerous, but they can be overcome. First among them is the complexity of the interrelationship of all of these challenges. When Sachs finished his keynote speech, one of my colleagues stood and asked a simple question: "If we could only focus on one aspect or facet to help going forward, what would that be?" Sachs admitted he was surprised by the question and stood quietly for several seconds. Finally he said, "I would say focus on protecting the water sources of the world." Since water is essential to life, it sounds like the right guidance, doesn't it? Well, if you do a relationship map of water, you immediately see that there is a direct relationship to climate change, which is influenced by CO_2 released into the atmosphere, which is directly affected by the use of hydrocarbon fuels in transportation and power generation—and the connections go on.

The current delicate state of balance is already stressing our economies and communities. The bloody struggle for resources, trading value, freedom, and prosperity touches every continent. Such unrest adds to the complexity of the problem and the complexity of the solution. Businesses can still make a big difference if they act quickly. Build sustainability into your corporate strategy. Review your entire value chain: How can your company move closer to being water- and carbon-neutral? What are the most critical issues facing the communities affected by your value chain? Find ways to make a positive impact. The models and methods described in this book will help you, but you have to start now.

Our last and most significant roadblock is the lack of engagement among the general public. Most people simply do not understand the challenges we face, and even if they do, there is no universal mechanism to help people contribute to solutions. Overcoming this hurdle will take education not just of our employees but also of people across the globe. We must help people understand what the issues are, what the solutions are, and what role they can play in building the solutions. I believe this may be the single most important contributor to our future, though it may be the most difficult to accomplish.

These are challenging goals, especially for small and midsized companies. But they are scalable. Make the default setting at your company one of action rather than one of waiting. Act now.

NATHALIE—If we rethink the system and act now, I truly believe we can have a very different and sustainable world in 2050. Just imagine: It's 2050, there are over nine billion people on this planet, and the middle class has, as expected, grown from one billion to four billion. Most businesses have changed their business model. Companies feel and act responsible for their products and services, from the very first ingredient until it's reused or recycled, in a fully closed product loop. Even better, the new trend is to leave a beneficial footprint on this planet—we are co-creating with the Earth.

Value circles (which used to be called value chains) are now fully sustainable. All over the world, companies take social aspects into account by providing work-life balance for their employees, offering fair and safe work environments, and ensuring healthy communities. Environmental aspects are integrated into the company's strategy and core decision making, and ecological costs are part of the balance sheet; the impact on the ocean and land ecosystems is on even footing with, for example, electricity costs when decisions are made about products or services. Most companies leave no footprint in carbon, water, and waste, and many are working toward a positive footprint: giving more back to the planet than they take from it. There are even some hopeful signs that the damage done by decades of abuse is slowly being reversed. Forests are expanding, and oceans are becoming less acidic.

Many leaders were astonished to find out how much they were saving in overall costs when implementing sustainable value circle efficiencies. Plus, product innovations focused on sustainability have opened whole new markets. Wall Street is very different today than it was in 2013; you might even say it is boring. Since analysts and investors are more concerned with the long-term impact of company activities, quarterly earnings reports went extinct years ago. Since business transparency has increased so significantly, anybody who is curious about what is going on with a company can simply visit the company's website and easily find up-to-date, accurate information. The savings realized by abandoning special quarterly reports and integrating data in day-to-day communication has surprised many.

Consumption patterns are totally different. A vibrant peer-to-peer economy allows people to share their assets, and it is commonplace for companies to rent or lease their products instead of selling them, providing maintenance services and ensuring that products will return to the value circle once they are no longer needed. Since companies are taking responsibility for the communities in their value circle, overall well-being has increased all over the world. Poverty has decreased, labor conditions have improved, gender equality is universal, and child labor has ended. In spite of the lingering effects of climate change and the environmental damage we are working to undo, the dismal projections of 1973 and 2013 now seem like a distant worry. The future is bright. This is what hope looks like.

GREG—I share Nathalie's dream and enthusiasm. For me, it boils down to one simple idea. My dream is for businesses to see that profits and ROI are a reward for global prosperity. That means that these organizations, through their own deliberate actions, have contributed to rebuilding the environment and are making significant contributions to sustainable communities. Most of all, I want companies to be trusted to take on this challenge. No longer reluctant, they are the active, engaged stewards of the public trust, and their social, economic, environmental, and ethical commitments create a profitable, sustainable future for us all.

Where will you start?

Never doubt that a small group of thoughtful, committed citizens
can change the world. Indeed, it's the only thing that ever has.
—Margaret Mead

APPENDIX A: SUSTAINABILITY LEADERS

The organizations covered in this book were chosen in a very deliberate manner, based on a set of specific and research-based criteria. In developing our approach, we focused on finding companies that have already recognized the need for dramatic changes. We hoped to find companies that were founded on the values of sustainability or that implemented strategic changes in response to global trends and thus repositioned themselves for a sustainable future.

Our research turned up many highly respected rating systems and initiatives that addressed the social, economic, environmental, and ethical axes in our SEEE model. After careful study, we selected several that complemented our systemic view of the strategic activity necessary to become a sustainable company. While no single system captured our view, the overall collection began to reveal the community of companies we wanted to study.

The rating systems and initiatives we selected fell into five specific areas (see Figure A.1):

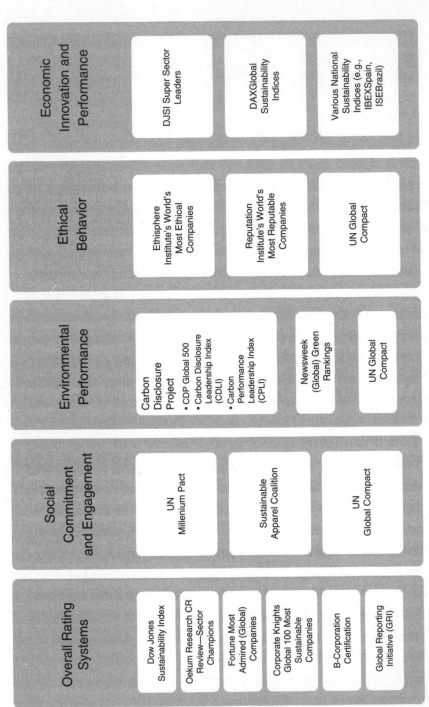

FIGURE A.1 The rating systems that established the criteria we used to identify the companies highlighted in this book.

1. Overall sustainability rating systems (e.g., Corporate Knights Global 100 Most Sustainable Companies)
2. Social commitment through action and collaboration (e.g., Sustainable Apparel Coalition, UN Millennium Goals Initiative)
3. Environmental performance (e.g., Carbon Disclosure Project)
4. Ethical behavior (e.g., Ethisphere Institute Assessments)
5. Economic innovation and performance (e.g., Dow Jones Sustainability Index)

We looked at five years of history and at how the companies acted and performed. In addition, we looked at multiple collaborative engagements over the last 10 years. The result was a group of nearly 30 organizations making a significant difference in their stakeholder communities and in the environment, as well as in the way they are perceived in the business world. In addition, we found that many of these companies were recognized as leaders not by one rating system but by several. These companies cover a wide range of types and activities:

- Small, large, and multinational companies
- Privately held, family-held, and publicly traded companies
- Social innovation companies
- Manufacturers, distributors, and retail aggregators

The full list of companies is provided below. The various sources for the rating systems, engagements, and activities are provided in Appendix B.

We were both surprised and excited by our choices. As our research and interviews progressed, we quickly found that these companies were making dramatic and innovative strategic changes throughout their supply chains, leading to impacts that could change entire industries. This is the kind of corporate performance and strategic change that we highlighted in this book. There are also companies driving change or social innovations that may not have been rated or perhaps are not yet leaders in their industry sectors. As a result, some companies highlighted in this book did not make the rating lists and have not been recognized by major media. However, they all have one thing in common: they have demonstrated innovative strategies that are profiting their organizations, our environment, and our communities.

As you review this list, keep a few things in mind. First, there are literally thousands of companies throughout the world making the transition to sustainability. It would be impossible to cover them all. The companies highlighted in this book are our top choices based on our investigation and based on their exemplary efforts to be sustainable and profitable. Second, and more important, we are not trying to separate the good from the bad or to predict the successes and failures. The characteristics of a "good" or "bad" company will be fodder for debates for generations to come. We want to show you the companies that are making a difference in the world and in their communities today and are highly profitable at the same time. You have to determine the best approach for your industry, country, or organization. We hope these examples will inspire you to start your own journey.

LIST OF COMPANIES

99designs Inc.
447 Battery Street 3rd Floor
San Francisco CA 94111
United States
www.99designs.com

Amanco
Av. Eng. Luis Carlos Berrini
1681 São Paulo
Brazil
www.amanco.com

Apple Inc.
1 Infinite Loop
Cupertino CA 95014
United States
www.apple.com

BASF SE
Carl-Bosch Straße 38
67056 Ludwigshafen
Germany
www.basf.com

Bayer International SA
Kaiser-Wilhelm-Allee 1
51373 Leverkusen
Germany
www.bayer.com

The BMW Group
Petuelring 130
80788 München
Germany
www.bmwgroup.com

City CarShare
1182 Market Street, Suite 300
San Francisco CA 94102
United States
www.citycarshare.org

The Coca-Cola Company
1 Coca Cola Plaza
Atlanta GA 30313
United States
www.coca-colacompany.com

Inter IKEA Group
Olof Palmestraat 1
2616 LN Delft
The Netherlands
www.inter.ikea.com

Interface Inc.
2859 Paces Ferry Road, Suite 2000
Atlanta GA 30339
United States
www.interfaceglobal.com

Johnson & Johnson
One Johnson and Johnson Plaza
New Brunswick NJ 08933
United States
www.jnj.com

Koninklijke Philips NV
Breitner Center
Amstelplein 2
1096 BC Amsterdam
The Netherlands
www.philips.com

Natura Cosméticos SA
Rodovia Régis Bittencourt
Km 293, Bldg. 1
Itapecerica da Serra
São Paulo 06850
Brazil
www.natura.net

Nokia Oyj
Keilalahdentie 2-4
FI-02150 Espoo
Finland
www.nokia.com

Patagonia Inc.
259 W Santa Clara Street
Ventura CA 93001
United States
www.patagonia.com

RelayRides Inc.
1035 Cambridge Street, Suite 9
Cambridge MA 02141
United States
www.relayrides.com

Ricoh Company Ltd.
8-13-1 Ginza, Chuo-ku
Tokyo 104-8222
Japan
www.ricoh.com

Suntory Holdings Ltd.
2-1-40 Dojimahama, Kita-ku
Osaka 530-0004
Japan
www.suntory.com

Tokio Marine Holdings Inc.
Tokio Marine Nichido Building
  Shinkan
1-2-1 Marunouchi, Chiyoda-ku
Tokyo 100-0005
Japan
www.tokiomarinehd.com

Unilever NV
Weena 455
3013 AL Rotterdam
The Netherlands
www.unilever.com

Wal-Mart Stores Inc.
702 SW 8th Street
Bentonville AR 72716
United States
corporate.walmart.com

Whole Foods Market Inc.
550 Bowie Street
Austin TX 78703
United States
www.wholefoodsmarket.com

**Zhangzidao Fishery Group
  Co. Ltd.**
26-28F Wanda Center
No. 6 Gangxing Road
Zhongshan District
Dalian 116001
P.R. China
www.zhangzidao.com

Zipcar Inc.
25 First Street 4th Floor
Cambridge MA 02141
United States
www.zipcar.com

APPENDIX B: SUSTAINABILITY INDEXES AND RATING SYSTEMS

Economic Innovation and Performance		
DJSI Supersector Leaders	Highlights the respective leader from "each of the 19 supersectors represented in the Dow Jones Sustainability Index."	www.sustainability -indices.com
DAXglobal Sustainability Indices	"Allow[s] investors to track numerous international markets and topics in a transparent, rule-based manner. . . . Combines regional indices from promising economies, global trends or topics of special interest such as alternative renewable energy sources."	www.dax-indices.com
Plus various indices such as . . .		
IBEX 35	Bolsa de Madrid's benchmark stock market index. Market value-weighted index including the 35 most liquid stocks traded in the Madrid Stock Exchange General Index.	www.ibex35.com

(continued on next page)

Solactive-ISE Brazilian Indices	Family of benchmark indices that allow investors to track Brazilian public companies active in certain sectors, such as financials and consumer products.	www.structured-solutions .de www.ise.com
MSCI Global Equity Indices	"Equity market coverage for over 70 countries in the Developed, Emerging and Frontier Markets." Provides "global views and cross regional comparisons across all market capitalization size, sector and style segments and combinations."	www.msci.com/products /indices

Ethical Behavior

Ethisphere Institute's World's Most Ethical Companies	"Recognizes companies that . . . promote ethical business standards and practices internally, exceed legal compliance minimums and shape future industry standards."	www.ethisphere.com
Reputation Institute's Global RepTrak Pulse	"The world's largest reputation study . . . measuring more than 2,000 companies from 25 industries across 40 countries." Provides a "global benchmark" and a "basis for continued thought leadership in reputation management."	www.reputationinstitute .com
UN Global Compact	"A platform for business and non-business entities to . . . network and engage in areas of human rights, labor, environment, anti-corruption and contribute to UN goals in order to . . . build a sustainable and inclusive global economy."	www.unglobalcompact .org

Environmental Performance

Carbon Disclosure Project (CDP)	Nonprofit organization that provides "the only global system for companies and cities to measure, disclose, manage and share vital environmental information." Focus on climate change, deforestation, water use, and supply chains.	www.cdproject.net

Newsweek Green Rankings (Global 500)	"Environmental ranking of the biggest companies in developed and emerging world markets." Takes into account "environmental footprints, management (policies, programs, initiatives, controversies), and reporting practices."	www.thedailybeast .com/newsweek /features/2012 /newsweek-green -rankings.html
UN Global Compact	"A platform for business and non-business entities to . . . network and engage in areas of human rights, labor, environment, anti-corruption and contribute to UN goals in order to . . . build a sustainable and inclusive global economy."	www.unglobalcompact .org
Social Commitment and Engagement		
UN Millennium Declaration	Adopted by the General Assembly on 8 September 2000. Outlines principles and goals that address "a collective responsibility to uphold the principles of human dignity, equality and equity at the global level."	www.un.org/millennium /declaration/ares552e .htm
Sustainable Apparel Coalition	"Industry-wide group of over 80 leading apparel and footwear brands, retailers, suppliers, nonprofits, and NGOs. . . . The focus of the SAC is the Higg Index that measures the environmental performance of apparel products."	www.apparelcoalition.org
UN Global Compact	"A platform for business and non-business entities to . . . network and engage in areas of human rights, labor, environment, anti-corruption and contribute to UN goals in order to . . . build a sustainable and inclusive global economy."	www.unglobalcompact .org
Overall Ratings Systems		
Dow Jones Sustainability Index	"The first global sustainability benchmark. . . . Tracks stock performance of the world's leading companies in terms of economic, environmental and social criteria."	www.sustainability -indices.com

(continued on next page)

Oekom Research Corporate Responsibility Review	"Annual review of global corporate responsibility . . . of around 3,100 companies" with a focus on "labor rights and human rights, corruption and environmental violations, the needs of an aging society and measures . . . to improve recycling."	www.oekom-research .com
Fortune World's Most Admired Companies	A "definitive report card on corporate reputations." Companies selected from the Fortune 1000 and Fortune's Global 500 database according to revenue.	money.cnn.com/ magazines/fortune/ most-admired
Corporate Knights Inc. Global 100 Most Sustainable Corporations in the World	A "data-driven corporate sustainability assessment" of the "world leaders in clean capitalism. . . . Inclusion is limited to a select group of the top 100 large-cap companies in the world."	www.global100.org
B Corp Certification	"Certified B Corporations . . . voluntarily meet higher standards of transparency, accountability, and performance." There are "more than 600 Certified B Corps from 15 countries and 60 industries."	www.bcorporation.net
Global Reporting Initiative (GRI)	Nonprofit organization that provides companies and organizations "with a comprehensive sustainability reporting framework" covering the "key areas of economic, environmental, social and governance performance."	www.globalreporting.org

Notes

Chapter 1

1. "21 Tropical Amazon Rainforest Facts," Dylan Linet, EcoLocalizer, July 20, 2011, http://www.ecolocalizer.com.
2. Maria L. Mendonça, "Impacts of Expansion of Sugarcane Monocropping for Ethanol Production" (English language research summary), *Co-operative Research on Environmental Problems in Europe*, October 2010, 4, http://crepeweb.net/?page_id=343. Extracted from the report "Impactos da produção de cana no Cerrado e Amazônia" ("Impacts of the production of sugarcane in the Cerrado and the Amazon"), published by The Pastoral Land Commission and the Network for Social Justice and Human Rights.
3. Lakshman D. Guruswamy and Jeffrey A. McNeely, eds., *Protection of Global Biodiversity: Converging Strategies* (Durham, NC: Duke University Press, 1998), 19–20.
4. For more information, see UN Collaborative Programme on Reducing Emissions from Deforestation and Forest Degradation in Developing Countries, http://www.un-redd.org.
5. The UN-REDD Programme website, November 2010, http://www.unep.org/forests/REDD/tabid/7189/Default.aspx.
6. Interactive data from UN Department of Economic and Social Affairs, Population Division, accessed January 2013, http://www.un.org/en/development/desa/population/.
7. *State of the World's Cities 2012/2013: Prosperity of Cities* (Nairobi: United Nations Human Settlements Programme [UN-HABITAT], 2012).
8. *The Millennium Development Goals Report 2012* (New York: United Nations, 2012), 4.
9. "Burgeoning Bourgeoisie," *Economist*, February 14, 2009, http://www.economist.com/node/13063298.
10. Eric D. Beinhocker, Diana Farrell, and Adil S. Zainulbhai, "Tracking the Growth of India's Middle Class," *McKinsey Quarterly*, no. 3 (2007): 56.

11. Mario Pezzini, "An Emerging Middle Class," *OECD Observer*, http://www
.oecdobserver.org/news/fullstory.php/aid/3681/An_emerging_middle_class
.html.
12. Homi Kharas, "The Emerging Middle Class in Developing Countries"
(Working Paper No. 285, The Brookings Institute, Washington, D.C.,
January 2010), http://www.oecd.org/dev/44457738.pdf.
13. "German Middle Class Shrinks by the Year, Study Says," *Deutsche Welle*
(Bonn: December 13, 2012), http://dw.de/p/171j1.
14. Ibid.
15. "The World in 2011: ICT Facts and Figures," (Geneva: International
Telecommunication Union, 2011), http://www.itu.int/ITU-D/ict/facts
/2011/material/ICTFactsFigures2011.pdf.
16. Louise Story and David Barboza, "Mattel Recalls 19 Million Toys Sent from
China," *New York Times*, August 15, 2007, New York Edition, A1.
17. Charles Duhigg and David Barboza, "In China, the Human Costs That Are
Built into an iPad," *New York Times*, January 26, 2012, New York Edition, A1.
18. Jørgen Randers, *2052: A Global Forecast for the Next Forty Years* (White River
Junction, VT: Chelsea Green Publishing, 2012), 6.
19. Randers, *2052*, xiv.
20. Randers, *2052*, 323.
21. Randers, *2052*, iii.

Chapter 2

1. American Association for the Advancement of Science, *AAAS Atlas of
Population & Environment*, s.v. "Freshwater" (Washington, D.C.: University
of California Press, 2001), http://atlas.aaas.org.
2. OECD, *Water and Agriculture: Sustainability, Markets and Policies* (Paris:
OECD, 2006), 295, doi:10.1787/9789264022577-en.
3. A. Ertug Ercin, Maite Martinez Aldaya, and Arjen Y. Hoekstra, "Corporate
Water Footprint Accounting and Impact Assessment: The Case of the Water
Footprint of a Sugar-Containing Carbonated Beverage," *Water Resources
Management* 25 (January 2011): 723, doi:10.1007/s11269-010-9723-8.
4. Tamim Younos, Rachelle Hill, and Heather Poole, "Water Dependency
of Energy Production and Power Generation Systems" (VWRRC Special
Report No. SR46-2009, Blacksburg, VA: Virginia Tech, 2009), http://www
.circleofblue.org/waternews/wp-content/uploads/2010/08/water_
dependency_of_energy.pdf.
5. United States Geological Survey (USGS), "Estimated Use of Water in the
United States in 2000," USGS Circular 1268, March 2004, http://pubs.usgs
.gov/circ/2004/circ1268/pdf/circular1268.pdf.
6. Ercin, et al., "Water Footprint."
7. SABMiller, WWF-UK, and Deutsche Gesellschaft fur Technische
Zusammenarbeit (GTZ), *Water Futures: Working Together for a Secure Water*

Future (Surrey, England: 2010), 1, http://www.waterfootprint.org/Reports/SABMiller-GTZ-WWF-2010-WaterFutures.pdf.

8. Beverage Industry Environmental Roundtable, "Water Use Benchmarking in the Beverage Industry: Trends and Observations, 2011" (2012), http://www.bieroundtable.com/files/BIER%20Benchmarking%20Publication%202012.pdf.

9. UN-Water, Food and Agriculture Organization (FAO), "Coping with Water Scarcity: Challenge of the Twenty-First Century," 2007, 10.

10. Potsdam Institute for Climate Impact Research and Climate Analytics, *Turn Down the Heat: Why a 4°C Warmer World Must be Avoided* (Washington, DC: World Bank, 2012).

11. Jonathan Hills and Richard Welford, "Coca-Cola and Water in India," *Corporate Social Responsibility and Environmental Management* 12, no. 3 (September 2005): 168–177, doi:10.1002/csr.97.

12. UN Water, *Managing Water Under Uncertainty and Risk (Executive Summary)* (Paris: UNESCO, 2012).

13. Ibid.

14. Royal Society of Chemistry, "Chemistry in Its Element—Tantalum," Interactive Periodic Table, http://www.rsc.org/chemistryworld/podcast/interactive_periodic_table_transcripts/tantalum.asp.

15. Maggie Koerth-Baker, "4 Rare Earth Elements That Will Only Get More Important," *Popular Mechanics*, http://www.popularmechanics.com/technology/engineering/news/important-rare-earth-elements#slide-1.

16. Kate Rockwood, "How a Handful of Countries Control the Earth's Most Precious Materials," *Fast Company*, November 1, 2010, http://www.fastcompany.com/1694164/how-handful-countries-control-earths-most-precious-materials.

17. International Telecommunication Union (ITU), *Measuring the Information Society, Executive Summary* (Geneva: ITU, 2012), 1, http://www.itu.int/dms_pub/itu-d/opb/ind/D-IND-ICTOI-2012-SUM-PDF-E.pdf.

18. Rockwood, *Fast Company*.

19. Greg Caramenico, "China's Rare Earth Metals Clampdown Drives New Trade, Mining Ties," *World Politics Review*, November 21, 2012, http://www.worldpoliticsreview.com/articles/12517/chinas-rare-earth-metals-clampdown-drives-new-trade-mining-ties.

20. United Nations Environment Program (UNEP), *Forest Resilience, Biodiversity, and Climate Change: A Synthesis of the Biodiversity/Resilience/Stability Relationship in Forest Ecosystems,* Technical Series no. 43 (Montreal: Secretariat of the Convention on Biological Diversity, 2009), 6, http://www.cbd.int/doc/publications/cbd-ts-43-en.pdf.

21. UN Food and Agriculture Organization (FAO), *State of the World's Forests 2012* (Rome: FAO, 2012), 5, http://www.fao.org/docrep/016/i3010e/i3010e.pdf.

22. UN FAO, "Key Messages: Forests for People," last updated March 2, 2011, http://www.fao.org/forestry/iyf2011/69186/en/.

23. United Nations website, s.v. "World Day to Combat Desertification," http://www.un.org/en/.

24. Carbon Disclosure Project (CDP), *CDP Supply Chain Report 2012—A New Era: Supplier Management in the Low-Carbon Economy* (London: CDP, 2012), https://www.cdproject.net/CDPResults/CDP-Supply-Chain-Report-2012.pdf.

25. Melissa Paschall and Don Seville, "Certified Cocoa: Scaling Up Farmer Participation in West Africa," case study (International Institute for Environment and Development/Sustainable Food Lab, 2012), 6, http://pubs.iied.org/pdfs/16034IIED.pdf.

26. Ibid., 7.

27. Jan Cappelle, *Towards a Sustainable Cocoa Chain: Power and Possibilities Within the Cocoa and Chocolate Sector*, Oxfam research report (Ghent, Belgium: Oxfam-Wereldwinkels, 2009), 4, http://www.oxfam.org/sites/www.oxfam.org/files/towards-a-sustainable-cocoa-chain-0901.pdf.

28. Edward Millard, "New Cocoa Business Model Catching On: Cocoa Certification Has Taken Off in the Last Few Years and Is Being Driven by the Need to Modernise the Industry," *Guardian*, November 5, 2012, http://www.guardian.co.uk/sustainable-business/business-model-cocoa-certification-growth.

29. Paschall and Seville, "Certified Cocoa," 3.

30. Unilever Global website, "Sustainable Cocoa & Sugar," http://www.unilever.com/sustainable-living/sustainablesourcing/cocoa-sugar/index.aspx.

31. International Cocoa Initiative (ICI) website, "History and Mission," http://www.cocoainitiative.org/en/about-ici/history-and-mission.

32. *CDP Supply Chain Report 2012*, 7.

CHAPTER 3

1. Joel Schectman, "Apple Removes Green Electronics Certification from Products," *Wall Street Journal*, July 6, 2012, http://blogs.wsj.com/cio/2012/07/06/apple-removes-green-electronics-certification-from-products/.

2. Apple website, "Letter from Bob Mansfield, Senior Vice President of Hardware Engineering" (press release), last updated July 13, 2012, http://www.apple.com/environment/letter-to-customers/.

3. Zach C. Cohen, "Apple Drops Environmental Certification; S.F. Drops Apple," *USA Today*, last updated July 11, 2012, http://content.usatoday.com/communities/technologylive/post/2012/07/apple-san-francisco-epeat/1.

4. Greenpeace, "How the Companies Line Up 17th Edition," last updated November 18, 2012, http://www.greenpeace.org/international/en/campaigns/toxics/electronics/Guide-to-Greener-Electronics/Previous-editions/How-the-companies-line-up-17/.

5. *2012 Edelman Trust Barometer Executive Summary* (Edelman, 2012), 1, http://trust.edelman.com/.
6. *2013 Edelman Trust Barometer Executive Summary* (Edelman, 2013), 1, http://www.edelman.com/insights/intellectual-property/trust-2013/.
7. Ibid., 6.
8. Reputation Institute, *2012 Global RepTrak 100: The World's Most Reputable Companies* (2012), 13, http://www.reputationinstitute.com.
9. Pagan Kennedy, "William Gibson's Future Is Now," *New York Times*, January 13, 2012, BR1, http://www.nytimes.com/2012/01/15/books/review /distrust-that-particular-flavor-by-william-gibson-book-review.html.
10. For examples, cf. NationMaster.com, s.v. "Government Statistics, Total businesses registered," (last updated May 7, 2013), and *Encyclopedia of the Nations*, s.v. "Total businesses registered (number)," http://www .nationsencyclopedia.com/WorldStats/WDI-trade-business-businesses -registered.html.
11. Global Reporting Initiative, http://www.globalreporting.org.
12. U.S. Securities and Exchange Commission (SEC) Form 10-K, "The Coca-Cola Company," Commission File No. 001-02217 (2011), http://www.sec .gov/Archives/edgar/data/21344/000002134412000007/a2011123110-k.htm.
13. World Wildlife Federation, "The Coca-Cola Company Pledges to Replace the Water It Uses in Its Beverages and Their Production" (press release), June 5, 2007, http://worldwildlife.org/press-releases/the-coca-cola -company-pledges-to-replace-the-water-it-uses-in-its-beverages-and-their -production.
14. The Coca-Cola Company, *The Water Stewardship and Replenish Report* (2012), http://www.coca-colacompany.com/our-company/water -stewardship-and-replenish-report-2012.
15. Adi Ignatius, "Shaking Things Up at Coca-Cola: An Interview with Muhtar Kent," *Harvard Business Review*, October 2011, http://hbr.org/2011/10 /shaking-things-up-at-coca-cola.
16. Morten T. Hansen, Herminia Ibara, and Urs Peyer, "The Best-Performing CEOs in the World," *Harvard Business Review*, January–February 2013, http://hbr.org/2013/01/the-best-performing-ceos-in-the-world.
17. Johnathan D. Rockoff, "James Burke 1925–2012: J&J CEO Amid Tylenol Scare," *Wall Street Journal*, October 1, 2012, http://online.wsj.com/article /SB10000872396390444592404578030681224799460.html.
18. Ibid.
19. Johnson & Johnson website, http://www.jnj.com/connect/about-jnj/jnj -credo/.
20. Tamar Lewin, "Tylenol Maker Finding New Crisis Less Severe," *New York Times*, February 12, 1986, http://www.nytimes.com/1986/02/12/business /tylenol-maker-finding-new-crisis-less-severe.html.

21. Richard W. Stevenson, "Johnson & Johnson's Recovery," *New York Times*, July 5, 1986, http://www.nytimes.com/1986/07/05/business/johnson -johnson-s-recovery.html.

22. "GBC Member Profiles: BMW Group," GBCHealth website, http://www .gbchealth.org/member_profiles/1457/.

23. "Supersector Leaders 2012," Dow Jones Sustainability Indices in collaboration with RobecoSAM, last updated September 24, 2012, http://www .sustainability-indices.com/review/supersector-leaders-2012.jsp.

24. *2012 Global RepTrak 100*, 8. *2013 Global RepTrak100*, 16, http://www .reputationinstitute.com.

CHAPTER 4

1. Susan Casey, "Patagonia: Blueprint for Green Business," *Fortune*, May 29, 2007, http://money.cnn.com/magazines/fortune/fortune_archive/2007/04 /02/8403423/index.htm.

2. "Our Reason for Being," Patagonia, http://www.patagonia.com/us /patagonia.go?assetid=2047.

3. Seth Stevenson, "Patagonia's Founder Is America's Most Unlikely Business Guru," *Wall Street Journal*, April 26, 2012, http://online.wsj.com/article /SB10001424052702303513404577352221465986612.html.

4. Casey, "Blueprint for Green Business," *Fortune*, 2007.

5. Stevenson, "Patagonia's Founder," *Wall Street Journal*.

6. http://www.patagonia.com/us/footprint/.

7. "Common Threads Partnership," Patagonia, http://www.patagonia.com/us /common-threads/.

8. 1% for the Planet website, http://www.onepercentfortheplanet.org.

9. Monte Burke, "Wal-Mart, Patagonia Team to Green Business," *Forbes*, May 6, 2010, http://www.forbes.com/forbes/2010/0524/rebuilding -sustainability-eco-friendly-mr-green-jeans.html.

10. Yvon Chouinard and Vincent Stanley, *The Responsible Company* (Ventura, CA: Patagonia Books, 2012), 11.

11. *The Responsible Company*, 12.

12. Sustainable Apparel Coalition website, "The Higg Index," http://www .apparelcoalition.org/higgindex.

13. Tom Zeller Jr., "Clothes Makers Join to Set 'Green Score,'" *New York Times*, March 1, 2011, http://www.nytimes.com/2011/03/01/business/01apparel .html.

14. Jessica Wohl, "Exclusive: After Fire, Wal-Mart Vows to Tighten Source Safeguards," Reuters, December 11, 2012, http://www.reuters.com /article/2012/12/11/us-bangladesh-fire-walmart-idUSBRE8BA06820121211.

15. Geoffrey Jones, "The Growth Opportunity That Lies Next Door," *Harvard Business Review*, July–August 2012, http://hbr.org/2012/07/the-growth -opportunity-that-lies-next-door/ar/1.

16. Carolyn Butler, "Soaps, Makeup and Other Items Contain Deadly Ingredients, Say Consumer Advocates," *Washington Post*, January 30, 2012, http://articles.washingtonpost.com/2012-01-30/national/35441321_1 _stacy-malkan-shampoos-cosmetics.

17. *Official Journal of the European Communities*, "Council Directive of 27 July 1976 on the Approximation of the Laws of the Member States Relating to Cosmetic Products (76/768/EEC)," No. L 262/169 (July 27, 1976), http:// eur-lex.europa.eu/LexUriServ/LexUriServ.do?uri=OJ:L:1976:262:0169 :0200:EN:PDF.

18. U.S. Food and Drug Administration (FDA) website, s.v. "Parabens," http:// www.fda.gov/Cosmetics/ProductandIngredientSafety/SelectedCosmetic Ingredients/ucm128042.htm.

19. Jones, "Growth Opportunity," *Harvard Business Review*.

20. Natura, *Annual Report* (2006), 15, http://natura.infoinvest.com.br/enu/s -15-enu.html.

21. Fabien Bronès, "Natura Brazil, a Life Cycle Management Experience in the Cosmetic Industry," paper presented at the LCM 2011 conference (Towards Life Cycle Sustainability Management), Berlin, August 2011.

22. Jones, "Growth Opportunity," *Harvard Business Review*.

23. Corporate Knights, "Global 100 Announced at the World Economic Forum in Davos," January 23, 2013, http://www.corporateknights.com/article /global-100-announced-world-economic-forum-davos.

24. Leonardo Yamamoto and Daniela Bouissou, "Natura: Exporting Brazilian Beauty," Case 1B-92, January 20, 2010 (Stanford: Stanford Graduate School of Business, 2010), downloaded via Scribd, http://www.scribd.com/doc /53082135/12/Natura.

25. Suntory, "Top Message: Striving to Become a Company 'Growing for Good,'" Nobutada Saji, http://www.suntory.com/csr/message/.

26. Ibid.

27. *Suntory Group Corporate Social Responsibility Report*, September 2012 (Tokyo: Suntory, 2012), http://www.suntory.com/csr/report/pdf/2012/report_all.pdf.

28. "Patagonia's Founder on Why There's 'No Such Thing as Sustainability,'" *Fast Company*, July 1, 2009, http://www.fastcompany.com/1298102/.

CHAPTER 5

1. "Plan G," *Hemispheres* magazine, April 2012, http://www.hemispheres magazine.com/2012/04/01/plan-g/.

2. Centre for Social Innovation website, "Social Innovation," http:// socialinnovation.ca/about/social-innovation.

3. It's surprisingly difficult to arrive at an accurate number of countries, not to mention the few scattered governments that interact with the international community (for example, the Palestinian Authority). As of this writing, the U.S. State Department recognizes 195 countries, including Kosovo

and South Sudan (but not Taiwan), there are 193 United Nations member states, and *Wikipedia* lists 206 sovereign states including disputed governments like Somaliland and Northern Cyprus. (Turkey doesn't even recognize Cyprus.) Israel still is not recognized by 33 nations. If we can't even agree who we are negotiating with, it's unlikely we will arrive at any truly global consensus.

4. "Strategic Analytics: Worldwide Smartphone Population Tops 1 Billion in Q3 2012," *BusinessWire*, October 17, 2012, http://www.businesswire.com/news/home/20121017005479/en/Strategy-Analytics-Worldwide-Smartphone-Population-Tops-1.

5. "All Eyes on the Sharing Economy," *Economist*, March 9, 2013, http://www.economist.com/news/technology-quarterly/21572914-collaborative-consumption-technology-makes-it-easier-people-rent-items.

6. "The Rise of the Sharing Economy," *Economist*, March 9, 2013, http://www.economist.com/news/leaders/21573104-internet-everything-hire-rise-sharing-economy.

7. Danielle Sacks, "The Sharing Economy," *Fast Company*, April 18, 2011, http://www.fastcompany.com/1747551/sharing-economy.

8. If you're curious about the Witkar's history and modern efforts to renew it, *Wikipedia* has an excellent entry on the subject (http://en.wikipedia.org/wiki/Witkar). There is a Witkar website up and running at www.witkar.nl as of this writing (Dutch only).

9. "GM Enters Carsharing Business; Teams Up with RelayRides," GM press release, October 5, 2011, http://media.gm.com/media/us/en/gm/news.detail.html/content/Pages/news/us/en/2011/Oct/1005_relay.html.

10. Carsharing.net website, "Volkswagen Pioneers Car Sharing," archived Volkswagen press release, October 3, 1997, http://www.carsharing.net/library/pr971003.PDF.

11. "Daimler Launches All-Electric Car2Go Carshare Service," *Mother Nature Network* website, Shea Gunther (blog), November 27, 2011, http://www.mnn.com/green-tech/transportation/blogs/daimler-launches-all-electric-car2go-carshare-service.

12. *The Economist*, "All Eyes on the Sharing Economy."

13. Andrew Martin, "Car Sharing Catches On as Zipcar Sells to Avis," *New York Times*, Deal Book, January 2, 2013, http://dealbook.nytimes.com/2013/01/02/avis-to-buy-zipcar-for-500-million/.

14. Tomjo Geron, "Airbnb and the Unstoppable Rise of the Share Economy," *Forbes*, February 11, 2013, http://www.forbes.com/sites/tomiogeron/2013/01/23/airbnb-and-the-unstoppable-rise-of-the-share-economy/.

15. Helen Goulden, "13 Predictions for 2013," *Nesta*, http://www.nesta.org.uk/news_and_features/13for2013/big_business_accelerates_collaborative_consumption_growth.

16. *The Economist*, "All Eyes on the Sharing Economy."

17. Ibid.
18. *2013 Edelman Trust Barometer*, 1.
19. Dana Gunders, *Wasted: How America Is Losing Up to 40 Percent of Its Food from Farm to Fork to Landfill*, NRDC Issue Paper IP:12-06-B (August 2012), http://www.nrdc.org/food/wasted-food.asp.
20. "The Comet Circle," http://www.ricoh.com/environment/management /concept.html.
21. "Towards the Circular Economy: Economy and Business Rationale for an Accelerated Transition," *Ellen MacArthur Foundation* website, January 2012, http://www.ellenmacarthurfoundation.org/case_studies/ricoh.
22. "History of Wikipedia," http://en.wikipedia.org/wiki/History_of_ Wikipedia.
23. David Tiltman, "Unilever to Crowdsource Content for 13 Global Brands," *Marketing*, April 20, 2010, http://www.marketingmagazine.co.uk /news/998122/Unilever-crowdsource-content-13-global-brands/.
24. Mark Sweney, "Unilever Goes Crowdsourcing to Spice Up Peperami's TV Ads," *The Guardian*, August 25, 2009, http://www.guardian.co.uk/media /blog/2009/aug/25/unilever-peperami-advertising-crowdsourcing.
25. Raz Godelnik, "Can Crowdsourcing Really Work for Unilever?" *TriplePundit*, April 6, 2012, http://www.triplepundit.com/2012/04 /crowdsourcing-really-work-unilever/.
26. Sarah Lacy, "Accel Invests $35M in 99designs . . . After Years of Trying," *TechCrunch*, April 28, 2011, http://techcrunch.com/2011/04/28/accel -invests-35m-in-99designs-after-years-of-trying/.
27. Associated Press, "Success of the 'Veronica Mars' Kickstarter Campaign Rattles Movie Industry," *The Washington Post*, March 22, 2013, http:// articles.washingtonpost.com/2013-03-22/entertainment/37923885_1 _kickstarter-veronica-mars-studio-project.

Chapter 6

1. Center for Creative Leadership, "History," http://www.ccl.org/leadership /about/history.aspx.
2. Ibid.
3. U.S. Securities and Exchange Commission (SEC) Form 10-K, "The Coca-Cola Company," Commission File No. 001-02217 (2011), http://www.sec .gov/Archives/edgar/data/21344/000002134412000007/a2011123110-k.htm.
4. "Culture Shift and Brands," presentation, Sustainable Brands Conference '10, Monterey, CA, June 7–10, 2010, Tom LaForge. Video of presentation is available at http://www.sustainablebrands.com/digital_learning/event-video /culture-shifts-and-brands-tom-laforge-coca-cola.
5. Ibid.
6. Ignatius, "Shaking Things Up at Coca Cola," *Harvard Business Review*, October 2011, http://hbr.org/2011/10/shaking-things-up-at-coca-cola.

7. Coca-Cola, "2020 Vision—Roadmap for Winning Together: TCCC & Our Bottling Partners," http://assets.coca-colacompany.com/22/b7 /ba47681f420fbe7528bc43e3a118/2020_vision.pdf.

8. Ignatius, *Harvard Business Review*, October 2011.

9. The Coca-Cola Company, *Sustainability Report 2011-2012*, http://www .coca-colacompany.com/sustainabilityreport/.

10. Coca-Cola, "Coca-Cola Announces Long-Term Partnership with DEKA R&D to Help Bring Clean Water to Communities in Need," press release, September 25, 2012, http://www.coca-colacompany.com/press-center /press-releases/deka-partnership-announcement.

11. For more information on Bonsucro, see website at http://www.bonsucro .com/.

12. 2011 BMW Sustainable Value Report, http://www.bmwgroup.com/d/0_0 _www_bmwgroup_com/verantwortung/kennzahlen_und_fakten/ sustainable_value_report_2010/einzelne_kapitel/11670_SVR_2010_engl _Online-Version.pdf.

13. BMW Group, *Sustainable Value Report*, English edition (Munich, Bayerische MotorenWerke, 2010), V1.

14. Ibid.

15. Peter Senge et al., *The Necessary Revolution: How Individuals and Organizations Are Working Together to Create a Sustainable World* (Crown Publishing Group, 2008).

16. BMW Group, "BMW i3 Concept," http://www.bmw-i.com/en_ww/bmw-i3/.

17. "Boeing/BMW Group to Collaborate on Carbon Fiber Recycling," *Multi Modal Journal* (Delhi: Ares Advisory Pvt. Ltd., 2012), http://www .multimodaljournal.com/Technology/Boeing_BMW_Group_to _collaborate_on_carbon_fiber_recycling.aspx.

18. *BASF Report 2011* (Ludwigshafen, Germany: BASF SE, 2011), http:// www.basf.com/report.

19. BASF, "Sustainable Development at BASF," http://www.basf.com /sustainability.

20. BASF, "Our Strategic Principles," http://www.basf.com/group/corporate /us/en/about-basf/worldwide/north-america/USA/about-basf/strategy /index.

21. BASF, "Verbund," http://factbook.basf.com/basf-the-chemical-company /verbund.html.

22. BASF, "Technology Blueprint," http://www.smartforvision.basf.com /#technology_blueprint.

23. Walmart, "Wal-Mart CEO Lee Scott Unveils 'Sustainability 360,'" press release, February 1, 2007, http://news.walmart.com/news-archive/2007 /02/01/wal-mart-ceo-lee-scott-unveils-sustainability-360.

24. Ibid.

25. Walmart, "Walmart Announces Sustainable Product Index," press release, July 16, 2009, http://news.walmart.com/news-archive/2009/07/16/walmart -announces-sustainable-product-index.
26. Lee Scott, "The Company of the Future," presentation at Walmart U.S. Year Beginning Meeting, Kansas City, MO, January 23, 2008. Full prepared text accessed at http://news.walmart.com/executive-viewpoints/company -of-the-future.

CHAPTER 7

1. *MIT/Sloan Management Review* and The Boston Consulting Group, "The Innovation Bottom Line: Findings from the 2012 Sustainability & Innovation Global Executive Study and Research Report" (Cambridge: MIT, 2013), available through http://sloanreview.mit.edu/sustainability. See also "The Benefits of Sustainability-Driven Innovation," *MIT Sloan Management Review* 54, no. 2 (Winter 2013), 69–73.
2. RobecoSAM and KPMG, *The Sustainability Yearbook 2013* (Zurich: RobecoSAM AG, 2013), 8, http://www.robecosam.com/images /sustainability-yearbook-2013.pdf.
3. Ibid., 12.
4. Ibid., 11.
5. Patricia Sellers, "Fortune's 40 Over 40," *Fortune Magazine*, October 2012, http://postcards.blogs.fortune.cnn.com/2012/10/11/40-under-40-marissa -mayer/.
6. For more information, see www.globalreporting.org.
7. For more information, see www.iso.org.
8. Carole Matthews, "Research Your Industry Through Trade Associations," *Inc.*, February 15, 2001, http://www.inc.com/articles/2001/02/22070.html.
9. The Gale Directory Library can be accessed online at http://www.gale .cengage.com/DirectoryLibrary/. Subscription is required, though some free trials are available as of this writing.
10. As of this writing, the most recent World Economic Forum report available is the *2013 Global Risks Report*, available online at http://www.weforum.org /reports/global-risks-2013-eighth-edition.

CHAPTER 8

1. R. Edward Freeman and William M. Evan, "Corporate Governance: A Stakeholder Interpretation," *Journal of Behavioral Economics* 19, no. 4 (1990): 337–359.
2. Daniel Hann, Jeroen Derwall, and Rob Bauer, "Corporate Environmental Management and Credit Risk," University of Maastricht (September 2010), doi:10.2139/ssrn.1660470.

3. Daniel Turban and Daniel Greening, "Corporate Social Performance and Organizational Attractiveness to Prospective Employees," *Academy of Management Journal* 40, no. 3 (1997): 658–672, doi:10.2307/257057.
4. Michael V. Russo and Paul A. Fouts, "A Resource-Based Perspective on Corporate Environmental Performance and Profitability," *Academy of Management Journal* 40, no. 3 (1997): 534–559, doi:10.2307/257052.
5. The Forum for Sustainable and Responsible Investment (U.S. SIF Foundation), "Report on Sustainable and Responsible Investing Trends in the United States" (November 2012), 12.
6. Global Sustainable Investing Alliance (GSIA), *Global Sustainable Investment Review*, January 2013, 9, www.gsi-alliance.org.
7. U.S. SIF Foundation.
8. SAM Research Group, "Alpha from Sustainability," white paper, (Zurich: SAM, 2011), 4, http://www.robecosam.com/en/sustainability-insights /library/study.jsp.
9. U.S. SIF Foundation.
10. Credit Suisse Research Institute, *Gender Diversity and Corporate Performance* (Zurich: Credit Suisse AG, 2012).
11. Jennifer Roberts, "Go Local, Go Global," *Stanford Social Innovation Review* 10, no. 2 (Spring 2012).
12. Ibid.
13. PriceWaterhouseCoopers for Carbon Disclosure Project (CDP), *Accelerating Progress Toward a Lower-Carbon Future*, CDP S&P 500 Climate Change Report 2012.
14. George G. Bouris and Peter Miscovich, "Corporate Real Estate Goes Green: Generating Shareholder Value, Boosting ROI, and Protecting the Environment," *The Leader*, July/August 2007, 34, http://www.deloitte.com /assets/Dcom-UnitedStates/Local%20Assets/Documents/us_consulting _so_cregoesgreen_211207.pdf.
15. The U.S. Green Building Council oversees the Leadership in Energy and Environmental Design (LEED) certification program to recognize achievement of high standards with respect to energy and environmental building project specifications. ENERGY STAR is a U.S. Environmental Protection Agency (EPA) program that helps businesses and individuals save money and protect the climate through better energy efficiency standards.
16. Norm Miller, Jay Spivey, and Andrew Florance, "Does Green Pay Off?" *The Journal of Real Estate Portfolio Management* 14, no. 4 (October–December 2008), 385–400.
17. Global Real Estate Sustainability Benchmark, *2012 GRESB Report*, 8.
18. Piet Eichholtz, Nils Kok, and Erkan Yonder, "Portfolio Greenness and the Financial Performance of REITs," *Journal of International Money and Finance*, 2012, doi:10.1016/j.jimonfin.2012.05.014.

19. Jones Lang LaSalle news detail, "Corporate Sustainability Programs Focus on Employee Productivity and Health as More Companies Say They Will Pay Extra for Green Leased Space," February 9, 2011, http://www.us.am .joneslanglasalle.com/UnitedStates/EN-US/Pages/Newsitem.aspx?ItemID =21199.

20. David Gardiner & Associates for the UNEP Finance Initiative, *Green Buildings and the Finance Sector*, February 2010, http://www.unepfi.org /fileadmin/documents/greenbuildings.pdf.

21. CalPERS, *Towards Sustainable Investment*, 2012, www.calpers-governance.org.

22. RobecoSAM, "Dow Jones Sustainability Indices (DJSI) February 2013," monthly presentation.

23. SAM Research (RobecoSAM), "Alpha from Sustainability," white paper, 2011, http://www.robecosam.com/en/sustainability-insights/library/study.jsp.

24. Ibid., 8.

25. Andres Gonzalez Rey, "Sustainable Management and Financial Performance: Sustainability Pays" (ARPEL website, September 2011), 2, http://www.arpel.org/media/apps/articles/attachments/Articulotecing.pdf.

26. Robert G. Eccles, Ioannis Ioannou, and George Serafeim, "The Impact of a Corporate Culture of Sustainability on Corporate Behavior and Performance" (Harvard Business School working paper 12-035, November 14, 2011), http://hbswk.hbs.edu/item/6865.html.

27. Ibid., 30–31.

28. Goldman Sachs Global Investment Research Report, *GS SUSTAIN* (May 7, 2012).

29. Ibid.

30. KPMG, *International Survey of Corporate Responsibility Reporting 2011*, 15.

CHAPTER 9

1. Martin Chilcott, "Could Collecting Supply-Chain Data Put Your Reputation at Risk?" 2degrees, *Supply Chain* (blog), March 13, 2013, http://www.2degreesnetwork.com/groups/supply-chain/resources/could-collecting -supply-chain-data-put-your-reputation-at-risk.

2. Economist Intelligence Unit, "Reputation: Risk of Risks," white paper (London: *The Economist*, 2005), 6, http://www.acegroup.com/eu-en/media -centre/research.aspx.

3. Ibid., 7.

4. Ibid., 6.

5. Harris Interactive, *The Harris Poll 2013 RQ® Summary Report*, February 2013, 4, http://www.harrisinteractive.com/Products/ReputationQuotient .aspx.

6. Ibid., 17.

7. BrandLogic/CRD Analytics, *2012 Sustainability Leadership Report: Measuring Perceptions vs. Reality for 100 Prominent Brands*, www.sustainability leadershipreport.com.

8. Ibid., 9.

9. *2013 RQ Summary Report*, 23.

10. Ibid., 24.

11. EIU, "Reputation: Risk of Risks," 19.

12. Interbrand, *Best Global Brands 2012: The Definitive Guide to the Best Global Brands*, 3, www.interbrand.com/best-global-brands.

13. Grahame Dowling and Peter Moran, "Corporate Reputations: Built in or Bolted On?" *California Management Review* 54, no. 2 (Winter 2012): 25–42, doi:10.1525/cmr.2012.54.2.25.

14. Ibid.

Chapter 10

1. Peter F. Drucker, "The Age of Social Transformation," *Atlantic Monthly*, November 1994, 53–80.

2. Kristie Lu Stout, "Can Social Media Clear Air over China?" *CNN*, April 19, 2013, http://edition.cnn.com/2013/04/19/world/asia/lu-stout-china -pollution/index.html.

3. "Social Responsibility Key to Attracting Top Talent," Kelly Services press release, October 28, 2009, http://ir.kellyservices.com/releasedetail.cfm ?ReleaseID=419383.

4. World Economic Forum, *More with Less: Scaling Sustainable Consumption and Resource Efficiency*, January 2012, 9, http://www.weforum.org/reports.

5. Nike, Inc., *FY10/11 Sustainable Business Performance Summary*, 49, http:// www.nikeresponsibility.com/report/.

6. Michael Conner, "Nike: Corporate Responsibility at a 'Tipping Point,'" *Business Ethics*, January 24, 2010, http://business-ethics.com/2010/01/24 /2154-nike-corporate-responsibility-at-a-tipping-point/.

7. Maria Shao, "Social Pressures Affect Corporate Strategy and Performance," *Stanford Graduate School of Business* website, December 1, 2009, http://www .gsb.stanford.edu/news/research/Baron_social.html.

8. Andrew C. Wicks, "Can Social Responsibility Sustain a Global Business?," *The Washington Post* online, March 2, 2013, http://articles.washingtonpost .com/2013-03-02/business/37390495_1_csr-activities-social-responsibility -human-rights.

9. Stephen Wright, "Nike Faces New Worker Abuse Claims in Indonesia," *Associated Press* wire story, *HuffPost Business* website, July 13, 2011, http:// www.huffingtonpost.com/2011/07/13/nike-faces-new-worker-abuse -indonesia_n_896816.html.

10. Nike, *FY10/11 Sustainable Business Performance*, 30.

11. Sam Beldona, Andrew C. Inkpen, and Arvind Phatak, "Are Japanese Managers More Long-Term Oriented Than United States Managers?," *Management International Review* 38, no. 3, 239–256, http://www.questia .com/library/1G1-21249265/are-japanese-managers-more-long-term -oriented-than.

12. Deborah Zabarenko, "Corporate Sustainability: Unilever CEO Polman on Ending the 'Three Month Rat-Race,'" *Reuters* online, October 26, 2012, http://blogs.reuters.com/macroscope/2012/10/26/corporate-sustainability -unilever-ceo-polman-on-ending-the-three-month-rat-race/.

13. Ray C. Anderson with Robin White, *Business Lessons from a Radical Industrialist* (New York: St. Martin's Press, 2010), 2.

14. David L. Scott, *The American Heritage Dictionary of Business Terms* (Boston: Houghton Mifflin Harcourt, 2009), 571.

15. Philips website, "EcoVision," http://www.usa.philips.com/about /sustainability/index.page.

16. Raz Godelnik, "Philips Makes the Business Case for Sustainability," *TriplePundit* website, March 2, 2012, http://www.triplepundit.com/2012/03 /philips-2011-report-great-example-business-case-sustainability/.

17. World Business Council for Sustainable Development (WBCSD), *Vision 2050*, February 2010, 4, http://www.wbcsd.org/vision2050.aspx.

18. "Disruptive innovation" is a phrase coined by Clayton Christensen, describing how an innovation gradually but "relentlessly" takes over a marketplace and changes the way established business models work. A good example is Napster: even though Napster eventually ran into legal issues, it forced the music industry to rethink distribution and, in conjunction with the equally disruptive iPod, spurred a change in consumer behavior for music listening and buying. For more on disruptive innovation, see Clayton Christensen's website: http://www.claytonchristensen.com/key-concepts/.

19. Dorothea Seebode, *Sustainable Innovation: Exploring a New Innovation Paradigm*, Philips, 2011, http://www.philips.com/shared/assets/global /sustainability/downloads/sustainable_innovation_paper.pdf.

20. Nike, *FY10/11 Sustainable Business Performance*, 49.

21. Jo Confino, "Paul Polman: 'The Power Is in the Hands of the Consumers,'" *The Guardian* online, November 21, 2011, http://www.guardian.co.uk /sustainable-business/unilever-ceo-paul-polman-interview.

CHAPTER 11

1. "The Annual Global Climate and Catastrophe Report," *Continuity Central* website, January 25, 2013, http://www.continuitycentral.com/news06626 .html.

2. World Nuclear Association, "Fukushima Accident 2011," last updated May 2013, http://www.world-nuclear.org/info/Safety-and-Security/Safety-of -Plants/Fukushima-Accident-2011/.

3. David Crossland, "German Public Reaction to Japan Nuclear Accident Close to Panic," *The National* online, March 17, 2011, http://www .thenational.ae/business/industry-insights/energy/german-public-reaction -to-japan-nuclear-accident-close-to-panic.

4. Bill Canis, *The Motor Vehicle Supply Chain: Effects of the Japanese Earthquake and Tsunami*, Congressional Research Service, R41831, 7-5700, May 23, 2011.

5. *Millea Group CSR Report 2005* (Tokyo: Millea Holdings, Inc., 2005), http:// www.tokiomarinehd.com/en/social_respon/report/.

6. "Contributing to the Preservation of Biodiversity Through Social Contribution Activities: Mangrove Planting Project," Tokio Marine Holdings website, http://www.tokiomarinehd.com/en/social_respon /environment/biodiversity.html.

7. Cari Tuna, "Pendulum Is Swinging Back on 'Scenario Planning,'" *The Wall Street Journal* online, July 6, 2009, http://online.wsj.com/article /SB124683295589397615.html.

8. Shell website, "Shell Celebrates 40 Years of Scenarios," press release, November 19, 2012, http://www.shell.com/global/aboutshell/media /news-and-media-releases/2012/shell-celebrates-40-years-scenarios -19112012.html.

9. The following reports may be useful for identifying potential driving factors and scenarios during scenario planning activities: World Business Council for Sustainable Development (WBCSD), *Vision 2050*, www.wbcsd.org; UNEP Global Environment Outlook (GEO), www.unep.org/geo/.

10. International Energy Agency (IEA), *World Energy Outlook 2011*, *Scenarios and Predictions* (Paris: IEA, 2011), worldenergyoutlook.org.

11. World Economic Forum (WEF), *Engineering and Construction: Scenarios to 2020* (Cologny, Switzerland: WEF, 2008), http://www.weforum.org/reports /engineering-construction-scenarios-2020.

12. Knut Haanaes, David Michael, Jeremy Jurgens, and Subramanian Rangan, "Making Sustainability Profitable: Lessons from Emerging Markets," *Harvard Business Review*, March 2013, http://hbr.org/2013/03/making -sustainability-profitable/.

13. Brandlogic, *Keys to Sustainability Leadership: Five Best Practices* (2012), http:// www.sustainabilityleadershipreport.com.

14. MIT Technology Review, "New Measure of Human Brain Processing Speed," *The Physics arXiv Blog*, August 25, 2009, http://www.technology review.com/view/415041/new-measure-of-human-brain-processing-speed/.

15. Julian Talbot, "What's Right with Risk Matrices?" Jakeman Business Solutions website, http://www.jakeman.com.au/media/whats-right-with -risk-matrices.

16. "Mars Promotes Sustainability, Warns of Cocoa Shortage," *Candy & Snack Today* website, June 24, 2011, http://www.candyandsnacktoday.com

/archives/2011/06/mars-promotes-sustainability-warns-of-cocoa-shortage
.shtml.

17. "International Cocoa Certification Workshop Details Announced,"
   International Cocoa Organization website, last updated May 2, 2013, http://
   www.icco.org/about-us/icco-news/225-international-cocoa-certification
   -workshop-details-announced.html.

18. Darrell Rigby and Barbara Bilodeau, "A Growing Focus on Preparedness,"
   Harvard Business Review, http://hbr.org/2007/07/a-growing-focus-on
   -preparedness.

19. MIT Sloan Management Review and the Boston Consulting Group,
   "Sustainability Nears a Tipping Point," Winter 2012, http://sloanreview
   .mit.edu/reports/sustainability-strategy/.

CHAPTER 12

1. Unilever Sustainable Living Plan (Rotterdam: Unilever N.V., 2010), 3.

2. cf. Eric Lowitt, *The Future of Value: How Sustainability Creates Value Through
   Competitive Differentiation* (San Francisco: Jossey-Bass, 2011).

3. Richard Anderson, "Unilever Says Sustainability Key to New Business
   Model," *BBC News* (November 15, 2010), http://www.bbc.co.uk/news
   /business-11755672.

4. Yvon Chouinard, *Let My People Go Surfing: The Education of a Reluctant
   Businessman* (New York: Penguin Group, 2005), reprinted at Patagonia.com,
   http://www.patagonia.com/us/patagonia.go?assetid=5625.

5. The Life Cycle Sustainability Assessment (LCSA) was created by the
   Society of Environmental Toxicology and Chemistry (SETAC) and the
   United Nations Environment Program (UNEP) and is available online at
   lifecycleinitiative.org. The International Organization for Standardization
   (ISO) series includes ISO 14040:2006, Environmental Management—Life
   Cycle Assessment—Principles and Framework, and is available online from
   iso.org.

6. For an excellent discussion of stakeholder engagement, see Jean-Philippe
   Renaut, *Practices and Principles for Successful Stakeholder Engagement*,
   SustainAbility, http://www.sustainability.com/library/successful
   -stakeholder-engagement.

7. Coca-Cola, "2020 Vision" Strategic Roadmap, http://assets.coca-colacompany
   .com/22/b7/ba47681f420fbe7528bc43e3a118/2020_vision.pdf.

8. Robert S. Kaplan and David P. Norton, "The Balanced Scorecard—
   Measures That Drive Performance," *Harvard Business Review* (January–
   February 1992).

9. Robert S. Kaplan and David P. Norton, *Strategy Maps: Converting Intangible
   Assets into Tangible Outcomes* (Boston: Harvard Business School Publishing,
   2004), 191–192.

10. "Production Sectors Cost Trillions in Damages to World Environment—UN-Backed Study," UN News Center, April 15, 2013, http://www.un.org/apps/news/story.asp?NewsID=44654.

11. For more on the illustrated process, see Robert G. Cooper, Scott J. Edgett, and Elko J. Kleinschmidt, *Portfolio Management for New Products* (Cambridge, MA: Basic Books, 2001).

Chapter 13

1. Randers, *2052*.

2. Charles Homans, "Energy Independence: A Short History," *Foreign Policy*, January/February 2012, http://www.foreignpolicy.com/articles/2012/01/03/energy_independence_a_short_history.

3. "US Boom Transforming Global Oil Trade," Associated Press, May 14, 2013, http://www.npr.org/templates/story/story.php?storyId=183999026.

4. Interbrand, *Best Global Brands 2012*, 96.

5. Hannah Miller, "Patagonia Founder Takes Aim: 'The Elephant in the Room Is Growth,'" *GreenBiz.com*, March 1, 2013, http://www.greenbiz.com/news/2013/03/01/patagonia-founder-takes-aim-elephant-room-growth.

6. Interview with Nick Folland (Kingfisher) by Hannah Clark Steiman, "The Net Positive Strategy: Where Environmental Stewardship Meets Business Innovation," *MITSloan Management Review*, May 10, 2013, http://sloanreview.mit.edu/article/the-net-positive-strategy-where-environmental-stewardship-meets-business-innovation/.

ACKNOWLEDGING THE POWER OF COLLABORATION

Judith W. Umlas, our good friend and colleague, is the author of three books on acknowledgment, including *Grateful Leadership*, which guided us in writing this section. To Judy, acknowledgment is not just about saying thanks or giving a pat on the back. It is about recognizing the unique value someone brings to a situation or a relationship, and sharing the benefits of that value. It is not easy to do so for this book, since literally dozens of professionals have collaborated with us to help us achieve a lifelong dream. However, we are going to try, since their work is a testament to the enthusiasm, honesty, openness, and dedication to excellence that created this book.

First of all, the leadership of the Project Management Institute (PMI) and their investment in scenario planning and strategic execution inspired us to continue this important conversation. Since 2006, PMI has used scenario planning to manage through uncertainty. That approach to strategic management prompted a critical analysis of key indicators or "mileposts" describing the alternate futures that might evolve. Continuous analysis of these mileposts with the leaders of PMI showed us the clear need for companies, businesses, and organizations to act now if they want to survive and thrive in the twenty-first century.

A project this large could not happen without a champion. Ours was International Institute for Learning, Inc. (IIL). In our opinion, no other for-profit educational institution has done more to prepare professionals for the challenges of project and program execution. IIL Founder, President, and CEO E. LaVerne Johnson possesses a unique capability to see opportunity where others see nothing but chaos. She approached Greg and asked him to write the book, agreed to bring in Nathalie as part of the team, and saw the need to continue the conversation after publication. LaVerne represents a remarkable balance between risk management and entrepreneurial freedom, between solid business sense and adaptive foresight. She believes, as we do, that the future of society, the planet, and business are all intertwined. She is the principal reason this book is in your hands.

Next we need to acknowledge the awareness and initiative of McGraw-Hill Professional. It reacted quickly and positively to our proposal, and then assigned one of the best editors we have ever worked with: Knox Huston. His enthusiasm, insight, and continuous communication to IIL, and in turn to us, helped us immensely in keeping the book on track. Without him, the project could have easily run aground.

The IIL team also provided critical support, feedback, guidance, and insight. Judy Umlas, IIL Publisher, believed in the project from the beginning and saw it as an important contribution to her goal to publish books that make a difference in the world. Judy led with her heart from the initial proposal (which she helped us shape) through the editing stages and provided the encouragement we needed to get the job done. Vanessa Nanchary Innes, the Associate Publisher, was nothing short of spectacular. Her day-to-day support was critical to our work. Vanessa's gentle nudging when we were late, and her dogged determination to get answers and approvals, were integral to our success and earned her the affectionate title of "Boss."

One of our greatest assets during development was our researcher, Kaylin Berry. Kaylin helped us sort, prioritize, and catalog hundreds of documents and references. She identified and sometimes summarized documents to expedite the inclusion (or exclusion) of a particular study. She was tireless when it came to cataloging resources and creating taxonomies for further research. Thanks also to Lori Milhaven, Executive VP of Marketing at IIL, for agreeing to "loan" Kaylin to us and for being so supportive throughout the project.

It was very important to us to make the book helpful to readers, which meant harmonizing our different writing styles into one clear voice. The conductor for this effort was DeAnna Burghart. For more than eight months, she guided, cajoled, pushed, and scolded us through this process on a daily basis. She was rigorous about deadlines, consistency, grammar, and readability. Her persona changed to match the situation; she was mother, coach, disciplinarian, wordsmith, therapist, and editor. Her commitment to the entire project was only surpassed by her sense of humor and her love of science fiction. She was nothing short of spectacular and constantly exceeded our expectations. We all bonded as a team from the first day and remain close friends.

One of the most difficult challenges and greatest roadblocks to embracing global sustainability has been the big question: Does it pay? To help answer that question, we asked Rebecca True, an award-winning certified investment manager, to research and provide insight into the relationship between overall financial performance and sustainable operations. She worked with us for nearly eight months to understand our approach and our premise. She then conducted a comprehensive study on the competitiveness and profitability of companies dedicated to sustainable operations. Rebecca's powerful treatise on the subject in Chapter 8 is a first for any book dedicated to this subject. We are profoundly grateful.

Before a single word of the book was written, and throughout the development of the book, we had dozens of interviews, contributions, and offers of help and assistance. We received unending feedback and direction on our proposal, outline, stories, and concepts, and every interaction added to the value and quality of the project. We hope we haven't left anyone off the list:

- Susan Stickley, scenario planner extraordinaire, for her continuous coaching and guidance on scenario development and interpretation over the last nine years.
- Ted Jackson, of Ascendant Strategy Management Group, for his continuous coaching and guidance on the Balanced Scorecard and its application, for over a decade.
- Scott Fass, Ed Hoffman, Beth Hand, Bonnie Halford, and Fred Payne for their friendship, personal reviews, and contributions to the book concept and proposal that helped us stay focused.
- Nancy Gabriel, for introducing and explaining the continuous contributions of Donella and Dennis Meadows to the systems work of global sustainability and leading us to a phenomenal intellect on the subject.
- Tom Esakin, Ryerson University, for his discussion of professional education and certification in the field of organizational sustainability.
- Deb Castellana, Director of Communications at Mission Blue/Sylvia Earle Alliance, and Carolina La Rotta Dratva, for arranging the meeting and interview with Sylvia Earle.
- Gregory Johnson, John Winter, and Kim Sienkiewicz, all of IIL, who dedicated time every week to be a sounding board to shape our ideas and our approaches in the book. Their ideas and feedback were always "out of the box" and were catalysts for innovative thinking.
- Nelson Mumma, Group Director of Global External Affairs, the Coca-Cola Company, for his unending support of our project, and for arranging interviews with seven key Coca-Cola executives throughout the world.
- April Rinne, for her insight into the collaborative consumption economy and the introduction to Shelby Clarke, founder of RelayRides.
- Sylvia Earle, award-winning researcher and explorer, for her interviews and her effort in preparing the foreword for the book.
- Shelby Clarke, founder of RelayRides, for an eye-opening introduction to the evolution of the peer-to-peer sharing economy.

- To the following executives at the Coca-Cola Company, who provided remarkable insight to Coca-Cola's strategic transformation into a global leader in sustainability:
  - Bea Perez, Chief Sustainability Officer
  - Charlotte Oades, Global Director, Women's Economic Empowerment
  - Carletta Ooten, VP and Chief Quality, Safety and Sustainable Operations Officer
  - Denise Knight, Director Sustainable Agriculture
  - Tom LaForge, Global Director of Human and Cultural Insights
  - Jeff Seabright, VP Environment and Water Resources

Finally, beyond the many professionals and friends that helped us, there remain a few people who are uniquely special to us:

- **From Nathalie Udo:** Thomas Watt, my life partner, for believing in me and supporting me during this project. His balanced perspective and sharp eye helped improve the quality of the book. In addition, he was patient, supportive, and took care of me while I was plugging away on this project for nearly 10 months with no time for fun activities. And of course my parents, for raising me to be a critical thinker who takes nothing for granted, and allowing their only daughter to travel the world—something that shaped who I am and my perspectives. I am eternally grateful for their support of me and my relentless curiosity to learn new things!
- **From Greg Balestrero:** Frances Higgins, my life partner and wife, for supporting me through this entire project, after 35 years of support and sacrifice during my busy career. She has remained my closest friend and ally in all phases of my life. In particular, her special effort to feed, coach, referee, and support us while we spent the last 10 days prior to submittal to McGraw-Hill, 18 hours per day, chained to the table in our dining room. It was nothing short of heroic.

Index

About the Authors

Gregory Balestrero is a Strategic Advisor on Leadership, Sustainability, and Corporate Consciousness for International Institute for Learning, Inc. (IIL), a global leader in training, consulting, and course development. He is a global advocate for excellence in performance management and business results with over 40 years of experience. In his career, he has served as a project engineer, project manager, and a senior 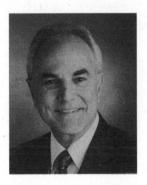 executive for several professional membership associations, including the Institute of Industrial Engineers (IIE), the Construction Specifications Institute (CSI), and the Project Management Institute (PMI).

Prior to joining IIL, Gregory served as the president and CEO of PMI for more than eight years. During that time he met with business and government leaders in more than 60 countries, advocating and promoting a project focus in engineering, construction, and a broad range of business sectors. This exposure has shaped his thinking and message, reinforcing the belief that organizations must transform to sustain themselves, integrating the values of community and the planet with their own corporate strategies and values. Through his work, Gregory aims to help global corporations discover how they can change their strategies to focus on serving their communities and the planet, while being or becoming market leaders.

In addition to his work with IIL and PMI, Gregory has served as Executive Director of the Institute of Industrial Engineers (IIE) and the Construction Specifications Institute (CSI). He has also served as an advisor to the National Ignition Facility (NIF), the American Society for Quality (ASQ), and the board of the Pediatric Brain Tumor Foundation (PBTF), as well as serving on the global advisory council to Interel Corporation, a global public affairs firm serving the European Community. He received the Friendship Award from the State Administration of Foreign Expert Affairs (SAFEA) of the People's Republic of China (PRC).

Gregory currently lives in Annapolis, Maryland, with his wife, Frances, and their two dogs. When he is not working, Gregory is an avid sailor, motorcyclist, and adventure traveler.

Nathalie Udo is a Strategic Advisor on Leadership, Sustainability, and Corporate Consciousness for International Institute for Learning, Inc. (IIL) and the founder of InDepth Strategies, LLC, a boutique global leadership and business consulting firm. She has more than 15 years of consulting and executive coaching experience, specializing in business strategy, program management, process improvement, and leadership development. She has a proven track record of leading successful projects for full lifecycle product development and enterprise implementations, using her infectious enthusiasm to inspire people to achieve things previously thought impossible. Her client list includes complex international companies like Royal Dutch Airlines, Boeing, Baan, Alcatel-Lucent, Autodesk, Kaiser Permanente, and Fireman's Fund.

Nathalie is a coauthor of *Scrappy Women in Business: Living Proof That Bending the Rules Isn't Breaking the Law* (Cupertino: Happy About, 2010), a collection of true stories about women who overcame obstacles in both their professional and personal lives to become extraordinary business leaders. She has written several papers on program management and global team interactions and presented at international conferences. She also served as chapter president of PMI San Francisco Bay Area Chapter and as an advisor on the PMI Leadership Advisory Group.

Nathalie has a master's degree in economics and business administration from University of Maastricht, The Netherlands. She is a Certified Professional Co-Active Coach (CPCC), a certified Project Management Professional (PMP), and a Certified ScrumMaster (CSM).

When she is not traveling the world, Nathalie lives in San Francisco and is an active scuba diver, motorcyclist, and skier.

Contributor

Rebecca True is Founder and President of True Capital Advisors, LLC, and has over 15 years of consultative and financial services industry experience, including eight years as a senior financial advisor with Bank of America/Merrill Lynch in New York City and Central Florida. She is a Certified Financial Manager (CFM) and holds a degree in economics from the University of South Florida. She currently serves as president of the Central Florida Women's League (CFWL) and resides in Windermere, Florida, with her husband and daughters.

About International Institute for Learning, Inc. (IIL)

With a wholly owned network of operating companies all over the world and clients in more than 150 countries, IIL is a global leader in training, consulting, coaching, and mentoring, as well as customized course development. Our core competencies include Project, Program, and Portfolio Management; Business Analysis; Microsoft Project and Project Server; Lean Six Sigma; PRINCE2; ITIL Agile; Leadership and Interpersonal Skills; and Corporate Consciousness and Sustainability.

In addition to innovative learning solutions, IIL's business divisions include:

- IIL Media, a full-service digital video production company
- IIL Printing, providing sustainable full-service digital printing, binding, and fulfillment
- IIL Speakers, a bureau of leading industry experts in the areas of Leadership, Sustainability, Project Management, and Business Analysis
- IIL Publishing, a focused full-scale publisher unit delivering unique, creative educational resources addressing a variety of business topics

Furthermore, IIL hosts two free web-based knowledge portals, allPM .com and TheBusyBA.com.

For more information about IIL's services and offerings, please visit www.iil.com, email learning@iil.com, or call 212-758-0177.